PROMOTING INCLUSION IN
EDUCATION ABROAD

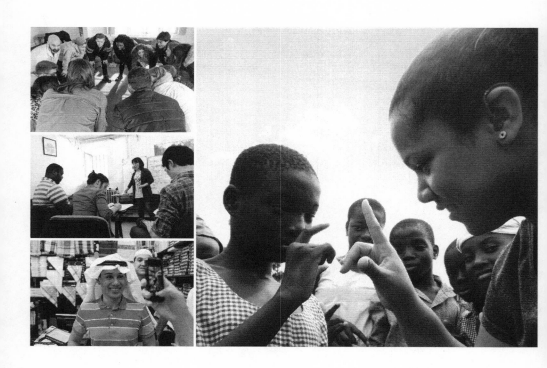

PROMOTING INCLUSION IN EDUCATION ABROAD

A Handbook of Research and Practice

EDITED BY

Heather Barclay Hamir

and *Nick Gozik*

Foreword by Esther D. Brimmer

Copublished with

STERLING, VIRGINIA

Published by Stylus Publishing, LLC.22883 Quicksilver Drive
Sterling, Virginia 20166-2102

Library of Congress Cataloging-in-Publication Data
Names: Hamir, Heather Barclay, editor. | Gozik, Nick, editor.
Title: Promoting inclusion in education abroad : a handbook of research
and practice / edited by Heather Barclay Hamir and Nick Gozik ;
Foreward by Esther Brimmer.
Description: First edition. | Sterling, Virginia : Stylus Publishing, 2017.
| Includes bibliographical references and index.
Identifiers: LCCN 2017024423 (print) |
LCCN 2017055455 (ebook) |
ISBN 9781620365571 (uPDF) |
ISBN 9781620365588 (ePUB, mobi) |
ISBN 9781620365557 (cloth : alk. paper) |
ISBN 9781620365564 (pbk. : alk. paper) |
ISBN 9781620365571 (library networkable e-edition) |
ISBN 9781620365588 (consumer e-edition)
Subjects: LCSH: Foreign study--Handbooks, manuals, etc. | Inclusive
education--Handbooks, manuals, etc.
Classification: LCC LB2376 (ebook) |
LCC LB2376 .P766 2017 (print) |
DDC 370.117--dc23
LC record available at https://lccn.loc.gov/2017024423

13-digit ISBN: 978-1-62036-555-7 (cloth)
13-digit ISBN: 978-1-62036-556-4 (paperback)
13-digit ISBN: 978-1-62036-557-1 (library networkable e-edition)
13-digit ISBN: 978-1-62036-558-8 (consumer e-edition)

Printed in the United States of America

All first editions printed on acid-free paper
that meets the American National Standards Institute
Z39-48 Standard.
A copublication of Stylus Publishing, LLC. and NAFSA: Association of
International Educators.

Bulk Purchases

Quantity discounts are available for use in workshops and for
staff development.
Call 1-800-232-0223
NAFSA: Call 1-866-538-1927 to order

First Edition, 2018

CONTENTS

FOREWORD

The expansion of access to international education is an important and timely endeavor. In our more globally integrated world in which trans-border phenomena affect daily lives, developing a greater understanding of conditions in other countries can provide students with cultural enrichment and academic expertise as well as help people to become more informed citizens, more empathetic neighbors, and more competent workers. The students themselves benefit from studying in another country, and their campuses, home countries, and future employers gain from the knowledge that they acquire. Yet, in the United States, too few students take advantage of these opportunities. This volume helps us learn why.

Currently, in the United States, less than 2% of higher education students participate in education abroad programs. Among that group, most of the participants are White and female (Institute of International Education, 2016). While honoring the commitment of those who have long cherished international education, we should also seek to widen the circle. Understanding the barriers that impede greater participation in education abroad is a prerequisite for addressing the problem of access. In this book, editors Heather Barclay Hamir and Nick Gozik provide university administrators, scholars, and the public with a crisp analysis of why different groups are underrepresented and offer ways to increase the diversity of students engaged in international education.

This book gathers together new research on a topic that has received more attention in recent decades as educators have recognized the need for greater diversity among U.S. students studying abroad. The editors acknowledge that many organizations, including NAFSA: Association of International Educators, the Institute of International Education, and the Council on International Educational Exchange, have been working toward increasing diversity in education abroad since the early 1990s. However, despite progress, the four Fs identified in 1991—faculty, finances, family, and fears—are still relevant today (Cole, 1991; p. 27, this volume). This book identifies and examines these and other barriers most salient to various underrepresented groups in the United States. While the editors frame the larger issue, contributors analyze different underrepresented groups, including ethnic minorities; men; first-generation college students; students majoring in the science, technology, engineering, and mathematics (STEM) fields; students at community colleges; students covered by Deferred Action for Childhood Arrivals (DACA); and students with disabilities. This book contributes to the field by examining the distinctive mix of barriers that may affect each group. NAFSA has been a leading voice in articulating the need for higher education institutions to address the institutional barriers that keep these underrepresented students from studying abroad and has long advocated for the creation of the federal Senator Paul Simon Study Abroad Program to encourage higher education institutions to prioritize this work. This important volume provides institutional policymakers with analyses that can contribute to institutional data-driven decision-making processes.

The rich array of examples provided in the chapters of this book highlight the insights of scholar-practitioners working in the field. These experts have valuable data at their fingertips to follow trends and pursue institutional change work. In international education, research can inform practice and practice can inform research. The book embeds education abroad in the context of the larger educational mission of colleges and universities. The advancement of international education requires collaboration among international education practitioners, faculty, and administrators.

This volume is timely. Changing demographics in the United States make the drive for greater diversity and inclusion even more imperative. Barclay Hamir and Gozik note that the United States will be a "majority minority" country within 30 years (Colby & Ortman, 2014; p. 4, this volume). They stress the importance of amplifying equal opportunity to education, using education abroad to deepen student learning, and including many different types of people in the mix of students studying abroad in order to enrich the experience for all students.

If international education enriches students' knowledge, then as educators we should endeavor to ensure that all students enrolled at our institutions have access to the programs we provide. If international education is beneficial to societies, then we as a polity must work to increase the number and types of students participating in this activity so that returned students can carry their gained knowledge to more parts of the country and different types of workplaces. Moreover, the United States needs to ensure that more people are gaining access to experiences that will allow the nation to remain economically successful.

The editors and contributors not only analyze the barriers preventing students' participation but also discuss steps to overcome them. Contributors underscore the value of developing the future research agenda and the power of organizations and other groups to convene.[1] NAFSA's Diversity and Inclusion in Education Abroad Subcommittee is one such group that provides educators with the tools and resources to support diverse populations. For more than three decades, through sessions at our annual and regional conferences, numerous publications, and advocacy with policymakers, NAFSA has supported the mission of finding ways to expand access to international education for each of the underrepresented populations identified in this book. This book makes an important contribution to that effort.

Esther D. Brimmer, DPhil
Executive Director & CEO
NAFSA: Association of International Educators

Note

1. Visit NAFSA's website at www.nafsa.org for more information.

References

Colby, S. L., & Ortman, J. M. (2014). *Projections of the size and composition of the U.S. population: 2014 to 2060. Current population reports.* Washington, DC: U.S. Census Bureau.

Cole, J. B. (1991). *Black students and overseas programs: Broadening the base of participation.* Introduction to the papers and speeches presented at the CIEE. Retrieved from ERIC database. (ED340323)

Institute of International Education. (2016). Open Doors Report on International Educational Exchange. Retrieved from www.iie.org/opendoors

ACKNOWLEDGMENTS

This book is a labor of love that started as a secret dream many years ago. I owe the fruition of this dream to my husband, best friend, and greatest champion, Zubair Hamir. This book would not have been possible without his faith in me, his occasional goading to keep me moving forward, and his generous support so that I could carve out the space to write. Thank you, Z, you've been as integral to this project as I have.

I'd also like to thank my fabulous coeditor, Nick Gozik. Nick is creative, compassionate, extremely organized, and a natural editor, all of which were necessary to create this volume that we're both so proud of. I'd also like to thank all the contributors to this work, those who wrote chapters and those who work every day to help us advance our efforts toward inclusion in education abroad.

And finally, I dedicate this book to my children, Zain and Tennyson. I hope that seeing my dream in print inspires them to strive for more than they believe they can achieve, and to embrace challenges with passion, enthusiasm, and determination.

Heather Barclay Hamir

I am so grateful to have been part of this project, resulting in the first book of its kind in the field of education abroad. None of this would have been possible without my coeditor, Heather Barclay Hamir, whose vision and passion for inclusion are highly inspirational and stem from more than a decade of work in this area. I have learned a tremendous amount from Heather and the other contributors to this volume, who have generously shared their knowledge and experience.

I would also like to express my gratitude to my colleagues at Boston College, whose support and enthusiasm for the project have been invaluable. Special thanks goes to Minna Ha for her research assistance at the beginning of the project.

Finally, I would like to thank the people who have been there for me in life, including my parents, and Rattaphol "Ahn" Onsanit, my best friend and partner in crime.

Nick Gozik

PART ONE

FRAMING THE DISCUSSION

MAKING THE CASE FOR INCLUSION IN EDUCATION ABROAD

Heather Barclay Hamir and Nick Gozik

Education is the most powerful weapon which you can use to change the world.
—Nelson Mandela

The education of students is an opportunity and a tremendous responsibility. As a nation, the United States relies on postsecondary institutions to prepare individuals for leadership, employment, and civic engagement. Despite substantial evidence of the outcomes of higher education (Mayhew et al., 2016; National Center for Education Statistics [NCES], 2017b), considerable debate continues over the foundational issues of who has access to educational opportunities and the extent to which students benefit. Institutions are under intense scrutiny to demonstrate their value through degree completion rates, learning outcomes, and alumni success to justify the investment of various entities including states, the federal government, families, and students themselves. Simultaneously, institutions are challenged to create equitable access to higher education among historically underserved groups through more inclusive recruitment and admissions practices. Significant attention has been focused on identifying effective educational practices as a means of improving educational quality and outcomes across demographic groups and disciplines.

Higher education aspires to prepare all students for their future lives and careers, which will continue to be influenced by the ease of global connectivity and interconnected global economies, while also seeking to reverse historical inequities in educational achievement at a societal level. At the time of this publication, the United States is within 35 years of becoming a majority-minority nation, with people of color making up the majority of the population for the first time in our history (Colby & Ortman, 2014). This population change is steadily shifting enrollment patterns throughout our educational system. As an example, students of color represented 41% of postsecondary enrollment in 2013 compared to only 16% in 1976 according to NCES (2017c) data. This is just one, although highly significant, shift that will have a great impact on higher education in the decades to come.

Against this backdrop, those involved in education abroad, including overseas study, research, internships, and service, grapple with many of the same concerns for equitable access. The importance of broader participation in education abroad stems from several intersecting beliefs about the education of students and intended outcomes of the educational process. It is no longer sufficient simply to admit a more diverse and representative population of college-going students across an expanding range of academic disciplines; instead, we are equally obligated to ensure that the many opportunities in higher education are apparent and available to all students. Participation in high-impact practices such as education abroad, service-learning, or capstone projects, among others, is a critical factor in student engagement, promotes deeper learning, and influences student retention (Kuh, Kinzie, Schuh, & Whitt, 2005). When considered in light of the reality of historical inequities in educational access, disparate participation rates in education abroad suggest one more layer of inequity within the bounds of higher education.

Although there has been significant attention on inclusion in education abroad, relatively little analytical work exists on the topic. Presentations at professional conferences and a scattering of articles and chapters advance knowledge and dialogue on the diversification of education abroad participation, yet to date there has not been a single volume focusing on research and practice to promote broader inclusion. With this book we fill this gap by providing a single resource designed for practitioners and researchers alike. This volume is not intended to provide an overview of all students underrepresented in education abroad. Instead, it provides a collection of chapters written by scholars and practitioners, with the goal of furthering a larger conversation on the barriers that students face and strategies to mitigate those barriers. We also hope that the chapters included here inspire more research and publications on the topic.

Education Abroad, Equity, and Learning Outcomes

On the surface, education abroad, equity, and learning outcomes might seem to have a tenuous relationship with each other. What can education abroad contribute to larger issues of access and equity in higher education or to improved student outcomes? We believe that the case for inclusion in education abroad rests on at least three main arguments related to student learning and success, equity of educational opportunity, and the impact of inclusion on learning.

Student learning and success is at the heart of discussions about the efficacy of higher education itself. Policy and public concern often focus on graduation rates, the quality of education, and employability. Historically, education abroad seemed tangential to these broader national and institutional concerns. Over the past two decades, though, multiple researchers have identified beneficial outcomes of education abroad participation that enhance student learning and success. Large-scale studies provide compelling evidence that participation in education abroad correlates with improved outcomes on several important measures of educational effectiveness, including degree completion (Kuh et al., 2005; O'Rear, Sutton, & Rubin, 2011; Sutton & Rubin, 2010) and integrative, or deep, learning (Kuh, 2008), which fosters the development of critical thinking skills. Although these gains exist for all students, they are particularly powerful among students historically underserved by higher education, including African American and Latino and Latina students (Kuh, 2008). Given that graduation rates for these groups have been consistently below the national average for decades (NCES, 2017a), this creates a compelling case for considering expanded participation in education abroad as a means for fostering greater student learning and success.

Inclusion in education abroad is also a matter of equity in terms of the educational opportunities students pursue within the bounds of their degrees. A college education consists of more than the sum of a student's courses. However, taking advantage of opportunities to pursue enriching educational activities such as research, internships, or education abroad requires students to know these opportunities exist, believe them to be valuable, and receive sufficient support in pursuing them. As an example, a first-generation college student is apt to matriculate with little familial guidance on navigating college. Once the student gets to college, he or she is likely to have even less assistance in pursuing additional activities that may seem unrelated to the overall goal of graduating and gaining employment. In contrast, a science major may be fully aware of a range of educational activities available beyond the classroom yet infer that participation is not valued because of a lack of faculty encouragement or sufficient assurance that transfer credit from abroad will fulfill necessary major, minor, or general education requirements. Similarly, a wheelchair user may be aware of and excited about education abroad, yet feel discouraged from participating when faculty or advisers seem hesitant about his or her ability to navigate a new physical environment. In each case, the net impact is a narrowing of educational opportunity within the context of the degree itself. Although not all students will be interested in education abroad, equity of opportunity requires that they are at least aware of the option and the potential benefits of participation, that institutional policies support participation, and that faculty and staff are equally supportive of participation by students from different backgrounds and disciplines. Failure to promote full access to any element of higher education equates to a failure to promote equity of educational opportunity, thereby perpetuating differential outcomes in student learning and success.

Another rationale for an inclusive approach to education abroad participation relates to the quality of learning for all students abroad. The positive impact of interactions with diversity on student development is well documented (Kuh et al., 2006; Mayhew et al., 2016; Pascarella, 2006). In this case, diversity takes on the broader meaning of "interactions with a diverse spectrum of people, ideas, values, and perspectives that are different from one's own and challenge one's assumed views of the world" (Pascarella, 2006, p. 511). Kuh (2008) categorizes education abroad as a high-impact practice that has the ability to foster global learning and interactions with individuals from diverse backgrounds. If the population going abroad is largely homogenous, however, participants miss one important opportunity to experience such diversity. This is especially true when contact with locals may be limited because of program design, as with short-term faculty-led programs or semester or academic-year programs where students spend much of their time in and out of the classroom with other U.S. students.

The Value of Education Abroad

Much of our argument is predicated on the assumption that education abroad is of value. If education abroad, as one high-impact practice, is known to be beneficial, it is not the only such practice. So why education abroad specifically? To be fair, not all key stakeholders, including parents, students, senior-level administrators, faculty, and lawmakers, necessarily buy into the argument that greater access to education abroad should be a priority. At some institutions with long-held commitments to internationalization, education abroad has gained wider acceptance and is considered part of the fabric of campus life. In other domains, overseas programming is not considered integral to the academic missions of institutions for a whole host of reasons. Even for those who are apt to support education abroad, realistic concerns have been raised over the cost, curricular fit, and ability of programs to deliver consistently on their stated promises (Twombly, Salisbury, Tumanut, & Klute, 2012).

We agree that education abroad should not be taken as a given and needs to be evaluated critically to determine whether it meets the needs of individual institutions and students. Indeed, it is necessary to question what students gain from education abroad and why it is relevant. The answer comes down in part to a long-standing debate over the purpose of higher education in the United States, which has pitted a seemingly lofty view of a liberal arts education, reduced to the notion of learning for learning's sake, against a more pragmatic vision of colleges and universities as training grounds for future careers (Berrett, 2015). For proponents of the liberal arts, college is designed to be a place of intellectual curiosity, where students learn academically and about themselves. Exposure to diverse perspectives in this context permits students to encounter others who are different from themselves and can lead to the promotion of critical thinking, an increase in one's knowledge base, greater worldliness, and the enhancement of social development (Hyman & Jacobs, 2009).

Intended outcomes of education abroad include a similar set of soft skills, with the goal that students become more adaptable, independent, globally minded, proficient in another language, and interculturally competent. It is true that many of these same skills can be developed on students' home campuses through classroom and extracurricular activities. Technology, moreover, has eroded many former boundaries, allowing instantaneous access to people and data from around the world. At the same time, one of the key distinctions in education abroad is the ability for students to be plunged into a different culture for a short, intense period. The cognitive dissonance created by such an experience can provide an opening for students to grow much more rapidly and deeply than they would at home (Che, Spearman, & Manizade, 2009).

From a pragmatic, career-oriented perspective, the soft skills discussed here are in fact equally relevant. To be sure, technical, or hard, skills are mandatory for many disciplines. None of us would want to hire, much less use the services of, a nurse or doctor who has not fully mastered his or her profession. In addition to this technical expertise, however, employers increasingly seek applicants with strong social skills, capable of interacting constructively with people who are different from themselves (Crossman & Clarke, 2010). Medical professionals must be able to interact with a diverse range of patients (Harden, 2006), often from other countries, whereas researchers and technicians are increasingly likely to collaborate with overseas partners, creating a need for scientists and engineers to become globally competent (Del Vitto, 2008; Downey et al., 2006; Grandin & Hirleman, 2009).

The types of skills developed abroad allow students to develop an intellectual curiosity and ability to think critically, while also preparing for a competitive and diverse workforce. Student growth is admittedly contingent on numerous factors, including students' own willingness and readiness to adapt to and learn from new surroundings; the training students receive throughout the advising, predeparture, on-site, and returning stages of education abroad programs; the ability of faculty and staff to challenge and mentor students; and academic and cocurricular offerings of programs. With adequate support, students' growth in a short amount of time nonetheless can be impressive—in their own words, life changing—and often more so for those who have not had previous access to international opportunities (McKeown, 2009).

Implications of Exclusion in Education Abroad

In addition to evaluating what students gain from going abroad, we might consider the risks associated with all students not having full access to such opportunities. Given what we know about the benefits of education abroad, one of the clearest hazards is that whole groups of students will have fewer opportunities to engage in the types of learning and development inherent to well-structured education abroad experiences. Some students will enhance global or intercultural competencies through coursework, on-campus activities, and interactions with students different from themselves. However, many others, to the detriment of their individual development and long-term ability to navigate interactions with differences of various kinds, will not.

At the institutional level, moreover, allowing disparities in access to education abroad opportunities to persist poses an ethical dilemma. Discussions of access often revolve around whether admissions policies are nondiscriminatory and allow recruitment of a diverse cohort of students. There is also, however, the reality of the students' experience after they arrive on campus. Depending on their financial aid package, for instance, high-need students may grapple with the basics of how to afford books, accommodations, and meal plans. On many campuses, this leads to a divide between the haves and have-nots, with wealthier students self-segregating in housing that is more expensive and taking greater advantage of activities on and off-campus (Lee, 2016; McGrath, 2013). The pressures placed on high-financial-need students put them at greater risk of attrition and simultaneously of potential delays in graduation. Because education abroad programs rarely come with a guarantee of degree progress, high-financial-need students may perceive that the risk of delayed graduation is too high to justify, despite research that demonstrates this is rarely the case (Barclay Hamir, 2011; Sutton & Rubin, 2010). Those who persevere may or may not have the mentorship necessary to take full advantage of opportunities that enhance their education, like internships, education abroad, or postgraduation fellowships, making it questionable then whether they are gaining the same benefits from their education, even when receiving a diploma in the same field as more affluent students.

Exclusion is not limited to income. Visible physical differences as well as invisible markers of difference, such as where and how students were raised, can lead to the belief that they do not belong. Even when these students meet the minimum requirements and have the necessary funding, they may not believe that activities like education abroad are important for or welcoming of them. As discussed in the upcoming chapters, a number of signals, explicit and implicit, affect the way various groups determine whether education abroad is perceived as relevant and attainable. This includes the images and text used to market programs, anecdotes from fellow students, recommendations from faculty and advisers, and policies related to financial aid, academic credit, and eligibility requirements.

Administrators of colleges and universities must juggle a number of priorities for their institutions to survive in an increasingly competitive environment. Such pressures have forced administrators to make their institutions act more like businesses by constantly monitoring the bottom line, implementing strategies that yield competitive advantages in the marketplace, and pursuing resource accumulation through capital campaigns. This is the case for public and private schools alike, including nonprofits (Bok, 2009; Slaughter & Leslie, 1997). At the same time, most institutions espouse the value of excellence in teaching and practice. To serve this objective, it is necessary to ensure that the entire student population is able and encouraged to participate in all activities, including education abroad. One could even argue that universities have an ethical obligation to do so.

Intersecting Frameworks: Inclusion and Inclusive Excellence

We have argued the need for *inclusion*, but what exactly do we mean by this term? Inclusion has been widely promulgated in higher education as a critical factor in the education of students, particularly through the construct of "inclusive excellence" proposed by the Association of American Colleges & Universities (AAC&U) (Milem, Chang, & Antonio, 2005). The AAC&U launched the Making Excellence Inclusive initiative in the early part of the twenty-first century as a new approach to address the integral nature of campus diversity and equity efforts in creating a high-quality learning environment for all students. Several of the chapters in this volume draw on inclusive excellence, which is composed of the following elements:

1. A focus on student intellectual and social development. Academically, it means offering the best possible course of study for the context in which the education is offered.
2. A purposeful development and utilization of organizational resources to enhance student learning. Organizationally, it means establishing an environment that challenges each student to achieve academically at high levels and each member of the campus to contribute to learning and knowledge development.
3. Attention to the cultural differences learners bring to the educational experience and that enhance the enterprise.
4. A welcoming community that engages all of its diversity in the service of student and organizational learning. (Milem et al., 2005, p. vi)

The emphasis on inclusive excellence addresses social inequities that play out in higher education from a strengths-based perspective as a means to enrich the educational community and learning environment. By acknowledging the benefit to the educational enterprise of cultural differences among learners, inclusive excellence reaffirms the foundational importance of diversity in higher education. The premise for this volume aligns with inclusive excellence where the discussion focuses on groups historically underserved in higher education. Because this volume also examines groups that typically are well represented on college campuses and may enjoy significant power and privilege (e.g., White males), we have adopted the broader term *inclusion* to avoid diluting the commendable intent of inclusive excellence as a guiding framework for change.

In its simplest form, *inclusion* in education abroad takes into account who does or does not participate relative to the student population at the institutional or national level. This definition creates important intersections and departures from higher education conversations about inclusion. As with higher education, studies of inclusion in education abroad identify students of color, students with disabilities, and first-generation college students among those who are underrepresented. At the same time, education abroad discussions of inclusion also encompass males and students in particular academic disciplines who are not historically underrepresented more broadly on university and college campuses yet who participate in fewer numbers in programming abroad. To denote the broader scope of inclusion in education abroad, we use the term *underrepresented* because it was originally used to indicate groups with disparate participation rates (Council on International Educational Exchange, 1991) versus other terms that may have connotations aligned with power and equity in society.

At a time when it is more common than ever before to work with diverse groups or across national borders virtually and in reality, notions of inclusion must encompass the full range of underrepresented populations in education abroad. Preparing students for life after college requires strategies to help them acquire a global perspective, which many institutions champion in mission statements and strategic plans (American Council on Education, 2012). Expanding beyond the historical junior year abroad model, new program types and locations have been developed to serve a much wider array of students. By linking such activities more closely to academic curricula and future employment prospects, faculty and staff have worked to make education abroad intentional and connected to learning in other aspects of students' academic trajectories.

Although the idea of inclusion is widely accepted in education abroad, more must be done to ensure inclusion in practice and intent. Organizations such as Diversity Abroad, The Forum on Education Abroad, Institute of International Education (IIE), and NAFSA: Association of International Educators provide leadership in national dialogue and action on this topic. Sessions on diversity and inclusion are common at national and regional conferences, yet the body of work dedicated to furthering these efforts is limited. This volume expands on the literature currently available to promote broader inclusion across a variety of student populations typically underrepresented in education abroad.

Scope of the Book

If not an exhaustive overview of all underrepresented populations, this project nonetheless is the first of its kind to bring together multiple perspectives on inclusion in education abroad in a single volume. By combining research and practice, and using sample case studies, the contributors shed light on the following groups: students of color, males, community college students, students with disabilities, first-generation college students, natural science majors, engineering majors, and undocumented students.

To determine which groups to include in this volume, we relied heavily on the IIE's Open Doors report (Farrugia & Bhandari, 2015), which traces participation in study abroad by academic level, gender, race and ethnicity, disability status, and field of study. These data demonstrate, for instance, a long-term trend of underrepresentation by males, who represented only 34.7% of participants in 2013–2014 compared to 43% of postsecondary enrollments (NCES, 2017c). Participation among other groups has increased over the past decade; African American students represented 5.6% of participants in 2013–2014 compared to 3.4% in 2002–2003, yet this is still far short of the 15% of all college students who identify as African American (Farrugia & Bhandari, 2015). The data reported annually by IIE point to some of the groups regarded for many years as underrepresented and that are included in this volume: males, students of color, students with disabilities, students at community colleges, and students with specific academic disciplines. Other chapters focus on groups commonly viewed as underrepresented for which we do not have benchmarking data at the national level, including first-generation and undocumented college students.

The broad definition of *inclusion* that underpins this book simultaneously precludes it from being a comprehensive volume. At the institutional level, underrepresentation varies based on institutional support, the student population, and available programming, among other factors. At the institutional and national levels, whom we define as *underrepresented* changes over time, as two chapters in this volume illustrate. As this book goes to press, the future of undocumented students in the United States is uncertain; soon it may simply be impossible to support education abroad participation for them without jeopardizing their ability to return to the United States. On the other end of the spectrum, the proportion of engineering majors in education abroad appears to have reached parity with their representation in higher education, demonstrating that long-term, multifaceted strategies can effect change.

Over time other groups identified in this book may also reach parity in their education abroad participation, some will make limited progress, and still others will be newly identified as underrepresented. Our intent is not to offer specific road maps to address issues of inclusion for all groups. Instead, we view this work as illuminating the challenges and detailing effective practice for a representative set of student groups historically underrepresented in education abroad. Although each group has unique characteristics influencing the likelihood that its members will go abroad, there are also commonalities that inhibit or promote participation across groups. This derives in part from the intersection of student identities—engineering is more highly populated by male students, for example—as well as our ability to identify larger systemic issues affecting a wide variety of students. Factors such as the need for academic certainty when selecting a program; the perceived relevance of education abroad to students' own goals for their education, finances, and institutional support; and inclusive marketing practices play a role for multiple underrepresented groups.

Overview of Subsequent Chapters

Subsequent chapters in this volume expand on the themes we have raised here and allow a more in-depth exploration of challenges and effective practices in mobilizing the underrepresented student populations outlined earlier. This volume is organized into three parts: Framing the Discussion, Research and Practice, and Next Steps.

In the first part, the contributors continue by framing the conversation around inclusion and education abroad. Chapter 2, "Underrepresentation in Education Abroad: A Review of Contemporary Research and Future Opportunities," by Lily Lopez-McGee, David Comp, and Eduardo Contreras, serves as a literature review for the volume. The contributors outline disparities in education abroad participation and recent efforts to study diversity in education abroad programming, with an emphasis on access and inclusion in terms of programming and student identity.

The second part of the book focuses on research and best practices in working with groups that have been traditionally underrepresented in education abroad. In Chapter 3, "Students of Color and Study Abroad: From Barriers to Results," Jinous Kasravi expands on her research exploring barriers to study abroad among students of color at the University of California, San Diego. Kasravi's work highlights the perspectives of students who do and do not go abroad and examines the experiences of those who have participated to illustrate how they have overcome obstacles. Michelle Tolan and Margaret S. McCullers then explore strategies to increase enrollment of first-generation college students in Chapter 4, "First-Generation College Students and Study Abroad: Examining the Participation Gap and Successful Strategies for Promoting Access," using case studies from the Institute for Study Abroad, Butler University and the University of Texas at Austin.

In Chapter 5, James M. Lucas investigates a group that is not often viewed as disadvantaged yet has historically been underrepresented in education abroad: males. "There and Back Again: A Study Abroad Journey With Men" summarizes research on males' perceptions of education abroad and their responses to marketing messages and then documents the application of these findings to the development, implementation, and assessment of programming for an all-male fraternity. Through their work at Mobility International USA, Ashley Holben and Monica Malhotra explore strategies to increase and enhance participation for students with disabilities in Chapter 6, "Commitments That Work: Removing Barriers for Students With Disabilities in Education Abroad." Rosalind Latiner Raby and Gary M. Rhodes similarly take a broader approach in Chapter 7, "Promoting Education Abroad Among Community College Students: Overcoming Obstacles and Developing Inclusive Practices," by outlining community college participation patterns, barriers to participation, and effective practices throughout the state of California.

The next two chapters serve as case studies illustrating effective programming for students in the science, technology, engineering, and mathematics fields. In Chapter 8, "Strategies for Mobilizing Students in the Sciences: A Case Study," Lynda Gonzales, Benjamin C. Flores, and Sarah Simmons present three approaches by the College of Natural Sciences at the University of Texas at Austin to increase and diversify participation in study abroad among natural science students. Chapter 9, "Engineers Abroad: Opportunities for Sophomores in International Education," by Amalia Pérez-Juez and Solomon R. Eisenberg, similarly details the successful efforts of Boston University to develop programs abroad that meet the needs of engineering students through careful consideration of curricular and linguistic limitations. Focusing on the case of Boston University's program in Madrid, they document strategies for combining engineering requirements with cultural and language immersion.

In the last of the chapters on underrepresented groups, Teri Albrecht, Arelis Palacios, and Daniel Siefken summarize approaches to working with undocumented students in Chapter 10, "Undocumented Students and Access to Education Abroad." Following an examination of the legal statutes at the national and state levels, they explore the ability of undocumented students to go abroad within existing legal structures. Much may change depending on the future of the Deferred Action for Childhood Arrivals and possible legislative actions. However, the contributors recognize that undocumented students are unlikely to disappear altogether on U.S. campuses, and that it is necessary for advisers to stay current on policies and be aware of the risks these students face to provide the best possible direction for those contemplating an abroad experience.

The third and last part of the book concludes by looking at future directions in research and practice. Chapter 11, "A Way Forward: Exploring Strategies at Multiple Levels," by Andrew Gordon, outlines strategies at the individual, institutional, and national levels to advocate for underrepresented students in education abroad. Gordon's analysis offers practical tips while also making the case for the need for more holistic and systemic approaches to advocacy. Last, in Chapter 12, "Expanding the Reach of Education Abroad: Recommendations for Research, Policy, and Practice," Heather Barclay Hamir and Nick Gozik summarize and discuss areas for future research and practice to foster inclusion in education abroad.

References

American Council on Education. (2012). *Mapping internationalization on U.S. campuses: 2012 edition.* Washington, DC: Author.

Barclay Hamir, H. (2011). *Go abroad and graduate on-time: Study abroad participa-tion, degree completion, and time-to-degree* (Doctoral dissertation). Available from ProQuest Dissertations and Theses database. (UMI No. 3450065)

Berrett, D. (2015, January 26). The day the purpose of college changed: After February 28, 1967, the main reason to go was to get a job. *Chronicle of Higher Education, 61*(20), 18–21.

Bok, D. (2009). *Universities in the marketplace: The commercialization of higher edu-cation.* Princeton, NJ: Princeton University Press.

Che, M., Spearman, M., & Manizade, A. (2009). Constructive disequilibrium. In R. Lewin (Ed.), *The handbook of practice and research in study abroad: Higher edu-cation and the quest for global citizenship* (pp. 99–116). New York, NY: Routledge.

Colby, S. L., & Ortman, J. M. (2014). *Projections of the size and composition of the U.S. population: 2014 to 2060. Current population reports.* Washington, DC: U.S. Census Bureau.

Council on International Educational Exchange. (1991). *Black students and overseas programs: Broadening the base of participation.* New York, NY: Author.

Crossman, J. E., & Clarke, M. (2010). International experience and graduate employability: Stakeholder perceptions on the connection. *Higher Education, 59,* 599–613.

Del Vitto, C. (2008). Cross-cultural "soft skills" and the global engineer: Corporate best practices and trainer methodologies. *Online Journal for Global Engineering Education, 3*(1). Retrieved from digitalcommons.uri.edu/ojgee/vol3/iss1/1

Downey, G. L., Lucena, J. C., Moskal, B. M., Parkhurst, R., Bigley, T., Hays, C., & Lehr, J. L. (2006). The globally competent engineer: Working effectively with people who define problems differently. *Journal of Engineering Education, 95,* 107–122.

Farrugia, C., & Bhandari, R. (2015). *Open doors 2015: Report on international educa-tional exchange.* New York, NY: Institute of International Education.

Grandin, J. M., & Hirleman, E. D. (2009). Educating engineers as global citizens: A call for action/A report of the national summit meeting on the globalization of engineering education. *Online Journal for Global Engineering Education, 4*(1). Retrieved from digitalcommons.uri.edu/ojgee/vol4/iss1/1

Harden, R. M. (2006). International medical education and future directions: A global perspective. *Academic Medicine, 81*(Suppl., 12), S22–S29.

Hyman, J. S., & Jacobs, L. (2009, August 12). Why does diversity matter at col-lege anyway? 8 ways meeting and working with different people in college can help you in the future. *U.S. News & World Report.* Retrieved from www.usnews.com/education/blogs/professors-guide/2009/08/12/why-does-diversity-matter-at-college-anyway

Kuh, G. D. (2008). *High-impact educational practices: What they are, who has access to them, and why they matter.* Washington, DC: Association of American of Colleges & Universities.

Kuh, G. D., Kinzie, J., Buckley, J. A., Bridges, B. K., & Hayek, J. C. (2006). *What matters to student success: A review of the literature.* Washington, DC: National Postsecondary Education Cooperative.

Kuh, G. D., Kinzie, J., Schuh, J. H., & Whitt, E. J. (2005). *Student success in college: Creating conditions that matter.* San Francisco, CA: Jossey-Bass.

Lee, E. M. (2016). *Class and campus life: Managing and experiencing inequality at an elite college.* Ithaca, NY: Cornell University Press.

Mayhew, M. J., Rockenback, A. N., Bowman, N. A., Seifert, T. A., Wolniak, G. C., Pascarella, E. T. & Terenzini, P. T. (2016). *How college affects students: 21st century evidence that higher education works.* San Francisco, CA: Jossey-Bass.

McGrath, M. (2013). The challenge of being poor at America's richest colleges. *Forbes.* Retrieved from www.forbes.com/sites/maggiemcgrath/2013/11/27/the-challenge-of-being-poor-at-americas-richest-colleges/#3d1ea1fe777d

McKeown, J. S. (2009). *The first time effect: The impact of study abroad on college student intellectual development.* Albany, NY: SUNY Press.

Milem, J. F., Chang, M. J., & Antonio, A. L. (2005). *Making diversity work on campus: A research-based perspective.* Washington, DC: Association of American Colleges & Universities.

National Center for Education Statistics. (2017a). *Annual earnings of young adults.* Retrieved from nces.ed.gov/programs/coe/indicator_cba.asp

National Center for Education Statistics. (2017b). *Graduation rate from first institution attended for first-time, full-time bachelor's degree-seeking students at 4-year postsecondary institutions, by race/ethnicity, time to completion, sex, control of institution, and acceptance rate: Selected cohort entry years, 1996 through 2009.* Retrieved from nces.ed.gov/programs/digest/d16/tables/dt16_326.10.asp

National Center for Education Statistics. (2017c). *Postsecondary education.* Retrieved from nces.ed.gov/programs/digest/d14/ch_3.asp

O'Rear, I., Sutton, R. C., & Rubin, D. L. (2011). *The effect of study abroad on college completion in a state university system.* Retrieved from glossari.uga.edu/wp-content/uploads/downloads/2012/01/GLOSSARI-Grad-Rate-Logistic-Regressions-040111.pdf

Pascarella, E. T. (2006). How college affects students: Ten directions for future research. *Journal of College Student Development, 47,* 508–520.

Slaughter, S., & Leslie, L. L. (1997). *Academic capitalism: Politics, policies, and the entrepreneurial university.* Baltimore, MD: Johns Hopkins University Press.

Sutton, R. C., & Rubin, D. L. (2010, May). *Documenting the academic impact of study abroad: Final report of the GLOSSARI project.* Paper presented at the annual conference of NAFSA: Association of International Educators, Kansas City, MO.

Twombly, S. B., Salisbury, M. H., Tumanut, S. D., & Klute, P. (2012). Study abroad in a new global century: Renewing the promise, refining the purpose. *ASHE Higher Education Report, 38*(4).

2

UNDERREPRESENTATION IN EDUCATION ABROAD

A Review of Contemporary Research and Future Opportunities

Lily Lopez-McGee, David Comp, and Eduardo Contreras

As participation in education abroad has expanded, the need to understand the nuances of the many types of students who participate has increased. Although education abroad has evolved over time, and the definition of *diversity* has widened, the research on certain student populations has not kept pace. Researchers are still striving to understand the differences in student expectations, experiences, and outcomes based on student identity as a result of going abroad. Despite these gaps in research and mismatch in pace, many scholars have contributed to strengthening our understanding of how diverse students come to access and ultimately experience education abroad.

This chapter begins with a brief historical review of underrepresentation in study abroad, provides a broad review of existing literature on specific student populations, and concludes with recommendations for future research. Through an overview of relevant literature, we make the case that the long-term development of research on various aspects of underrepresentation in education abroad is essential and ought to continue. The research reviewed not only documents the stagnancy or growth of diversity in education abroad but also illuminates how students of different backgrounds can learn and succeed on overseas study programs and how various institutions can foster greater access while maintaining best practices.

Underrepresentation in Education Abroad: Looking Back

The first junior year abroad program started at the University of Delaware in 1923, and the model was quickly adopted by institutions such as Smith College, Marymount College, and Rosary College (Council on International Educational Exchange [CIEE], 1988; Hoffa, 2007; University of Delaware, 2013). These early programs were largely intended for White female liberal arts students, helping to set the stage for what are still common assumptions regarding who should (and should not) go abroad.

Over time the demographics in study abroad have changed and so too have the designs and destinations of study abroad programs. The 1960s brought about significant change across the United States and higher education. President Lyndon B. Johnson signed the Immigration and Nationality Act (1965), which ended the long-standing national origin immigration quotas, and the Higher Education Act (1965), which established the Federal Work-Study Program and other federal higher education loans and grants for financially disadvantaged students. These two legislative actions had a significant impact on higher education in the United States and began to change the composition of its college students (Stallman, Woodruff, Kasravi, & Comp, 2010). As the examples in this section demonstrate, a growing body of literature emerged over the next few decades focusing on foreign language and area studies by so-called minority and community college students.

In the late 1970s, several initiatives began to focus on diversifying the U.S. education abroad student population. For instance, the President's Commission on Foreign Language and International Studies during the Carter administration recommended the establishment of a nationally competitive federal grants program for "the development or improvement of integrated International Studies Programs (ISPs) at U.S. colleges and universities, including community colleges and colleges with high minority enrollments," which "should offer vocationally as well as culturally oriented options to the students" (Ward, 1979, p. 155). Additionally, in 1979 the University of California system's Education Abroad Program (UCEAP) and Michigan State University began promoting diversity by providing scholarships to students of color for research and study. The UCEAP received a $50,000 grant from the U.S. International Communication Agency in an effort to "stimulate enrollment of and provide orientation for minority and disadvantaged students in study abroad" (Shorrock, 1979, p. 6). Of the 187 scholarships awarded, 100 were distributed to minority students (Shorrock,

1979). Returning study abroad participants were surveyed about their experiences abroad, the need for more minority student mentors, and representation of minority students in UCEAP promotional materials (G. Woodruff, personal communication, June 13, 2008).

Charles Gliozzo (1980), director of Michigan State University's Office of Overseas Study, published the first known article devoted exclusively to underrepresentation and international education. Gliozzo described a new international study and research minority scholarship established by a $15,000 grant from the U.S. International Communication Agency that awarded $350 to $500 to 6 graduate students and 18 undergraduate students for research and study activities in 12 countries, primarily to be used toward airfare. A review of the scholarship program found that overseas study enhanced the academic careers of minority students and included a number of brief student examples illustrating this impact.

During the early 1990s, education abroad professionals renewed their focus on diversity in education abroad, led in part by CIEE, NAFSA: Association of International Educators (NAFSA), and the Institute of International Education (IIE). Several landmark reports were issued by CIEE, beginning with one in 1988, which was the first major publication to recommend that

> special efforts should be made to identify and encourage both students from underrepresented academic and social groups and students with potential leadership ability to incorporate study abroad in their academic programs, and to do so in a greater range of subject areas. (CIEE, 1988, p. 5)

Following up on this article, CIEE established a Committee on Underrepresented Groups in Overseas Programs and dedicated several annual conferences to focus on diversity in education abroad. These events led to the subsequent publication by CIEE (1991) containing key papers and resources presented and discussed at the 1991 annual conference. This conference included an opening address by Spelman College President Johnnetta B. Cole (1991), who introduced the concept of the four Fs, the four significant barriers faced by African American students: faculty, finances, family, and fears.

Although IIE reported fields of overseas study among U.S. participants from the inception of its annual Open Doors report in 1954, race and ethnicity data were included for the first time in 1994–1995 (Bu, 2003; IIE, 2005), and data on students with disabilities were added in 2006–2007 (IIE, 2015a). Such additions to Open Doors enhanced the literature on diverse groups of U.S. students studying abroad by providing an annual snapshot of the current state of affairs in the field and, more important, longitudinal data to inform future research and initiatives in the field.

These early efforts have led to numerous initiatives and reports over the years that highlight the need to diversify the U.S. study abroad student profile and make recommendations for this to happen. Significant reports include those from the Commission on the Abraham Lincoln Study Abroad Fellowship Program (2005); Herrin, Dadzie, and MacDonald (2007); the American Institute for Foreign Study (2010); and IIE (2014b). To be sure, there have been many other efforts focusing on diversifying the study abroad student profile, and these efforts have contributed greatly to the literature and research base in the field.

Student Identities

Understanding student identity is one of the most important and complex aspects of research in education abroad today. Even as data have demonstrated that multiple student populations are considerably underrepresented, much of the scholarship on diversity in education abroad programming largely examines participation rates and barriers to accessing education abroad based on gender, major, and ethnic or racial background (Norfles, 2003; Obst, Bhandari, & Witherell, 2007; Salisbury, Paulsen, & Pascarella, 2011). Fewer studies have explored the differences in student expectations, experiences, and outcomes based on student identity as a result of going abroad (Hospod, 2016). Consequently, the research on underrepresented students in education abroad is relatively limited in scope even as the publications centered on this topic have increased over the past decade.

The scholarship that has sought to examine how student identity intersects with the study abroad experience generally falls into three categories: reports on participation rates of specific populations (Hembroff & Rusz, 1993; IIE, 2015b; Obst et al., 2007; Simon & Ainsworth, 2012); assessments of the accessibility of study abroad to certain groups, including the barriers to and decision-making process in going abroad (Kasravi, 2009; McKinley, 2014; Salisbury, Paulsen, & Pascarella, 2010; Salisbury, Umbach, Paulsen, & Pascarella, 2009; Stroud, 2010); and examinations of the experiences of diverse students throughout the process of studying abroad (Penn & Tanner, 2009; Sweeney, 2014; Williams, 2007; Willis, 2015). These areas of inquiry have practical implications for how students are recruited and supported in education abroad programming and provide a window into the areas of research that require more attention.

It has been demonstrated that students enter college with nearly equal interest in pursuing international opportunities, but acting on those interests is not the same across student populations (Kim & Goldstein, 2005; Luo & Jamieson-Drake, 2014; Markow & Pieters, 2010; Stroud, 2010). In exploring the motivating factors for study abroad based on race and ethnicity, Salisbury and colleagues (2011) found that White students with higher family incomes have higher odds of intending to study abroad than other student populations; arguments that study abroad would increase intercultural development are generally not sufficient in persuading underrepresented students to study abroad; and Asian American and Hispanic students are more likely to study abroad if they received a grant, whereas White students are less likely to do so. Finances are reported across the board as a challenge for students interested in going abroad; however, other factors have been shown to affect whether students consider an education abroad experience viable, including their major (e.g., accessibility of curriculum, sequential coursework), cultural and social capital (e.g., knowledge of study abroad process), interest in learning more about other cultures, and having traveled or knowing people who have traveled abroad (Anderson, 2007; Brux & Fry, 2010; Bryant & Soria, 2015; Kasravi, 2009; Klahr, 1998; McKinley, 2014; Norfles, 2003; Simon & Ainsworth, 2012).

Next we provide a few examples of underrepresented student identities in education abroad. Although this is not an exhaustive list by any means, these samples nonetheless demonstrate some of the common themes that run throughout these identity groups, as well as some of the key nuances that help to differentiate them.

Race and Ethnicity

Race and ethnicity have consistently been the subject of U.S. higher education scholarship, in part as a result of the reliable availability of data and salience to the U.S. higher education experience. Moreover, the U.S.'s contentious and significant history of systematic discrimination and marginalization of racial and ethnic minority groups, which persists today and is the subject of many scholars' writings, continues to influence the importance of addressing gaps in education access and opportunity. Most research on student identity, however, does not disaggregate underrepresented populations to explore the experiences of students with intersecting identities. For example, where much work has focused on detailing Black student experiences abroad (e.g., Bruce, 2012; Jackson, 2006; Morgan, Mwegelo, & Turner, 2002; Trimble, 2016; Willis, 2015), less is known about the intragroup differences of Black students based on gender, socioeconomic status, major, or study abroad program type, among other areas. Data from IIE (2015d) show that study abroad participation rates of students from racial and ethnic minority groups have steadily increased over the past two decades. Overall participation of racial and ethnic minority students in 2003–2004 was 16% and increased to 26% in 2013–2014 (IIE, 2015d). Table 2.1 shows the past 10 years of student participation by race and ethnicity.

TABLE 2.1

Study Abroad Participation by Race and Ethnicity From IIEE Open Doors Report, 2003–2014

Race/Ethnicity	2003/ 2004	2004/ 2005	2005/ 2006	2006/ 2007	2007/ 2008	2008/ 2009	2009/ 2010	2010/ 2011	2011/ 2012	2012/ 2013	2013/ 2014
White	83.7%	83.0%	83.0%	81.9%	81.8%	80.5%	78.7%	77.8%	76.4%	76.3%	74.3%
Hispanic or Latino(a)	5.0%	5.6%	5.4%	6.0%	5.9%	6.0%	6.4%	6.9%	7.6%	7.6%	8.3%
Asian, Native Hawaiian, or Other Pacific Islander	6.1%	6.3%	6.3%	6.7%	6.6%	7.3%	7.9%	7.9%	7.7%	7.3%	7.7%
Black or African American	3.4%	3.5%	3.5%	3.8%	4.0%	4.2%	4.7%	4.8%	5.3%	5.3%	5.6%
Multiracial	1.3%	1.2%	1.2%	1.2%	1.2%	1.6%	1.9%	2.1%	2.5%	3.0%	3.6%
American Indian or Alaska Native	0.5%	0.4%	0.6%	0.5%	0.5%	0.5%	0.5%	0.5%	0.5%	0.5%	0.5%

Source. From Profile of U.S. Study Abroad Students, 2004/05–2013/14, by Institute of International Education, 2015d, www.iie.org/opendoors

Hispanic and Latino student participation has increased in the past 10 years, from 5.6% in 2004–2005 to 8.3% in 2013–2014 (IIE, 2015d), and is now the highest among underrepresented students in education abroad. Multiracial students have seen the fastest growth in the past 10 years (from 1.3% to 3.6%), and Black students' participation has increased steadily (from 3.4% to 5.6%). Although Asian American students have the second highest participation rate among minority students, the growth of participation has been modest (6.1% to 7.7%). Native American students' participation has notably remained nearly identical for the past decade even as general participation in study abroad has grown .5% (IIE, 2015d). Annual changes are important to note as well, as there were years where some groups saw no growth, and other years where growth was rapid.

For racial and ethnic minority students, there are persistent challenges to accessing international opportunities that often mirror the concerns other populations (e.g., first-generation college, high financial need) face in regard to going abroad. In line with Cole's (1991) four *F*s, the cost and perceived cost of going abroad have, for some time, been the top concern with pursuing education abroad opportunities (e.g., Brux & Fry, 2010; CIEE, 1991; Hembroff & Rusz, 1993). As Salisbury and colleagues (2011) found, for example, Latino students who received federal aid were much more likely to go abroad than their Latino peers who did not receive aid. Similarly, Black and Latino students may have less information about the study abroad process and the true costs of going abroad, perpetuating the perception that study abroad is prohibitively expensive and not worth considering (Hembroff & Rusz, 1993; Hospod, 2016; Norfles, 2003; Salisbury et al., 2011).

Fear of racial discrimination abroad, lack of family support or understanding of what the potential benefits of study abroad are or what it entails, and faculty and staff's lack of support or failure to discuss international opportunities are other aspects that influence whether racially and ethnically diverse students opt to go abroad (Ganz, 1991; Gutierrez, 2015; Hembroff & Rusz, 1993; Kasravi, 2009; Norfles, 2003). In some studies, students' cultural and social capital (i.e., their prior experience with overseas travel and study, networks of friends and family members who have traveled overseas, and exposure to international issues and cultures) have been found to be mismatched with the social and cultural capital needed to gain access to education abroad opportunities (Lu, Reddick, Dean, & Pecero, 2015; Salisbury et al., 2011; Simon & Ainsworth, 2012). These students often enter college with different social networks, experiences with higher education structures, and community support systems that may act as benign or counterfactors in engaging in international programming (Bryant & Soria, 2015; Luo & Jamieson-Drake, 2014; Yosso, 2005). Furthermore, marketing and recruitment information and resources may be perpetuating stereotypes about who goes abroad and the kind of experiences one can expect while abroad (Bishop, 2013). The messages about study abroad, then, may compel underrepresented students to believe that such opportunities are not for them (Bishop, 2013; Bryant & Soria, 2015). These findings suggest that underrepresented students make decisions about going abroad differently from their peers.

Challenges aside, study abroad has been shown to lead to compelling outcomes for racially and ethnically diverse students. Black, Latino, and Asian American students have been shown to have generally positive experiences abroad and have expressed a perceived growth in their social and cultural capital (Guerrero, 2006; Jackson, 2006; Ng, 2004; Sweeney, 2014; Wick, 2011; Willis, 2015). Such experiences also help these students develop a greater openness to diversity and a heightened awareness of ethnic, racial, and U.S. identity (Bruce, 2012; CIEE, 1991; Day-Vines, Barker, & Exum, 1998; Harden, 2007; Lu et al., 2015; Morgan et al., 2002; Trimble, 2016). Beyond immediate outcomes from going abroad, students may be more likely to persist and graduate from college in a timely manner than those who remain at home (Barclay Hamir, 2011; O'Rear, Sutton, & Rubin, 2011; Sutton & Rubin, 2004; Sutton & Rubin, 2010). A handful of institutional and statewide studies have demonstrated that students who go abroad may be more inclined to complete their university degree and complete it more quickly than those who do not, and it is important to note that the effects may be more significant for racial and ethnic minority and first-generation college students.

Socioeconomic and First-Generation Status

National data on study abroad participation rates for low-income students and students who are the first in their family to go to college (first-generation) are currently not available. Nonetheless, there are efforts at the institutional level to collect, analyze, and better understand the needs of first-generation students in study abroad (Andriano, 2011; Callihan, Francis, Lochner, & Tolan, 2016). IIE (2015b) provides data on funding sources for education abroad, although information about student household income or Pell Grant eligibility, a proxy for low-income status, is available only at the institutional level. The exception to this are data collected for students who receive Benjamin A. Gilman International Scholarship Program grants, and who must be Pell Grant eligible (IIE, 2015c). The program awarded 2,763 scholarships in 2013–2014, representing about 1% of all students who went abroad; 9,164 applications were received, suggesting there could be as much as 30% of study abroad students who are Pell Grant eligible (IIE, 2015c). In higher education generally, about one-third (36%) of all U.S. undergraduate students receive Pell Grant funding (College Board, 2013), and the estimated percentage of first-generation college students enrolled in higher education is as high as 50%, with the National Center for Education Statistics reporting that 30% of incoming freshmen identify as first-generation (First Generation Foundation, 2013; U.S. Department of Education, 2013).

As mentioned earlier, low-income students often face challenges in accessing education similar to those of racial and ethnic minority students. Although the actual and perceived costs of study abroad are viewed as barriers by many student populations, students with high financial need report that finances are a consistent concern in assessing study abroad opportunities (Hospod, 2016; Thompson-Jones, 2012; Williams, 2007). Low-income students are more likely to report having to work in addition to going to school and often must consider the loss of potential income as a result of not working while abroad (Hembroff & Rusz, 1993; Simon & Ainsworth, 2012). Although low-income and first-generation college students generally arrive at college with close family ties and work experience (Bui, 2002; Phinney, Dennis, & Chuateco, 2005), these attributes may also act as counterfactors to going abroad as students feel pressure from family obligations and work to forgo studying abroad (Andriano, 2011; Hembroff & Rusz, 1993; McKinley, 2014; Ng, 2004).

Students With Disabilities

The information related to participation rates for students with disabilities in education abroad has improved significantly over the past two decades since data collection began through IIE (2015a) in 2006–2007; however, most institutions that respond to the survey still do not report such data (IIE, 2015a; Malmgren, 2016; Mobility International USA, 2015; Soneson & Fisher, 2011). Study abroad participants reporting a disability increased from 2.6% in 2007 to 5% in 2012, with the largest proportion of students reporting a learning disability (43.4%) or mental health disability (28%; IIE, 2015a). Although participation seems to have increased, many scholars point to underreporting as a concern for students going abroad, suggesting that more students with disabilities are likely participating than are reflected in the data. As Malmgren (2016) notes, underreporting could "indicate there is too little collaboration among faculty, study abroad, and disability services professionals to encourage participation and enable students to disclose and plan for accommodation abroad" (p. 261).

Beyond participation rates, students with disabilities face multiple challenges to accessing education abroad, including insufficient knowledge about available programs, lack of assistive devices and services, and financial barriers (Hameister, Matthews, Hosley, & Groff, 1999; Matthews, Hameister, &

Hosley, 1998). Students report challenges to requesting appropriate accommodations either as a result of a reluctance to ask or concern that the same level of accommodations in the United States may not be available abroad (Hameister et al., 1999; Soneson, 2009). Other students have expressed concern for how they will be perceived overseas and report having little support or encouragement from family, faculty, and staff for going abroad (Matthews et al., 1998; Soneson & Fisher, 2011).

Many students with disabilities report a preference for participating in programs that can accommodate their needs rather than programs that are designed specifically for students with disabilities (Mobility International USA, 2015). To this end, study abroad practitioners have been working toward developing more inclusive curricula to ensure that programs are accessible to a wider range of students (Malmgren, 2016; Soneson & Fisher, 2011). Soneson and Cordano (2009) have recommended four categories of functional differences in ability as a way to better assess the programmatic considerations that must be considered for students with disabilities: physical, sensory, cognitive, and emotional or behavioral. By working closely with other campus units, the study abroad provider, and faculty on the ground, it is argued that students with disabilities can thrive abroad. Additional practitioner guides also have been created to provide practical guidance on advising and accommodating students with disabilities and methods to evaluate programs and feasible accommodations such as NAFSA's guide (Soneson, 2009) and the University of Minnesota's online guide (Learning Abroad Center, 2015).

Gender

In 2013–2014, 65.3% of study abroad participants were women (IIE, 2015b), demonstrating a long-held historical pattern toward more females going abroad dating from the early roots of U.S. education abroad programming in the 1920s (Walton, 2010). Many have consequently asked how more males can be encouraged to go abroad. The research on gender representation in study abroad largely reflects differences between women and men (Bryant & Soria, 2015; Talburt & Stewart, 1999; Twombly, 1995). Only in recent years has the national discourse on gender included transgender and genderqueer identities (Diversity Abroad Network, n.d.; NAFSA Rainbow Special Interest Group, n.d.). For now, data on gender for study abroad are available only on the participation of women and men.

In terms of access, conversations often explore the different decision-making processes of women and men when considering options for study abroad (Bryant & Soria, 2015; Lucas, 2009; Obst et al., 2007; Salisbury et al., 2011; Stroud, 2010). It has been found, for example, that women may be influenced by a wider variety of factors, including authority figures, peer interactions, decisions on a major, and whether courses fit into their larger academic plans. Men, however, may take into account fewer considerations and may be most heavily influenced by their peers (Bryant & Soria, 2015; Schmidt, 2009). Additionally, women may tend to start the study abroad decision-making process earlier by meeting with academic advisers, faculty, and staff who can assist them in identifying programs that fit with their academic plans (Lucas, 2009, 2013).

Women and men may also learn differently while abroad. A large-scale study facilitated by Michael Vande Berg, then at Georgetown University, and colleagues from partner institutions found that women demonstrate greater and faster growth in terms of intercultural competence (Vande Berg, Connor-Linton, & Paige, 2009), as measured by the Intercultural Development Inventory (Hammer & Bennett, 2003), and greater foreign language oral proficiency gains according to the Simulated Oral Proficiency Interview (Stansfield, 1996). Male and female students demonstrated, on average, more gains in both areas compared to students who did not study abroad (Vande Berg et al., 2009), but the study illustrates that there is a gap in what is known about what and how female and male students learn while abroad.

Disciplines and Majors

Although a student's identity may not be defined by a major or discipline, these aspects of a student's academic career can serve as a significant factor in the decision to study abroad. In the past decade the curricula available for students interested in studying abroad have rapidly expanded (IIE, 2015b). The expansion of institutional exchanges, third-party provider programs, and faculty-led programs has made study abroad more accessible to students from diverse disciplines (Rodman & Merrill, 2010). Still, there are disciplines that remain underrepresented in education abroad, particularly those in fields with more rigid curricula or emphasis on domestic credentials such as education, public health, and nursing. Although all underrepresented disciplines are relevant to the discussion of accessibility in education abroad, emphasis in recent years has centered on the underrepresentation of science, technology, engineering, and math (STEM) majors (Leggett, 2011; Oguntoyinbo, 2015). STEM student participation has grown in recent years and in the 2014–2015 academic year approached parity with the number of students majoring in STEM at U.S. institutions (Chen, 2013; IIE, 2015b; Oguntoyinbo, 2015). The increase in STEM student participation provides a notable case of how curriculum integration, program design, a wider variation of program options, and expanded campus engagement can lead to parity in campus enrollment and study abroad participation rates (Leggett, 2011; Luo & Jamieson-Drake, 2014; McKinley, 2014; Oguntoyinbo, 2015).

Although representation of STEM majors has improved significantly over the past decade, the barriers to participation are still relatively similar to those of other underrepresented disciplines. Students from underrepresented disciplines receive different and often conflicting messages about going abroad, and decisions for going abroad are multifaceted (Klahr, 1998; Luo & Jamieson-Drake, 2014; McKinley, 2014; Salisbury et al., 2010). Faculty encouragement, the availability of coursework abroad in English, and the sequencing of coursework at the home institution are frequently cited barriers to study abroad for students from underserved majors (Klahr, 1998; Luo & Jamieson-Drake, 2014; McKinley, 2014; Salisbury et al., 2010). Savicki and Brewer (2015) and Brewer and Cunningham (2010) provide additional insight into the existing literature on access based on discipline in study abroad.

Institutional Types

Disparities in participation among different institutional types underpins any discussion of diverse groups in education abroad. As Green, Luu, and Burris (2008) reported, 91% of American campuses in 2006 provided some form of study abroad for their undergraduates. It can be assumed that the percentage has continued to increase since then. Despite this success, participation in education abroad is still lower at certain types of institutions, including community colleges and minority-serving institutions (MSI).

Community colleges play a major role in supporting postsecondary education for a large number of U.S. undergraduates; consequently, it follows that these institutions should have great potential to provide access to study abroad to a wide array of students. According to the American Association of Community Colleges (2016), in the fall of 2014, 7.3 million students enrolled for credit at community colleges in the United States, which represents 45% of the total number of U.S. undergraduates. Of these 7.3 million students, 49% were White; 22% Hispanic; 14% Black; 6% Asian American or Pacific Islander; 1% Native American; 3% two or more races; 4% other or unknown, and 1% nonresident alien (American Association of Community Colleges, 2016). In terms of study abroad, IIE (2015b) reported that of the 304,467 total students who studied abroad in 2013–2014, only 6,404 (2%) were from associate-degree-granting colleges or community colleges.

Community colleges have developed education abroad options considerably over the second half of the twentieth century, and the number of students participating has increased steadily, yet the extent to which community colleges provide access to study abroad remains limited by the many challenges unique to these institutions. Rosalind Latiner Raby (2008) reports that community colleges face the following major barriers to expanding international education: "serving the diverse community college student body; institutional constraints; and the need for further professionalization" (p. 18). Students often face work and family obligations or lack of funding. From an institutional standpoint, education abroad suffers from a lack of stakeholder support (e.g., from upper administration), minimal funding, limited staffing, and a peripheral status (e.g., education abroad is not considered a core mission of community colleges). Finally, many community colleges lack the professionalization on campus to serve various aspects of education abroad such as risk management, legal issues, ethics, evaluation, and predeparture and reentry programming. For education abroad to be bolstered on community college campuses, Raby emphasizes the need for study abroad to be established as an "integral component of the mission of each institution" (p. 24) by emphasizing the benefits of international education to gain stakeholder acceptance from various campus constituents.

MSIs represent another type of postsecondary institution that has served to democratize U.S. higher education since their inception. Although many of the institutions that now fall under this distinction existed since the nineteenth century, the MSI designation emerged from the Higher Education Act of 1965 and today includes historically Black colleges and universities, Hispanic-serving institutions, tribal colleges and universities, Alaska Native– or Native Hawaiian–serving institutions, predominantly Black institutions, Asian American and Native American Pacific Islander–serving institutions, and Native American–serving nontribal institutions (U.S. Department of Education, n.d.). The Department of Education determines an institution's particular status based on whether enrollments of specific student populations reach certain percentages. By definition, *MSIs* serve the needs of specific groups of students, defined primarily by race and ethnicity, who are underrepresented in American higher education on the whole. Moreover, they serve the needs of many low-income students (Gasman & Conrad, 2013).

MSIs have received increasing attention for their role in fostering access to study abroad. For example, in 2014, in conjunction with IIE's (2014a) Generation Study Abroad Initiative, more than 20 MSIs joined the pledge to increase the total number of students studying abroad to 600,000 by 2020. Additionally, in 2015 California State University, Fullerton, an HSI and an Asian American and Native American Pacific Islander–serving institution, launched a six-week program in Mexico intended for low-income and first-generation students with the explicit intention of exposing underrepresented students to another country (Zalaznick, 2016). MSIs have been providing an important pipeline to study abroad for students of color. Study abroad providers have also worked with MSIs in recent years to promote inclusive excellence for all students. The Institute for the International Education of Students (IES Abroad) formed a partnership with Diversity Abroad in 2016 to introduce the inaugural MSI Global Education Summit with more than 70 administrators and faculty from 30 MSIs to discuss ways to break down barriers for students at these institutions (IES Abroad, 2016). In March 2016, CIEE (2016) collaborated with the University of Pennsylvania's Graduate School of Education's Center for MSIs to provide workshops, training, and scholarships for MSI faculty and students. As a result of this partnership, a research team produced a report outlining the current landscape of study abroad for MSIs, the challenges to inclusive excellence for these institutions, broad strategies for moving forward, and the ways MSIs already contribute to the current diversification of study abroad (Esmieu et al., 2016).

Research on Retention, Persistence, High-Impact Learning, and Equity in Learning

Some assume that education abroad is a luxury, resulting in the question of whether it is necessary to ensure that the previously mentioned groups, as well as others underrepresented in education abroad, really do need to be accommodated in education abroad programming. The scholarship demonstrates that, in fact, students from a wide variety of backgrounds can gain much by an overseas experience, making it clear that education abroad does need to be open to all students, regardless of background or identity.

As mentioned at the beginning of this chapter, research on education abroad has been descriptive (e.g., documenting slow demographic change) and illuminating (e.g., highlighting the intersection of student identity and international education). Research reveals how education abroad activities may have broader impacts in higher education. A growing body of literature has concentrated on the intersection of study abroad and retention, persistence, high-impact programming, and equity in learning. Although not all of this literature focuses exclusively on diversity or access, the implications of this research can be considered in light of the long-term goal of expanding access to various types of students. In a broad sense, Kuh (2008) has argued that study abroad programs augment students' learning through engagement with cultures and worldviews different from their own. More specifically, studies on pathways to graduation and retention (Barclay Hamir, 2011; Malmgren & Galvin, 2009; Sutton & Rubin, 2004) have found positive correlations with studying abroad and academic performance and graduation. Sutton and Rubin have reported, for example, that study abroad is correlated with improved academic performance after returning and higher graduation rates. In their study of graduation rates at the University of Minnesota Twin Cities, Malmgren and Galvin discovered that study abroad did not negatively affect graduation rates for students, and participation in study abroad was correlated with higher graduation rates for at-risk undergraduates and students of color. Barclay Hamir's research similarly found that students who studied abroad with The University of Texas at Austin graduated at higher rates than applicants and nonparticipants. These studies reveal intriguing correlations among studying abroad, stronger academic performance, and graduation rates. Although such correlations are not tantamount to causation, they have prompted some researchers and professionals to advocate for education abroad as a retention strategy for underrepresented student groups (Metzger, 2006). The findings are consistent with other research that shows that students on the whole are more engaged with their academic work after their study abroad experiences (Dolby, 2007; Hadis, 2005).

For several decades, researchers have also examined the implications of study abroad on students' personal and intercultural development (Anderson, Lawton, Rexeisen, & Hubbard, 2006; Bennett, 2010; Clarke, Flaherty, Wright, & McMillen, 2009; Landis, Bennett, & Bennett, 2004; Vande Berg, Paige, & Lou, 2012). Although beneficial, most of the scholarship has focused specifically on gender differences (Vande Berg et al., 2009) and not done nearly as much to help our understanding of how students who identify with a specific race, ethnicity, sexual orientation, or socioeconomic class undergo personal or intercultural growth while abroad.

In this context it is important to recognize that higher education in the United States is idiosyncratic, and institutions have varying missions, policies, demographics, and profiles. As a result, it is impossible to engage in research that is all encompassing or will affect colleges and universities equally. Recognizing such differences, Picard, Bernardino, and Ehigiator (2009) surveyed the landscape of study abroad to find case studies that demonstrate success in meeting the needs of underrepresented students. This work has allowed us to identify a few factors that have enabled success on campuses, including defining the profile of underrepresented students on campus and identifying their personal and academic needs, pinpointing obstacles for these students in going abroad, locating the necessary financial and human institutional resources, and developing a comprehensive strategy for meeting students' needs (Picard et al., 2009).

Beyond this, it is important to consider that students may have multiple motivations for studying abroad and that there is no one single solution for an entire group of students. For example, developing programs for students who seek to study abroad in destinations related to their ancestry, also known as *heritage seekers*, may be a good way to reach some underrepresented students, yet others within the same group may not share this interest or may face challenges that are not addressed alone by the creation of a program. Comp (2008) notes that heritage seekers do not always have their parents' support, nor do they experience seamless integration into the host nation. In general, program directors who seek to expand access must consider how the costs, educational outcomes, and support structures (predeparture, while abroad, and on return) meet the varied needs of all students.

Summary and Recommendations for Future Research

Research shows gradual, long-term growth in study abroad with an increasing number of program types and greater access for students of different backgrounds. Most of this innovation has taken place in the past 25 to 30 years, with strategies that include better and more inclusive communication about study abroad, collaborative partnerships with campus units and offices that work with diverse student populations, more inclusive and accessible programming, and better data collection to draw a more representative picture of the students who go abroad. There has been a trend in developing more inclusive programming and training programs for faculty and staff to better serve the students who are going abroad. As the narrative of study abroad has largely been dominated by White middle- or upper-class constituents, the support structures for students while abroad may need to be reconsidered as more diverse students go abroad. Several efforts by national organizations have been launched to fill the need for practical guidance on serving diverse student populations including the Diversity Abroad Network's (n.d.) repository of tools and resources available online and in person and NAFSA's (n.d.) Diversity and Inclusion in Education Abroad Subcommittee.

This broad overview of the literature suggests that there are several areas of opportunity for future research and scholarship centered on access to international opportunities and the experiences of diverse and underrepresented students in education abroad. It is clear there is a need for better and more robust institutional- and national-level data that reflect the increasingly diverse student populations participating in international programming. It is easier to evaluate student and programmatic needs when the basic information of who the students are, where they go, and the type of programs they are participating in is readily available. Additionally, more work needs to include the systematic investigation of the differences in student experiences while abroad based on student identity. As noted earlier, much of the research and resources available on this subject are largely focused on students' intents and decisions to go abroad. This work has given the field a foundational understanding of what prevents and encourages students from going abroad; now attention should be paid to the unique experiences students have while abroad. In a similar vein, future scholarship should examine differences in learning outcomes based on student demographics that is, whether students from certain demographic populations have different outcomes in intercultural competencies, language acquisition, and other competencies after going abroad. It is also important to consider, per the recommendation of Engle and Engle (2003), the learning outcomes associated with program type and student identity. The demand for international opportunities is only expected to increase, and it is imperative for the research to keep pace with this growth.

References

American Association of Community Colleges. (2016). *2016 fact sheet.* Retrieved from www.aacc.nche.edu/AboutCC/Documents/AACCFactSheetsR2.pdf

American Institute for Foreign Study. (2010). *Diversity in international education hands-on workshop: Summary report.* Washington, DC: Author.

Anderson, B. D. (2007). *Students in a global village: The nexus of choice, expectation, and experience in study abroad* (Doctoral dissertation). Available from ProQuest Dissertations and Theses database. (UMI No. 3274739)

Anderson, P. H., Lawton, L., Rexeisen, R. J., & Hubbard, A. C. (2006). Short-term study abroad and intercultural sensitivity: A pilot study. *International Journal of Intercultural Relations, 30,* 457–469. doi:10.1016/j.ijintrel.2005.10.004

Andriano, B. R. (2011). *Study abroad participation and engagement practices of first-generation undergraduate students* (Doctoral dissertation). Available from ProQuest Dissertations and Theses database. (UMI No. 3417953)

Barclay Hamir, H. (2011). *Go abroad and graduate on-time: Study abroad participation, degree completion, and time-to-degree* (Doctoral dissertation). Available from ProQuest Dissertations and Theses database. (UMI No. 3450065)

Bennett, M. J. (2010). A short conceptual history of intercultural learning. In W. W. Hoffa & S. C. DePaul (Eds.), *A history of U.S. study abroad: 1965–present* (pp. 419–450). Carlisle, PA: Frontiers Books.

Bishop, S. C. (2013). The rhetoric of study abroad perpetuating expectations and results through technological enframing. *Journal of Studies in International Education, 17,* 398–413. doi:10.1177/1028315312472983

Brewer, E., & Cunningham, K. (Eds.) (2010). *Integrating study abroad into the curriculum: Theory and practice across the discipline.* Sterling, VA: Stylus.

Bruce, A. I. (2012). *Beyond the Black horizon: Perspectives of African American collegians who studied abroad* (Doctoral dissertation). Available from ProQuest Dissertations and Theses database. (UMI No. 3505969)

Brux, J. M., & Fry, B. (2010). Multicultural students in study abroad: Their interests, their issues, and their constraints. *Journal of Studies in International Education, 14,* 508–527. doi:10.1177/1028315309342486

Bryant, K. M., & Soria, K. M. (2015). College students' sexual orientation, gender identity, and participation in study abroad. *Frontiers, 25*, 91–106.

Bu, L. (2003). *Making the world like us: Education, cultural expansion, and the American century. Perspectives on the twentieth century.* Westport, CT: Praeger.

Bui, K. V. T. (2002). First-generation college students at a four-year university: Background characteristics, and reasons for pursuing higher education, and first-year experiences. *College Student Journal, 36*(1), 3–12.

Callihan, L., Francis, J., Lochner, S., & Tolan, M. (2016). *Family outreach of first generation college students: Best practices.* Retrieved from www.diversitynetwork .org/blogpost/1437725/265318/Family-Outreach-of-First-Generation-College-Students-Best-Practices

Chen, X. (2013). *STEM attrition: College students' paths into and out of STEM fields.* Washington, DC: National Center for Education Statistics.

Clarke, I., Flaherty, T. B., Wright, N. D., & McMillen, R. D. (2009). Student intercultural proficiency from study abroad programs. *Journal of Marketing Education, 31*, 173–181. doi:10.1177/0273475309335583

Cole, J. B. (1991). Black students and overseas programs: Broadening the base of participation. *Introduction to the papers and speeches presented at the CIEE.* Retrieved from ERIC database. (ED340323)

College Board. (2013). *Trends in student aid 2013.* Retrieved from trends .collegeboard.org/sites/default/files/student-aid-2013-full-report.pdf

Commission on the Abraham Lincoln Study Abroad Fellowship Program. (2005). *Global competence & national needs: One million Americans studying abroad.* Washington, DC: Author.

Comp, D. (2008). US heritage-seeking students discover minority communities in Western Europe. *Journal of Studies in International Education, 12*, 29–37. doi: 10.1177/1028315307299417

Council on International Educational Exchange. (1988). *Educating for global competence: The report of the Advisory Council for International Educational Exchange.* New York, NY: Author.

Council on International Educational Exchange. (1991). *Black students and overseas programs: Broadening the base of participation.* New York, NY: Author.

Council on International Educational Exchange. (2016). *CIEE and Penn Center for Minority Serving Institutions announce three-year partnership to expand study abroad for students of color.* Retrieved from news.ciee.org/2016/04/ciee-and-penn-center-for-minority-serving-institutions-announce-100000-scholarship-to-expand-global-.html

Day-Vines, N., Barker, J. M., & Exum, H. A. (1998). Impact of diasporic travel on ethnic identity development of African American college students. *College Student Journal, 32*, 463–471. Retrieved from connection.ebscohost.com/c/articles/1209045/impact-diasporic-travel-ethnic-identity-development-african-american-college-students

Diversity Abroad Network. (n.d.). *Diversity & Inclusion Resource Center.* Retrieved from www.diversitynetwork.org/page/resourcecenter

Dolby, N. (2007). Reflections on nation: American undergraduates and education abroad. *Journal of Studies in International Education, 11*, 141–156. doi:10.1177/1028315306291944

Engle, L., & Engle, J. (2003). Study abroad levels: Toward a classification of program types. *Frontiers, 9*, 1–20.

Esmieu, P., Mullen, S., Samayoa, A. C., Gasman, M., Perkins, C., Wolff, M., & Beazley, M. (2016). *Increasing diversity abroad: Expanding opportunities for students at minority serving institutions.* Retrieved from www.ciee.org/downloads/MSI_Study_Report.pdf

First Generation Foundation. (2013). *Supporting first generation college students.* Retrieved from www.firstgenerationfoundation.org

Ganz, M. (1991). The Spelman experience: Encouraging and supporting minority students abroad. In Council on International Exchange (Ed.), *Black students and overseas programs: Broadening the base of participation* (pp. 29–34). New York, NY: Author.

Gasman, M., & Conrad, C. F. (2013). *Educating all students: Minority serving institutions.* Retrieved from www.gse.upenn.edu/pdf/cmsi/msis_educating_all_students.pdf

Gliozzo, C. (1980). The international education of minority students. *Minority Education, 2*(5), 6–7.

Green, M., Luu, D. T., & Burris, B. (2008). *Mapping internationalization on US campuses: 2008 Edition.* Washington, DC: American Council on Education.

Guerrero, E. (2006). *The road less traveled: Latino students and the impact of studying abroad* (Doctoral dissertation). Available from ProQuest Dissertations and Theses database. (UMI No. 3249418)

Gutierrez, D. (2015). *Latino male college students in study abroad programs: The role of identity and culture, family, and faculty in making the decision to attend* (Doctoral dissertation). Available from ProQuest Dissertations and Theses database. (UMI No. 10001641)

Hadis, B. (2005). Gauging the impact of study abroad: How to overcome the limitations of a single-cell design. *Assessment & Evaluation in Higher Education, 30*(1), 3–19.

Hameister, B., Matthews, P., Hosley, N., & Groff, M. (1999). College students with disabilities and study abroad: Implications for international education staff. *Frontiers, 5*, 81–100.

Hammer, M. R., & Bennett, M. J. (2003). Measuring intercultural sensitivity: The Intercultural Development Inventory. *International Journal of Intercultural Relations, 27*, 421–443.

Harden, R. (2007). *Identities in motion: An autoethnography of an African American woman's journey to Burkina Faso, Benin, and Ghana* (Doctoral dissertation). Retrieved from etd.ohiolink.edu

Hembroff, L. A., & Rusz, D. L. (1993). *Minorities and overseas studies programs: Correlates of differential participation* (Occasional Papers on International Educational Exchange: Research Series 30). New York, NY: Council on International Educational Exchange.

Herrin, C. A., Dadzie, S., & MacDonald, S. A. (Eds.). (2007). *The proceedings for the colloquium on diversity in education abroad: How to change the picture.* Washington, DC: Academy for Educational Development, Center for Academic Partnerships.

Higher Education Opportunity Act of 1965, 3078 U.S.C. §§ 110-315 (2008).

Hoffa, W. W. (2007). *A history of US study abroad: Beginnings to 1965.* Carlisle, PA: Frontiers Books.

Hospod, T. J. (2016). *World class(ed) talk: The reflective discourse of Pell Grant students about their study abroad experience* (Doctoral dissertation). Available from ProQuest Dissertations and Theses database. (UMI No. 10100299)

IES Abroad. (2016). *Recap: Minority-Serving Institutions Global Education Summit, Diversity Abroad Conference & Forum Conference.* Retrieved from www.iesabroad .org/study-abroad/news/recap-minority-serving-institutions-global-education-summit-diversity-abroad

Immigration and Nationality Act, 1151 U.S.C. §§ 89-236 (1965).

Institute of International Education. (2005). *Open doors 1948–2004* [CD-ROM]. New York, NY: Author.

Institute of International Education. (2014a). *IIE Generation Study Abroad announces new partners and scholarships.* Retrieved from www.iie.org/Why-IIE/ Announcements/2014-IIE-Generation-Study-Abroad-Announces-New-Partners-Scholarships

Institute of International Education. (2014b). *What will it take to double study abroad? A "green paper" on the big 11 ideas from IIE's generation study abroad think tank.* New York, NY: Author.

Institute of International Education. (2015a). *Students with disabilities, 2006/07– 2013/14. Open doors report on international educational exchange.* Retrieved from www.iie.org/Research-and-Insights/Open-Doors/Data/US-Study-Abroad/ Students-with-Disabilities

Institute of International Education. (2015b). *Fast facts: Open doors data.* Retrieved from www.iie.org/-/media/Files/Corporate/Open-Doors/Fast-Facts/ Fast-Facts-2015.ashx?la=en&hash=20A4162472A8C6E2EB2E4171C17B 16F535499631

Institute of International Education. (2015c). *Program statistics.* Retrieved from www.gilmanscholarship.org/program/program-statistics

Institute of International Education. (2015d). *Profile of U.S. Study Abroad Students, 2004/05–2013/14.* Retrieved from www.iie.org/opendoors

Jackson, M. J. (2006). *Traveling shoes: Study abroad experiences of African American students participating in California State University international programs* (Doctoral dissertation). Available from ProQuest Dissertations and Theses database. (UMI No. 3227519)

Kasravi, J. (2009). *Factors influencing the decision to study abroad for students of color: Moving beyond the barriers* (Doctoral dissertation). Available from ProQuest Dissertations and Theses database. (UMI No. 3371866)

Kim, R. I., & Goldstein, S. B. (2005). Intercultural attitudes predict favorable study abroad expectations of U.S. college students. *Journal of Studies in International Education, 9*, 265–278. doi:10.1177/1028315305277684

Klahr, S. C. (1998). *A descriptive study of the barriers to study abroad in engineering undergraduate education and recommendations for program design* (Doctoral dissertation). Available from ProQuest Dissertations and Theses database. (UMI No. 9904259)

Kuh, G. D. (2008). *High-impact educational practices: What they are, who has access to them, and why they matter.* Washington, DC: Association for American Colleges & Universities.

Landis, D., Bennett, J. M., & Bennett, M. J. (Eds.). (2004). *Handbook of intercultural training* (3rd ed.). Thousand Oaks, CA: Sage.

Learning Abroad Center. (2015). *Access abroad: Access abroad overview.* Retrieved from umabroad.umn.edu/professionals/accessabroad

Leggett, K. (2011). Encouraging STEM students to study abroad. *International Educator, 20*(4), 44–47. Retrieved from www.nafsa.org/_/File/_/ie_julaug11_edabroad.pdf

Lu, C., Reddick, R., Dean, D., & Pecero, V. (2015). Coloring up study abroad: Exploring Black students' decision to study in China. *Journal of Student Affairs Research and Practice, 52*, 440–451. doi:10.1080/19496591.2015.1050032

Lucas, J. M. (2009). *Where are all the males?: A mixed methods inquiry into male study abroad participation* (Doctoral dissertation). Available from ProQuest Dissertations and Theses database. (UMI No. 304949857)

Lucas, J. M. (2013, January 10). *Masculinity in study abroad: Male participation in education abroad* [Webinar]. Retrieved from diversitynetwork.org/events/104/Masculinity-in-Study-Abroad:-Male-Participation-in-Education-Abroad#sthash.eKAp0k9x.dpuf

Luo, J., & Jamieson-Drake, D. (2014). Predictors of study abroad intent, participation, and college outcomes. *Research in Higher Education, 56*, 29–56. doi:10.1007/s11162-014-9338-7

Malmgren, J. (2016). Succeeding with access: Studying abroad for students with disabilities. In D. Gross, K. Abrams, & C. Z. Enns (Eds.), *Internationalizing the undergraduate psychology curriculum: Practical lessons learned at home and abroad* (pp. 259–275). Washington, DC: American Psychological Association.

Malmgren, J., & Galvin, J. (2009). Effects of study abroad participation on student graduation rates: A study of three incoming freshman cohorts at the University of Minnesota, Twin Cities. *NACADA Journal, 28*(1), 29–42.

Markow, D., & Pieters, A. (2010). *The MetLife survey of the American teacher: Preparing students for college and career.* Retrieved from www.metlife.com/assets/cao/contributions/foundation/american-teacher/MetLife_Teacher_Survey_2010.pdf

Matthews, P. R., Hameister, B. G., & Hosley, N. S. (1998). Attitudes of college students toward study abroad: Implications for disability service providers. *Journal of Postsecondary Education and Disability, 13*(2), 67–77.

McKinley, K. E. (2014). *Identifying barriers to study abroad program participation* (Doctoral dissertation). Available from ProQuest Dissertations Theses and database. (UMI No. 1526510827)

Metzger, C. A. (2006). Study abroad programming: A 21st century retention strategy? *College Student Affairs Journal, 25*, 164–175.

Mobility International USA. (2015, November 16). *Statistics on U.S. college-level study abroad students with disabilities.* Retrieved from www.miusa.org/resource/tipsheet/opendoorstats

Morgan, R. M., Mwegelo, D. T., & Turner, L. N. (2002). Black women in the African diaspora seeking their cultural heritage through studying abroad. *NASPA Journal, 39*, 333–353.

NAFSA: Association of International Educators. (n.d.). *Resources for supporting diversity in education abroad.* Retrieved from www.nafsa.org/Find_Resources/Supporting_Study_Abroad/Resources_for_Supporting_Diversity_in_Education_Abroad

NAFSA: Association of International Educators Rainbow Special Interest Group. (n.d.). Retrieved from www.rainbowsig.org

Ng, H. (2004). *Sojourners' truth: Intergenerational conflict and racial identity attitudes among second-generation Asian American participants in college study abroad programs in Asia* (Doctoral dissertation). Available from ProQuest, Dissertations and Theses database (UMI No. 3118441)

Norfles, N. (2003). *Toward equal and equitable access: Obstacles in international education.* Paper presented at the Global Challenges and U.S. Higher Education Research Conference, Duke University, Durham, NC.

Obst, D., Bhandari, R., & Witherell, S. (2007). *Current trends in U.S. study abroad and the impact of strategic diversity initiatives.* Washington, DC: Institute for International Education. Retrieved from www.iie.org/en/Research-and-Publications/Publications-and-Reports/IIE-Bookstore/Current-Trends-in-US-Study-Abroad-and-The-Impact-of-Strategic-Diversity-Initiatives

Oguntoyinbo, L. (2015, June 17). STEM students leading charge to study abroad. *Diverse Issues in Higher Education.* Retrieved from diverseeducation.com/article/73887

O'Rear, I., Sutton, R. C., & Rubin, D. L. (2011). *The effect of study abroad on college completion in a state university system.* Retrieved from glossari.uga.edu/wp-content/uploads/downloads/2012/01/GLOSSARI-Grad-Rate-Logistic-Regressions-040111.pdf

Penn, E. B., & Tanner, J. (2009). Black students and international education: An assessment. *Journal of Black Studies, 40*, 266–282. doi:10.1177/0021934707311128

Phinney, J. S., Dennis, J. M., & Chuateco, L. I. (2005). The role of motivation, parental support, and peer support in the academic success of ethnic minority first-generation college students. *Journal of College Student Development, 46*, 223–236. doi:10.1353/csd.2005.0023

Picard, E., Bernardino, F., & Ehigiator, K. (2009). Global citizenship for all: Low minority student participation in study abroad-seeking strategies for success. In R. Lewin (Ed.), *The handbook of practice and research in study abroad: Higher education and the quest for global citizenship* (pp. 321–345). New York, NY: Routledge.

Raby, R. L. (2008). *Expanding education abroad at U.S. community colleges.* New York, NY: Institute of International Education. Retrieved from p.widencdn.net/gu1iiu/Expanding-Education-Abroad-at-U.S.-Community-Colleges

Rodman, R., & Merrill, M. (2010). Unlocking study abroad potential: Design models, methods and masters. In W. W. Hoffa & S. C. DePaul (Eds.), *A history of U.S. study abroad: 1965–present* (pp. 199–252). Carlisle, PA: Frontiers Books.

Salisbury, M. H., Paulsen, M. B., & Pascarella, E. T. (2010). To see the world or stay at home: Applying an integrated student choice model to explore the gender gap in the intent to study abroad. *Research in Higher Education, 51,* 615–640. doi:10.1007/s11162-010-9171-6

Salisbury, M. H., Paulsen, M. B., & Pascarella, E. T. (2011). Why do all the study abroad students look alike? Applying an integrated student choice model to explore differences in the factors that influence White and minority students' intent to study abroad. *Research in Higher Education, 52,* 123–150. doi:10.1007/s11162-010-9191-2

Salisbury, M. H., Umbach, P., Paulsen, M., & Pascarella, E. (2009). Going global: Understanding the choice process of the intent to study abroad. *Research in Higher Education, 50,* 119–143. Retrieved from doi.org/10.1007/s11162-008-9111-x

Savicki, V., & Brewer, E. (Eds.). (2015). *Assessing study abroad: Theory, tools, and practice.* Sterling, VA: Stylus.

Schmidt, P. (2009, November 6). Men and women differ in how they decide to study abroad, study finds. *Chronicle of Higher Education.* Retrieved from chronicle.com/article/MenWomen-Differ-in-How/49085

Shorrock, H. (1979). *Report on the University of California Education Abroad Program's project: To stimulate enrollment and provide orientation for minority and disadvantaged students.* Santa Barbara CA: University of California, Education Abroad Program.

Simon, J., & Ainsworth, J. W. (2012). Race and socioeconomic status differences in study abroad participation: The role of habitus, social networks, and cultural capital. *International Scholarly Research Notices, 2012,* 1–21. doi:10.5402/2012/413896

Soneson, H. M. (2009). Education abroad advising to students with disabilities. Retrieved from www.nafsa.org/Shop/detail.aspx?id=120E

Soneson, H. M., & Cordano, R. J. (2009). Universal design and study abroad: (Re-)designing programs for effectiveness and access. *Frontiers, 18,* 269–288.

Soneson, H. M., & Fisher, S. (2011). Education abroad for students with disabilities: Expanding access. *New Directions for Student Services, 134,* 59–72. doi:10.1002/ss.395

Stallman, E, Woodruff, G. A., Kasravi, J., & Comp, D. (2010). The diversification of the student profile. In W. W. Hoffa & S. C. DePaul (Eds.), *A history of U.S. study abroad: 1965 present* (pp. 115–160). Carlisle, PA: Frontiers Books.

Stansfield, C. (1996). *Test development handbook: Simulated Oral Proficiency Interview (SOPI).* Washington, DC: Center for Applied Linguistics.

Stroud, A. H. (2010). Who plans (not) to study abroad? An examination of U.S. student intent. *Journal of Studies in International Education, 14,* 491–507. doi:10.1177/1028315309357942

Sutton, R. L., & Rubin, D. C. (2004). The GLOSSARI Project: Initial findings from a system-wide research initiative on study abroad learning outcomes. *Frontiers, 10,* 65–82.

Sutton, R. C., & Rubin, D. L. (2010, June). *Documenting the academic impact of study abroad: Final report of the GLOSSARI Project.* Paper presented at the NAFSA Annual Conference, Kansas City, MO. Retrieved from glossari.uga.edu/datasets/pdfs/FINAL.pdf

Sweeney, K. L. (2014). *Race matters: An examination of the study abroad experiences of African American undergraduates* (Doctoral dissertation). Available from ProQuest Dissertations and Theses database. (UMI No. 3642032)

Talburt, S., & Stewart, M. A. (1999). What's the subject of study abroad? Race, gender and "living culture." *Modern Language Journal, 83,* 163–175.

Thompson-Jones, M. (2012). *Not for kids like me: How the Gilman Program is changing study abroad* (Doctoral dissertation). Available from ProQuest Dissertations and Theses database. (UMI No. 3530066)

Trimble, M. J. (2016). *Non-traditional study abroad: African American collegiate women navigating service learning in Indonesia* (Doctoral dissertation). Available from ProQuest Dissertations and Theses database. (UMI No. 10092253)

Twombly, S. B. (1995). Piropos and friendships: Gender and culture clash in study abroad. *Frontiers, 1,* 1–27.

University of Delaware. (2013). *Institute for Global Studies: Study abroad: Our history.* Retrieved from www1.udel.edu/global/studyabroad/information/brief_history.html

U.S. Department of Education (2013). *Total fall enrollment in degree-granting postsecondary institutions, by attendance status, sex, and age: Selected years, 1970 through 2023* [Table 303.40.]. Retrieved from nces.ed.gov//programs/digest/d13/tables/dt13_303.40.asp

U.S. Department of Education. (n.d.). *Lists of postsecondary institutions enrolling populations with significant percentages of undergraduate minority students: Overview.* Retrieved from www2.ed.gov/about/offices/list/ocr/edlite-minorityinst.html

Vande Berg, M., Connor-Linton, J., & Paige, R. M. (2009). The Georgetown Consortium Project: Interventions for student learning abroad. *Frontiers, 18,* 1–75.

Vande Berg, M., Paige, R. M., & Lou, K. H. (Eds.). (2012). *Student learning abroad: What our students are learning, what they're not, and what we can do about it.* Sterling, VA: Stylus.

Walton, W. (2010). *Internationalism, national identities, and study abroad: France and the United States, 1890–1970.* Stanford, CA: Stanford University Press.

Ward, R. E. (1979). Statement on advanced training and research in international studies. In U.S. Department of Health, Education & Welfare, National Institute of Education (Ed.), *President's Commission on Foreign Language and International Studies: Background papers and studies* (pp. 135–167). Washington, DC: U.S. Government Printing Office.

Wick, D. (2011). *Study abroad for students of color: A third space for negotiating agency and identity* (Unpublished doctoral dissertation). San Francisco State University, San Francisco, CA.

Williams, F. D. (2007). *Study abroad and Carnegie doctoral/research extensive universities: Preparing students from underrepresented racial groups to live in a global environment* (Doctoral dissertation). Available from ProQuest Dissertations and Theses database. (UMI No. 3286526)

Willis, T. Y. (2015). "And still we rise": Microaggressions and intersectionality in the study abroad experiences of Black women. *Frontiers, 26*, 209–230.

Yosso, T. J. (2005). Whose culture has capital? A critical race theory discussion of community cultural wealth. *Race Ethnicity and Education, 8*, 69–91. doi:10.1080/1361332052000341006

Zalaznick, M. (2015, December 31). New initiatives aim to close "study abroad gap." *University Business, 19*(1), 14. Retrieved from www.universitybusiness.com/article/new-initiatives-aim-close-%E2%80%98study-abroad-gap%E2%80%99

PART TWO

RESEARCH AND PRACTICE

3

STUDENTS OF COLOR AND STUDY ABROAD

From Barriers to Results

Jinous Kasravi

Institutions of higher education, students, and government leaders in the United States have frequently touted the benefits and value of an international experience during a student's time in college. Although the number of U.S. undergraduate students studying abroad has increased continually since the 1980s, the share of participating students of color remains low. To address this concern, scholars and practitioners are forced to consider the barriers to study abroad that exist for many students.

Using Fishbein and Ajzen's (1975) theory of reasoned action, in this chapter we address the personal, social, and institutional factors influencing the decision of students of color to study abroad, how the factors differ by demographics, and the barriers applicants and nonapplicants encounter in their decision. Rather than focusing only on those who did not go abroad, as previous studies have done, this chapter also investigates students of color who have successfully overcome hurdles to participate in an overseas study experience at the University of California, San Diego (UCSD). In doing so, we learn not only what does not work but also the factors that can positively affect a student's path toward an overseas experience.

Definition of Terms

For the purpose of this chapter, it is necessary to differentiate between the terms *underrepresented students* and *students of color* as they pertain to the field of study abroad. Students identified as Asian American, African American,

Latino or Hispanic American, and Native American are referred to here as students of color. Underrepresented students, by contrast, belong to any student group that has not had a significant number of its members participate in study abroad programs (Council on International Educational Exchange, 1991) and includes groups that might be considered to be in the majority or have a privileged status outside education abroad. Examples of underrepresented groups include but are not limited to students of color; males; science, technology, engineering, and math majors; and students with disabilities. This chapter focuses on students of color as one underrepresented group.

Barriers to Study Abroad

This chapter contributes to a growing body of literature focusing on the barriers encountered by students of color in their decision to participate in study abroad. Before proceeding to the research study that addressed this issue, we begin by looking at four barriers that have been raised as particularly dominant in these students' decision-making: financial barriers, family support or cultural capital, institutional and academic barriers, and fear or racism. Empirical studies using mixed methods that have been conducted on this topic are rare. In addition, the majority of the empirical research has focused on African American or Asian American students (Comp, 2003). The most prominent literature on the barriers for students of color has been comprised of anecdotal articles and presentations by professionals in international education.

Financial Barriers

Scholars and practitioners alike have recognized that one of the largest barriers for students of color is cost. In one of the initial studies conducted at Michigan State University on factors influencing students' decisions to study abroad, Hembroff and Rusz (1993) found that African American students identified the cost of study abroad as the key hurdle along with language difficulties, lack of information about study abroad, and cultural concerns. According to the same survey, more than 81% of African American students responded that a lack of finances was a significant factor in their decision to not study abroad, whereas only 69.2% of their Caucasian peers responded similarly.

Subsequent research has pointed out that students with high need are dependent on financial aid to cover their educational and living expenses (Kasravi, 2009). The cost of airfare, passport, visa, travel insurance, and other expenses incurred while overseas largely contribute to these students' decision not to go abroad. The burden of work to help pay for tuition, related educational costs, and the need to financially help their families also restricts students from taking time off from work to study abroad (Andriano, 2010; Brux & Fry, 2010).

Financial barriers are compounded by a lack of knowledge about financial aid availability and scholarships. On some campuses, students of color report they are unaware that financial aid can be applied to study abroad (Carroll, 1996; CIEE, 1991). Salisbury, Umbach, Paulsen, and Pascarella (2009) found that those with less awareness about financial resources are often the ones who decide not to go abroad. Their work also revealed nuances among various subgroups, reminding us that we cannot bundle all students of color (see also Van Der Meid, 1999, 2003). Salisbury, Paulsen, and Pascarella (2011) found, for example, that Asian and Latino and Latina students who receive a federal grant for overseas study are more likely to participate, whereas Latino and Latina students are less likely to do so if offered a loan. Although some student populations display knowledge about funding opportunities, their intention to go overseas varies by the type of financial aid received and their perceptions about each type of aid.

Family Support or Cultural Capital

Lack of knowledge is interconnected with lack of family support and fear of the unknown. Students of color in certain subgroups indicate that study abroad is not supported by their family and community and is not regarded as a valuable educational experience (Andriano, 2010; Doan, 2002; Salisbury et al., 2011; Van Der Meid, 2003). The increase in students wanting to return to the countries from which their families emigrated, also known as heritage-seeking destinations, has ameliorated some parental fears and been viewed as a way of protecting and enhancing students' connections with their cultural heritage. In other cases, parents may not understand the desire to return to a country that they left for better opportunities in the United States (Brux & Fry, 2010). Family and social constraints to stay in the United States and help the family establish itself often inhibit newly arrived immigrant groups from participation in study abroad (Andriano, 2012).

Students are also affected by the extent to which their peer groups have had access to overseas experiences (Brux & Fry, 2010; Salisbury et al., 2009; Sweeney, 2013; Van Der Meid, 2003). Salisbury and colleagues found, for example, that the intent to study abroad for students from certain demographic groups did not differ; in particular, African American and Latino and Latina students were equally likely to indicate intent to study abroad compared to White students. As with their White peers, those with previous international experiences are more likely to indicate intent to study abroad (Salisbury et al., 2011).

Institutional and Academic Barriers

Admission and acclimation to a higher education institution can be a significant accomplishment for students of color, especially those who are the first in their family to go to college or who come from a disadvantaged background. The thought of going abroad to a new country with a new language may seem like an unattainable goal (Norfles, 2003). Many of these students have not had the opportunity to travel outside the country, nor have they grown up in communities in which international travel and study are common (Bailey-Shea, 2009; Brown, 2002). It is often not until they first arrive at college that these students first begin contemplating the idea of study abroad.

Whether students actually go abroad depends largely on the messages and support they receive from institutional leaders and advisers, as well as the policies put in place for international programming. For students for whom finances are a concern, faculty and staff may not promote study abroad to these students but rather focus on degree completion and adjustment to their home university (Brux & Fry, 2010; Sweeney, 2013). Although financial or other constraints need to be taken into account, the research indicates that targeted messaging is necessary to reach students who may not feel that study abroad is for them.

Since the 1990s numerous campuses have worked to increase the number of students of color studying abroad by ramping up recruitment efforts, updating marketing materials to be more inclusive, increasing short-term programs that appeal to heritage seekers, and promoting funding sources such as the Benjamin A. Gilman International Scholarship. With an increased focus on internationalization of the campus, many have argued that a positive racial climate on campus that supports all students, faculty, and staff has the added benefit of creating a space where students of color feel supported in going abroad (Schulze, 2016). Recruitment for students of color by students and faculty of color is a strategy that remains underused (Sweeney, 2013).

Fear and Racism

The fear of the unknown and concerns over racism abroad may also prevent students of color from studying abroad. Hembroff and Rusz (1993) found that 2.3% of Caucasian respondents compared to 14.3% of African American respondents stated that fear of discrimination while abroad had an impact on their decision to not participate. Today African American students are still more likely to report fearing and actually experiencing racism while abroad (Brux & Fry, 2010). This is a message that quickly circulates among other students back on the home campus, dissuading those already uneasy about a fear of the unknown. The lack of a support system from another student, staff, or other administrator while overseas is daunting. Andriano (2010) found that students who already struggle with the racial climate on their home university campus as a minority will rarely put themselves in a similar situation overseas with a foreign culture and language. Heritage-seeking destinations have become more common and can assuage some fears of racism while overseas (Brux & Fry, 2010).

A new layer has been added to students' fear of going abroad with the current global climate of terrorist attacks and threats, which have extended to destinations historically viewed as safe in Europe. Students not only of color but also from various ethnic and racial backgrounds fear anti-Americanism while overseas (Jackson, 2006). The attacks in places like Paris and Brussels, cities with reputations for being safe, have confirmed for some students their worst anxieties in living overseas, regardless of the color of their skin.

About the Research Study

This study explores whether the barriers cited in the literature are still relevant to students of color and what factors might influence their decision to participate in an overseas program, including variations by race, gender, generational status in college, generational status in the United States, socioeconomic status, and financial aid status. Rather than looking at only students who do not go abroad, as has been done in many previous studies, this study focuses on students who have and have not opted to participate, thus filling a key gap in the literature.

This study focused on students of color at UCSD who had made the decision to participate in a summer, fall, or academic year program through the Programs Abroad Office (PAO). In addition, students who explored study abroad opportunities and made the decision to not study abroad were surveyed and interviewed to explore the barriers that prevented participation. Although the population of Asian and Asian American students enrolled at UCSD may be higher than at other institutions in the United States, leading to a different sample population from other U.S. campuses, it was helpful for the purpose of this study to explore in depth the issues and decision factors of various ethnic groups of students, including Asian Americans as the factors affecting their decision may be similar to other students of color

California served as an ideal place to carry out the research. The U.S. Census Bureau (2007) reported that California's population included more people of American Indian and Alaska Native, Asian, Latino and Hispanic, Native Hawaiian and Pacific Islander, and biracial and multiracial descent compared to the rest of the United States. The diverse population in California, found in similar proportions at UCSD, provided a perfect laboratory for drawing substantive conclusions.

Methodology

This study employed an explanatory mixed-methods design and a two-phase sequential design method (Creswell & Plano Clark, 2007, 2009). The quantitative methods phase used Fishbein and Ajzen's (1975) theory of reasoned action as the basis for two surveys that explored the personal, social, and institutional factors influencing the decision to study abroad for students of color. Two different survey instruments were administered to students who did study abroad and those who did not. Survey results helped inform the format of interview questions for the second phase of the study. During the second phase, focus groups and individual interviews were conducted to explore the factors and issues in more depth.

The population for this study consisted of two groups. Group 1, the applicants, was composed of undergraduate students of color who had been accepted to a study abroad program for the summer, fall, or 2008–2009 academic year either through the University of California Education Abroad Program, Opportunities Abroad Program (third-party provider), or Global Seminars (faculty-led programs). Criteria for participant selection for Group 1 were students self-identifying with any racial or ethnic category other than Caucasian regardless of undergraduate standing, gender, or duration of program. Participants in Group 2, the nonapplicants, were sophomore students and above of all ethnicities who had decided to not study abroad after attending an introductory meeting offered through the PAO during the 2007–2008 academic year. Students of all ethnicities were included in Group 2 to allow more comparison and analysis of the barriers to participation.

The first phase of the study relied on two versions of an online survey instrument. The survey for Group 2 measured the personal, social, and institutional barriers these students encountered in their decision to not study abroad. Statistical analysis of the survey items was run and organized according to research questions and social, personal, and institutional factors from the theoretical framework. In the qualitative phase of the study, the theoretical framework and factors presented in the literature review served as baseline data in forming the protocol for the focus group interviews with students in Group 1. For students in Group 2, the interview protocol was semistructured and based on the theoretical framework and preliminary results of the survey data for this group of students. Analysis of the qualitative data occurred in stages and involved interview transcription, notes based on transcriptions, a memo for each interview, open coding, and topic coding to allow for emergent themes in the final code book. Main themes from the code book were organized to answer research questions. In the final phase, results were triangulated from the quantitative and qualitative data to draw some interpretations to answer the research questions.

The population for the first survey consisted of 349 students of color who had made the decision to participate in a summer, fall, or academic year program through the PAO during 2008–2009. The total number of survey respondents for Group 1 was 80, resulting in a 23% response rate. The top destinations for those in Group 1 were France, Spain, and China, with the majority of students going abroad for one semester to a year. Table 3.1 displays the complete population by frequency and percentages for students in Group 1 (applicants).

The response rate for Group 2 was significantly lower with a total of 35 students, even though the UCSD PAO sent several recruitment e-mails to all students who had attended an introductory meeting during that year but decided not to go overseas. The majority of students in Group 2 were

TABLE 3.1

Complete Population by Frequency and Percentage (Group 1, Applicants)

Ethnicity	Total response by population	Frequency of response
Chinese	108	30.1%
Latino/A, Hispanic, Chicano/a, Mexican, other Spanish	75	21.0%
Korean	46	12.8%
Caucasian/Middle Eastern	33	9.1%
Filipino	26	7.2%
Vietnamese	18	5.0%
Japanese	14	3.9%
Indian/Pakistani	11	3.1%
African American	5	1.4%
Pacific Islander/Polynesian	3	0.8%
American Indian	1	0.3%
Other Asian	10	2.8%
Other	9	2.5%
Total	359	100%

Caucasian (45.7%), and the second largest group by ethnicity was Asian and Asian American (45.7%). Students identifying themselves as Chinese or Chinese American (20%) and Korean or Korean American (14.3%) were the second and third largest groups of respondents by ethnicity.

Findings

Surveys and interviews with applicants revealed the complex interplay of influences on the decision-making process for all racial and ethnic groups. Although the sample size is too small to generalize broadly, the findings illuminated the variety of factors that positively and negatively influence the decision of students of color to study abroad and the wide variation in how those influences work. For the purpose of retaining confidentiality, all student names in this section have been changed. Among the personal factors examined, the impact of cultural norms and family expectations differed depending on the student's ethnicity, generational status in college, generational status in the United States, socioeconomic status, and financial aid status.

Broadly speaking, family and work or internship obligations were more of a barrier for males compared to females. Language of study, taking classes at a host institution, and heritage seeking were more important personal factors for second-generation college students. Of the three potential sources of influence on students' decision to study abroad—personal, institutional, or social—personal factors were the largest influencers of students of color in this study with respect to their decision-making process. For those students in Group 1, their internal drive and anticipated outcomes of personal growth and learning about another culture were the main personal factors positively influencing their decision to study abroad. Seventy-five percent of survey respondents in Group 1 stated that one of their anticipated outcomes of study abroad was to learn about themselves, and qualitative data analysis revealed that becoming more independent was the second most frequently cited personal factor for applicants.

Internal drive was a recurring personal characteristic that emerged from the interviews with applicants. Themes related to this code were students' ambition, personal motivation, determination, resiliency, and curiosity. Casey, a biracial student identifying herself more as African American than Caucasian, discussed her internal drive as it related to her decision to study abroad.

> Study abroad is something you can't really push upon someone else. I mean people can share their experiences and everything with other people to try to get them to start thinking about it. But to actually motivate them to do it, and to actually follow through with it; I think would be hard because a lot of it I think is internal. It has to do with what your personal desires are.

> I mean it's something I've always wanted to do and always driven myself to do it. Because no matter where I am, if I tell myself I'm going to do something, then I *have* to do it. I won't talk about it if it's not going to happen.

Applicants' internal drive connected highly with overcoming some of the barriers. Those in this population knew that they ultimately wanted to study abroad; they weighed their options and found solutions to the barriers, so their internal drive positively influenced their decision to study abroad.

At this stage of their college experience, applicants very much wanted to take advantage of the study abroad opportunity while in school; they were aware of the fact that as students they had fewer obligations than they would in the future and were interested in new experiences in a new environment. A survey respondent identifying herself as Chicana stated, "The value of study abroad as a student of color is to represent a minority that is rarely heard of in higher [education] institutions."

Peers and past participants were the main social factors positively influencing students' decisions to study abroad. Students who had an external messenger validating the value of study abroad and supporting them felt more confident in their decisions and became more resilient when encountering barriers. Alan, an aerospace engineering major, described the influence of one of his peers from his engineering courses:

> So, when he went and he told me about his experience, it kind of encouraged me to think, "Why not go?" Because if I'm going to end up spending a lot of money in the end and be an engineering major, trying to have the four-year plan can't stop me from doing something that I really wanted and can do.

For a few of the students who had negative external messengers and experienced various forms of resistance in their decision to study abroad, these invalidating experiences had the exact opposite effect and actually made them more determined to go and be successful. This correlates with their internal drive to have an overseas experience, exhibiting the interplay of the social and personal factors influencing their decision. Casey described her own internal drive and resiliency in the following:

> I think it depends on the person too. Like do you *want* to be like everyone else? Do you want to do stuff just because other people are doing it? Or is it something you want to do? As far as *my* decisions, I don't think anyone else influenced me in anyway. I could have friends who say the most negative things and tell me not to go, but regardless, I probably still would have gone anyway. I don't care what people say about it.

The perceived social pressures and external influences on the participant's decision to study abroad differed by race, and in some cases by ethnicity. More than 50% of Korean and Korean American respondents in Group 1 felt that study abroad was something their family expected them to do for their academics, which was a much larger percentage in comparison to the other Asian and Asian American ethnic subgroups. Latino and Hispanic American participants were less likely to know a friend who had studied abroad, whereas those in all the other ethnic groups indicated they did. Peers were the largest social factor and influence on the decision to study abroad for all racial groups.

A larger number of Latino and Hispanic American respondents felt that study abroad was not encouraged by the campus, and there were fewer sources of funding for students from their background. Although in the survey a low percentage of applicants stated their professors were not influential, students in the interviews named high school teachers and college professors as significant factors in their decision to go abroad. The significant resources, marketing, and positive campus culture supporting study abroad were the main institutional factors positively influencing their decision.

Several personal, social, and institutional barriers were encountered by applicants in Group 1 in their decision to study abroad. Program cost and delaying graduation were the main barriers and risks that students identified. Despite this, applicants found an avenue to obtain additional financial aid, loans, family support, or work to help offset costs in their decision to study abroad. The survey and interviews for Group 1 revealed additional personal barriers, such as anxiety related to home, like the strain on relationships with significant others and homesickness.

Family resistance and students going outside of the cultural norm were additional personal and social barriers that applicants had to face in their decision-making process. Respondents identifying as Latino or Hispanic and Middle Eastern were more likely to disagree that "participating in study abroad is the norm for people from [their] culture" compared to respondents from other racial backgrounds. Julia, a student identifying herself as Armenian, encountered a lot of resistance from her family at first: "They struggled to come here, to settle here, and to go to school here. So their goal in life was to be here. They don't understand why I would leave here and go somewhere else. To them, here is the goal." Several students mentioned labeling by their family and others in their culture because of their decisions. Laura, a student identifying herself as El Salvadoran and Mexican, explained this labeling as follows: "When you do things, like if you do the American things, you're kind of 'Whitewashed.' I've always been called that. I'm 'Whitewashed' because I go to college and now because I'm going to study abroad." Although students discussed labeling, and often felt a cultural divide between their decisions and their culture, their own internal drive and ambition helped them to overcome this barrier.

Some of the students from collectivist cultures, such as Latino and Hispanic American and African American, experienced higher levels of family support. Their families supported them in their decision to pursue higher education and to go overseas because they did not want them bound to the typical cultural norms. At the same time, other students from the same cultures reported that their families resisted decisions that fell outside the expected norms. As a result, family resistance is still a barrier for some students of color who would like to study abroad, but it cannot be generalized as a barrier to all students of color; many of their families do encourage and support them to take advantage of such opportunities.

The main barrier that nonapplicants (Group 2) identified in their decision to not study abroad was the personal factor of finances. Again, the non-applicant group included students of all ethnicities, with a substantial subset of Caucasian students. As a whole, findings reveal that cost continues to be the primary obstacle for applicants and nonapplicants regardless of ethnicity, immigration status in the United States, financial aid received, or generational status in college when making the decision to study abroad. Academics was the second largest barrier cited by nonapplicants.

Despite the low response rate and difference in demographics between applicants and nonapplicants, the two groups had a number of barriers in common, including a lack of family support, not meeting grade point average requirements for study abroad programs, fear of delaying graduation, work or internship obligations, and restrictions on financial aid for study abroad. Surprisingly, applicants identified more personal barriers in their decision compared to nonapplicants. Applicants stated they had researched options, completed the application and selection process, and discussed their decision with family and friends, and this may have affected their reporting a larger number of barriers because they had navigated the system. In contrast, nonapplicants had only begun the primary research process and may not have progressed far enough to have encountered some of the other barriers and influences reported by students who applied.

Discussion

This study created an adapted model of the decision to study abroad drawn from Fishbein and Ajzen's (1975) theory of reasoned action. We see that several of the factors influencing the students' decisions are more promi-nent than others. Cost continues to be the primary barrier for applicants and nonapplicants, but the interplay of students' personal and social factors helped overcome the cost barrier. Students' internal drive and social messengers helped influence their decision and seek other avenues to overcome the cost barrier. Norfles (2006) discussed graduation from college and survival in college as main priorities for first-generation college students; in this study several of these students did not see graduation from college as the primary goal for their time there. One interesting result from this study reveals that many students of color are not as concerned about graduating in the typical four years. Rather, staying in school for an additional year is becoming more common, more socially acceptable, and allows them to partake of other extracurricular or academic opportunities. At this level of education and stage of their college experience, these students really wanted to take advantage of the opportunity to have a new experience in a new environment while they are in school and have fewer obligations.

A lack of knowledge about study abroad opportunities and fear of racism were not significant barriers for those surveyed in this study. This finding indicates that several of the barriers in the previous literature need to be reevaluated. The previous literature was limited when discussing or exploring the factors influencing biracial and multiracial students' decision to study abroad. It is important to include these groups as their populations are increasing on college campuses throughout the nation.

A key finding that was consistent in student responses was that internal drive and determination play a significant role in helping students overcome barriers in going abroad. The literature did not extensively discuss student personal characteristics of internal drive, but other research conducted by Fishbein and Ajzen (1975), Peterson (2003), and Booker (2001) does help us interpret the results by applying the theory of reasoned action. As illustrated in this adapted model (see Figure 3.1), students' internal drive corresponds with the personal factors affecting their attitudes in their decision to study abroad. Furthermore, a student's personal characteristics and internal drive were more influential in affecting their attitudes and ultimately their decision. Booker (2001) explored the relationship between attitudinal and social variables and how they weighed in students' decisions, but the specific student's personal characteristics such as internal drive and personal motivation were not examined. As a result, using the theory of reasoned action, findings from this study reveal that the attitudes of students of color—their behavioral beliefs and evaluation of outcomes—are more influential in their decision to study abroad than the social and external influences that create their subjective norm; although in this study, the subjective norm influences their attitudes.

These findings are related to Steele's (1997) discussion of stereotype threat. He stated that students from historically underrepresented populations

Figure 3.1. Adapted model of decision to study abroad.

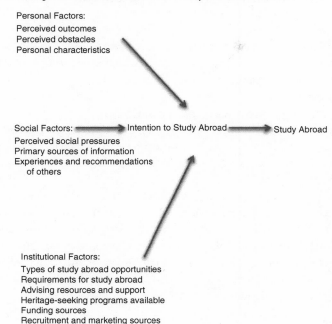

Note. Adapted from Peterson (2003) and Booker (2001).

who encounter negative stereotypes in school that pertain to their academic success begin to perform lower. Findings from the present study challenge Steele's theory by demonstrating that students actually became even more resilient and motivated, regardless of stereotype threats from members of their community or family who were apt to label students as Whitewashed for opting to go abroad. Although family resistance is still a barrier, it cannot be generalized to all students of color. Many families do encourage and support their children, even if they do not completely understand what study abroad may entail.

Next Steps and Conclusions

This study attempted to move beyond the literature on barriers to study abroad and to draw conclusions that can inform policy and practice by examining the experiences of students of color who made the decision to participate in an overseas program. It has several limitations, which include the limited sample size of respondents, low response rate, and a small population of male and African American students. Further studies might include more universities and colleges from various geographic regions in the United States that vary in size and competitiveness to allow a more diverse sample of student demographics and permit more comparison. Another recommendation for further study is to include more research and discussion centered on biracial and multiracial students because this student demographic is growing in higher education.

Since this study was conducted, the UCSD PAO continues to increase its efforts to promote diversity in participant numbers with the help of the various academic units on campus. The PAO has set an annual goal to increase underrepresented minorities in its programs by 10%. Among many initiatives, the PAO has since conducted mobile advising in all the community centers on campus, consulted with Diversity Abroad, encouraged the University of California's central office on education abroad to commit to a systemwide membership in Diversity Abroad, designated study abroad scholarship funds specifically for underrepresented students, and worked with campus development officers to raise additional scholarship funds for underrepresented students. In 2015–2016 the numbers of study abroad participants through the UCSD PAO closely mirrored the overall student population at UCSD, with 12% Mexican, Mexican American, and Chicano and Chicana; 6.32% Filipino and Filipino American; 5.36% Vietnamese and Vietnamese American; 2.04% African American; 1.39% other Asian; 0.64% American Indian and Alaska Native; 0.11% Latino and other Spanish; and 0.11% Pacific Islander (K. O'Sullivan Sommer, personal communication, October 25, 2016).

Because finances and academics continue to be obstacles for students who made the decision not to apply, this reveals that some of the previous barriers addressed in the literature remain. Current efforts, initiatives, and policies should be evaluated in light of students' perceptions and attitudes in the decision-making process, as should the resources dedicated to reducing financial barriers to participation. The barriers affect not only the student's decision to apply or not apply but also their personal drive or motivation in college and social influences need to inform the efforts to increase participation. Marketing and outreach efforts should rely on messaging through peer advisers, returned study abroad students, and mentorship in college, high school, or college preparation programs. In particular, the academic and practical outcomes of study abroad should be stressed, as well as the personal outcomes for students. It is critical to reach students during their senior year of high school and first year of college so that they have adequate time to prepare mentally and academically for the experience.

The ways we talk about issues of access and diversity in study abroad also need to be reevaluated to reflect some of the cultural norms and expectations, family resistance, self-negotiation, and student personal development issues that students of color encounter when they are deciding to apply or not apply for study abroad. All of this could increase the opportunity for the profile of the study abroad participant to become more diverse and representative of our U.S. and higher education population.

References

Andriano, B. R. (2010). *Study abroad participation and engagement practices of first-generation undergraduate students* (Doctoral dissertation). Available from ProQuest Dissertations and Theses database. (ED 523703)

Andriano, B. R. (2012). Engagement practices and study abroad participation of first-generation American college students. In T. Hicks & A. Pitre (Eds.), *Research studies in higher education: Educating multicultural college students* (pp. 119–160). Lanham, MD: University Press of America.

Bailey-Shea, C. (2009). *Issues that affect American college students' participation in study abroad* (Doctoral dissertation). Available from ProQuest Dissertations and Theses database. (3395372)

Booker, R. W. (2001). *Differences between applicants and non-applicants relevant to the decision to apply to study abroad* (Unpublished doctoral dissertation). University of Missouri, Columbia, MO.

Brown, L. M. (2002). Going global: Traditionally, the percentage of African American students who studied abroad has been low; however, university officials are looking into ways to increase those numbers. *Black Issues in Higher Education, 19*(6), 28–31.

Brux, J. M., & Fry, B. (2010). Multicultural students and study abroad: Their interests, their issues, and their constraints. *Journal of Studies in International Education, 14*, 508–527.

Carroll, A. V. (1996). *The participation of historically underrepresented students in study abroad programs: An assessment of interest and perception of barriers* (Unpublished master's thesis). Colorado State University, Fort Collins, CO.

Comp, D. (2003). *Research on underrepresentation in education abroad: An annotated bibliography*. Retrieved from www.nafsa.org/_/file/_/underrepresentation_in_2 .doc

Council on International Educational Exchange. (1991). *Increasing participation of ethnic minorities in study abroad*. Retrieved from ERIC database. (ED346784)

Creswell, J., & Plano Clark, V. (2007). *Designing and conducting mixed methods research*. Thousand Oaks, CA: Sage.

Creswell, J., & Plano Clark, V. (2009). *Understanding research: A consumer's guide*. Upper Saddle River, NJ: Prentice Hall.

Doan, T. M. (2002). *Asian American students: Study abroad participation, perspectives, and experiences* (Unpublished master's thesis). University of Minnesota, Minneapolis, MN.

Fishbein, M., & Ajzen, I. (1975). *Belief, attitude, intention, and behavior: An introduction to theory and research.* Reading, MA: Addison-Wesley.

Hembroff, L. A., & Rusz, D. L. (1993). *Minorities and overseas studies programs: Correlates of differential participation.* New York, NY: Council on International Educational Exchange.

Jackson, M. J. (2006). *Traveling shoes: Study abroad experiences of African American students participating in California State University international programs* (Doctoral dissertation). Available from ProQuest Dissertations and Theses database. (UMI No. 3227519)

Kasravi, J. (2009). *Factors influencing the decision to study abroad for students of color: Moving beyond the barriers* (Doctoral dissertation). Available from ProQuest Dissertations and Theses database. (UMI No. 3371866)

Norfles, N. (2003). *Toward equal and equitable access: Obstacles in international education.* Paper presented at the Global Challenges and U.S. Higher Education Research Conference, Duke University, Durham, NC.

Norfles, N. (2006, May). *What we know about diversity in education abroad: Obstacles and opportunities.* Paper presented at the Colloquium on Diversity in Education Abroad: How to Change the Picture, Washington, DC.

Peterson, D. L. (2003). *The decision to study abroad: Contributing factors and implications for communication strategies* (Unpublished doctoral dissertation). Michigan State University, East Lansing, MI.

Salisbury, M. H., Paulsen, M. B., & Pascarella, E. T. (2011). Why do all the study abroad students look alike? Applying an integrated student choice model to explore differences in the factors that influence white and minority students' intent to study abroad. *Research in Higher Education, 52,* 123–150.

Salisbury, M. H., Umbach, P. D., Paulsen, M. B., & Pascarella, E. T. (2009). Going global: Understanding the choice process of the intent to study abroad. *Research in Higher Education, 50,* 119–143.

Schulze, W. L. (2016). *Best practices for increasing diversity in study abroad: A manual for small private co-ed universities in the United States* (Unpublished master's thesis). University of San Francisco, San Francisco, CA.

Steele, C. M. (1997). A threat in the air: How stereotypes shape intellectual identity and performance. *American Psychologist, 52,* 613–629.

Sweeney, K. (2013). Inclusive excellence and underrepresentation of students color in study Abroad. *Frontiers, 23,* 1–21.

U.S. Census Bureau. (2007). *State and country quick facts.* Retrieved from quickfacts.census.gov/qfd/states/06000.html

Van Der Meid, J. (1999). *Asian Americans: Factors influencing the decision to study abroad* (Unpublished master's thesis). Lesley College, Cambridge, MA.

Van Der Meid, J. (2003). Asian Americans: Factors influencing the decision to study abroad. *Frontiers, 9,* 71–110.

4

FIRST-GENERATION COLLEGE STUDENTS AND STUDY ABROAD

Examining the Participation Gap and Successful Strategies for Promoting Access

Michelle Tolan and Margaret McCullers

A critical tenet of *inclusive excellence*, a term developed by the Association of American Colleges & Universities, is the engagement of inclusion as an academic practice rather than a focus on access and numbers alone (Milem, Chang, & Antonio, 2005). For educators, inclusive excellence means not only reimagining the square-hole, round-peg puzzle of access but also learning how to engage constituencies with diverse backgrounds, learning styles, communication norms, and personal obligations for the benefit of all students in the learning community. This topic becomes particularly imperative when considering first-generation college students (FGCSs) who often fall into multiple at-risk categories for disengagement and attrition and notably represent a substantial portion of today's college enrollment.

According to the National Center for Education Statistics, FGCSs constitute upward of 40% of undergraduates in the United States (Skomsvold, 2014). This figure can vary depending on parameters such as institution type (i.e., four year versus two year, nonprofit versus for profit) and definition (parents with no college, parents with some college). For the purpose of this chapter, *FGCS* refers to a student for whom no custodial parent has completed a four-year college degree.

Beyond the basic definition of the term, it can be challenging to define a *first gen* as they are particularly heterogeneous, and each institution's FGCS population is influenced by factors like local and state demographics, feeder school districts, tuition, financial aid award rates, and entrance requirements. More complicated yet, many FGCSs do not identify themselves as first-generation or see themselves as having unique needs in relation to their peers (Orbe, 2004). There are, however, macrolevel patterns that emerge among the FGCS population in the United States, including a greater likelihood to pursue vocation-oriented majors, be a student of color, come from the lowest income quartile, spend twice as much time working on and off campus during school (Billson & Terry, 1982; Chen & Carroll, 2005; Choy, 2001), and—conspicuously to international educators—be far less likely to participate in study abroad (National Survey of Student Engagement, 2007). As a program disproportionately popular among White female humanities majors at elite institutions of higher education, how study abroad is perceived by FGCSs presents a distinct challenge and requires international educators to reexamine the value propositions they put forward in the context of the needs and interests of a new constituency.

As a high-impact educational practice, study abroad is a considerable opportunity to influence the academic and sociocultural trajectory of students and their families. Educational research suggests high-impact practices—which demand extensive time and effort, faculty engagement, and collaboration with diverse others—increase rates of student retention, engagement, and deep learning (Kuh, 2008). Among the world's developed nations, the United States currently has one of the lowest rates of intergenerational mobility; our citizens are disproportionately constrained by their parents' social class and access to education opportunities when compared to the rest of the industrialized world (Causa & Johansson, 2011). As our society becomes increasingly preoccupied by class mobility—or lack thereof—the imperative also rises to ensure FGCSs have equitable access to, and facilitation of, high-impact educational practices such as study abroad.

This chapter explores two case studies of institutions that engage FGCSs in study abroad: the Institute for Study Abroad at Butler University (IFSA-Butler), which is a nonprofit education abroad program provider, and the University of Texas at Austin (UT Austin), a large state university. These cases demonstrate several research-grounded approaches to relationship building, retention strategies, and infrastructure (financial and pastoral) that most benefit FGCSs.

Case 1: IFSA-Butler

As a nonprofit education abroad organization affiliated with a private university based in Indianapolis, IFSA-Butler has traditionally attracted high-achieving participants from the nation's elite colleges, in part because of its rigorous academic requirements, institutional partnerships, and substantial support services. IFSA-Butler's low staff-to-student ratio and commitment to tailored academic guidance and individualized learning represent a study abroad program model that largely attracts students with significant support systems at home and on their own campuses that mirror standards they are accustomed to.

Although access to appropriate support can be integral to the success of every student abroad, paradoxically, education abroad professionals tend to direct students who may benefit most from enhanced support systems toward programs that offer lower levels of support, which is tied directly to the cost of delivery. Research suggests support may be especially important for FGCSs, who particularly benefit from individual faculty and staff engagement (Lohfink & Paulsen, 2005), access to academic resources, and help making the transition to college and beyond (Terenzini, Springer, Yaeger, Pascarella, & Nora, 1996). IFSA-Butler is an organization with an established reputation for an individualized approach to pastoral care and academic services, which presented an opportunity to use its strong student support structures for a population that might need it most overseas.

IFSA-Butler launched in 2012 what would become the first of many FGCS-oriented initiatives, the First Generation College Student Program. The program had four primary goals: align how scholarships are awarded with the unique needs of FGCSs in mind, address inequities in traditional scholarship application processes, increase the overall enrollment of FGCSs in IFSA-Butler programs, and contribute narratives of FGCSs studying abroad for prospective students and education abroad practitioners.

Funding Structure

Prior to 2012 nearly all IFSA-Butler's scholarships were disbursed as tuition discounts, mirroring traditional university scholarship structures. Reaching more FGCSs, however, required retooling processes, particularly with IFSA-Butler's core sending institutions in mind, a number of which provide fixed financial aid policies and access to institutional funding for students with established need. The organization had to address the pertinent question of where funds would be most helpful to students who have found the means to attend college but may not be able to afford a parking pass. The IFSA-Butler FGCS scholarship that emerged was designed to alleviate upfront costs and unanticipated expenses rather than discount tuition. The award covers international airfare and visa and passport fees and credits $500 toward room and board for a maximum value of $2,500. Twelve scholarships are awarded each year, five per semester and, since 2016, two per summer session.

Reasons for the cost-coverage approach were threefold. First, because FGCSs have been found to be more likely to work during the academic year (Pascarella, Pierson, Wolniak, & Terenzini, 2004; Terenzini et al., 1996), the mechanism allows students to save more of their earnings and safeguard financial stability while abroad rather than exhaust their bank account prior to departure. Second, it maximizes student financial aid packages by complementing rather than undermining tuition-based aid like institutional scholarships and federal grants. Third, it is an attempt to alleviate some of the bureaucratic fatigue students might encounter while preparing to go abroad. Requirements such as procuring a passport, navigating the foreign visa process, and booking an international flight can be burdensome and daunting for any student, especially for those who have never traveled internationally. This scholarship eases the financial pressure of such tasks and allows students to concentrate on the preparation itself with guidance from their IFSA-Butler advising team in addition to their home campus.

Marketing

For many, costs associated with study abroad are not purely financial; they also include the cost of lost opportunities involved in foregoing other activities. Considering the monetary investment of U.S. higher education and the tightening labor market, undertaking an activity without a clear preprofessional value might be perceived as frivolous or wasteful. This can be especially true for FGCSs, for whom subsequent employment is a key motivator for attending college (Saenz, Hurtado, Barrera, Wolf, & Yeung, 2007). To reach a more career-focused student, IFSA-Butler began to add nuances to what had been aspiration-oriented visuals in its promotional materials. Nearly every education abroad catalog, including some at IFSA-Butler, has featured photos of a backpack-clad student looking pensively into a beautiful landscape. Staff began to question whether this approach would resonate with students who entered college with more concrete objectives than self-discovery.

While creating marketing materials for the IFSA-Butler FGCS scholarship, marketing staff took the concept of self-discovery (i.e., a sprouting plant) built on a foundation (i.e., stacked books) of concrete information such as program length and number of options while employing results-oriented language such as *enhanced résumé* (see Figure 4.1). In digital resources it was equally critical for academic-relevant and asset-centered language to be used to attract FGCSs; indeed, IFSA-Butler as an organization values FGCSs' ability to navigate multiple landscapes in new environments

Figure 4.1 First Generation College Students graphic.

Note. From the Institute for Study Abroad, 2012.

(Orbe, 2004) and seeks to deploy that skill set as educators. The IFSA-Butler scholarship booklet, for example, states that "first gens have some of the lowest study abroad participation rates," and that "we know their work ethic and cultural navigation skills make them ideal study abroad candidates, and we want to help make the study abroad dream a reality" (Institute for Study Abroad, 2016d). These materials attempt to break down perceptions that study abroad is not intended for FGCSs while highlighting the fact that study abroad is an extension of the academic and preprofessional preparation that all students, including FGCSs, undertake on campus.

FGCS Narratives

Some of the most compelling advocates for study abroad are students themselves through storytelling. It is much more convincing for FGCSs to hear peers speak about their experiences abroad and how these experiences have positioned them for success. To increase marketable narratives on FGCSs abroad and learn from the students themselves, scholarship recipients are required to chronicle their time abroad via blogs or articles for IFSA-Butler's online publication *Unpacked: A Study Abroad Guide for Students Like Me* (Institute for Study Abroad, 2017), using the lens of their generational status. Recipients are given several prompts on topic areas like family, program cohort dynamics, and academics, such as the following:

> Adjusting to a new educational landscape: As the first person in your family to attend college, you are a seasoned academic pioneer. How is this adjustment to yet another new academic system? Are you using skills you gained

your first year on campus? Any unexpected surprises? What challenges have
you encountered? How do you navigate learning a new system so quickly?

The chronicles are not always cheerful, as the study abroad experience
is not positive every day, but they challenge assumptions that study abroad
is for someone else and provide concrete student stories not captured in the
conventional landscape photo. In addition to content marketing, these narratives serve as an internal barometer for IFSA-Butler as real-time snapshots of
life on the ground and have allowed staff to respond to students and address
inequities that may arise while they are abroad.

Application Process and Recipient Selection

Tracking the success of this project required identifying FGCSs as early as
possible. Prior to the scholarship's inception, no mechanisms existed to track
FGCS participants at IFSA-Butler. The query "Do one or more of your
custodial parents hold a four-year college degree?" was inserted into the initial application phase, along with questions for other perfunctory information such as e-mail address, major, and program of interest. Many FGCSs
may be hesitant to self-identify or merely do not think of themselves as a
first-generation college student (Orbe, 2004), so alongside this question is a
simple check box and an accompanying statement that lets applicants know
that they may be eligible for additional scholarships. It is important to note
that, at the same time, it allows IFSA-Butler program advisers to monitor
FGCSs' applicant retention rate and modify communication and support
strategies as necessary.

There is emergent research that U.S. universities' focus on student independence may undermine the success of underrepresented populations,
including FGCSs (Murphy, Walton, & Stangor, 2013). Indeed, many study
abroad advisers approach students with the expectation, even insistence, of
autonomy while working through program selection and the bureaucratic
paperwork of application, course selection, and visa procurement. After all,
if students cannot navigate the application and predeparture process, how
will they navigate the new systems abroad? Although well meaning, this tactic may alienate students unfamiliar with such processes and send a message that this isn't for them (Murphy et al., 2013). Embedding expectations
of autonomy in the predeparture phase, moreover, may inadvertently spotlight FGCSs' cultural capital gaps and undermine the very real skill sets they
bring to study abroad. Indeed, it may help to consider that many FGCSs are
uniquely positioned for success in study abroad as they are already familiar
with multiple-identity negotiation, that is, navigating new landscapes as the
other while developing a nuanced sense of self (Orbe, 2004). Although they

may need more support in some areas, in other ways they can be better prepared than their peers.

The IFSA-Butler FGCS scholarship application was designed to be simple and to take account of the critical timing of award disbursement and varied experiences. Notably, the grade point average (GPA) requirement of 2.7 is lower than most merit-based scholarships, resulting from research that FGCSs tend to have lower GPAs regardless of major (Chen, 2005). The application does *not* require students to choose an active IFSA-Butler program, and deadlines are set before program applications are due to reach students whose funding for the program is make or break.

The application itself has three parts, which are intended to be easy to complete: a 500-word essay, a résumé, and a one-page financial aid form. The application's brevity is an acknowledgment that FGCSs are more likely to have multiple obligations in addition to college, so the application is quickly navigable and realistic. The résumé component was added after the pilot year as it became obvious that applicants with weaker writing skills were at a significant disadvantage, and it now makes up 50% of the applicant's total score. Résumés also showcase skills that may not be so readily available in a typical program application yet are valuable for students in technical and preprofessional fields.

Results and Areas for Further Research

Enrollments

Response to the scholarship was positive in student enrollments. Only five students receive the scholarship per semester, but overall FGCS enrollment in IFSA-Butler programs jumped quickly from 4% of participants in fall 2012 to 9% in spring 2013, and then 14% by fall 2013 (see Table 4.1).

Numbers have risen most steadily for spring semesters, which have peaked and been maintained at 16% of total enrollment; fall is consistently lower, including an unexplained dip in fall 2015 (see Figure 4.2). The fluctuation may stem from key sending institutions and their enrollment

TABLE 4.1
First-Generation College Student Enrollment, 2012–2015

U.S. Term	2012	2013	2014	2015
Fall	4%	14%	13%	7%
Spring	N/A	9%	16%	16%

Note. From Institute for Study Abroad (2016a).

Figure 4.2. First-generation college student enrollment.

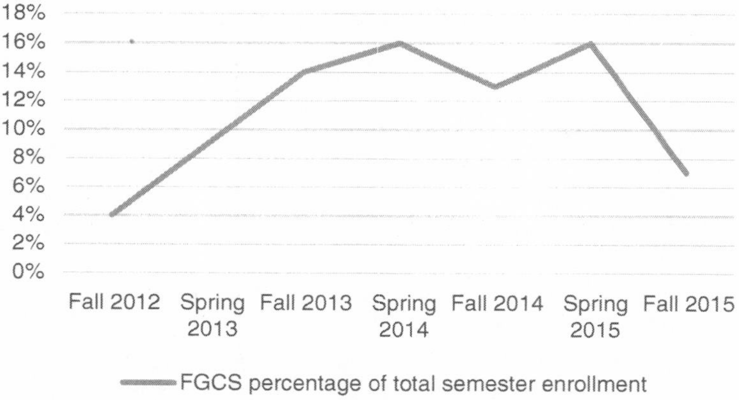

Note. FGCS = first-generation college student. From Institute for Study Abroad (2016a).

patterns. One point worth noting is the elevated attrition rate among FGCS applicants. From 2012 to 2015, 85% of students who completed an IFSA-Butler application went on to participate in that program after acceptance. Only 81% of FGCS applicants during that period, however, enrolled after acceptance. Although the data are insufficient to track reasons or timing for attrition, this is certainly an area for future investigation.

Majors

FGCSs in IFSA-Butler programs do not choose drastically different study abroad locations from students in the overall enrollment; however, their majors reflect more concrete academic interests, aligned with national trends. Among the top 10 majors in IFSA-Butler programs, neuroscience, education, and business stand out as distinctive to FGCSs when compared to total participants (see Table 4.2).

Academic Performance

Also in alignment with national statistics, FGCSs possessed lower GPAs on applying, a trend that continued while these students were abroad. Compared to continuing-generation students, FGCSs applying to an IFSA-Butler program from 2012 to 2015 had significantly lower (less than 0.60) grade point averages, whereas FGCS participants earned slightly lower GPAs abroad than students overall (see Table 4.3).

The story underlying these numbers, however, is just how much better FGCSs perform abroad. Continuing-generation students had a GPA decline

TABLE 4.2
TABLE 4.2
Comparison of Top Majors for First-Generation College Students Versus Overall

Top 10 Majors, IFSA-Butler FGCS Participants	Top 10 Majors, IFSA-Butler Total Participants
Psychology	Psychology
Economics	Economics
Biology	English
Political science	Biology
History	History
English	Political science
Sociology	Math
Neuroscience	Anthropology
Education	Sociology
Business	Other

Note. From Institute for Study Abroad (2016b). FGCS = first-generation college student; IFSA = Institute for Study Abroad.

TABLE 4.3
Academic Performance by Generational Status

	GPA at Application	GPA on IFSA-Butler Program	Average Difference
All students	3.85	3.32	-0.53
FGCSs only	3.33	3.18	-0.16
Excluding FGCSs	3.91	3.33	-0.58

Note. From Institute for Study Abroad (2016c). FGCS = first-generation college student; GPA = grade point average; IFSA = Institute for Study Abroad.

of nearly 0.60 in their program, whereas FGCSs had just a 0.16 dip. In other words, although both groups had decreased GPAs abroad, FGCSs did significantly better than their peers when compared to their previous academic performance. This may support the supposition that FGCSs are uniquely positioned for success in study abroad thanks to their experience navigating new academic landscapes.

Case 2: UT Austin

Although the first case examined a provider organization catering to students at a variety of universities, we next turn to the example of a large state university serving a wide array of students on one campus. UT Austin is the flagship campus of a statewide system enrolling 51,331 students, 40,168 of which are undergraduates. In 2016, 79.4% of all students were in-state residents and represented a great diversity of backgrounds and academic interests from across the state (UT Austin, 2016). Within the incoming class of 2016, for example, the university had a majority-minority student body, and 24% were FGCSs (UT Austin, 2012).

Within this context, study abroad staff at UT Austin discovered the need to support FGCSs after determining that only 8% of FGCSs at the university studied abroad, although they represented 18% of the student body (Barclay Hamir, 2011). This revealed a larger participation gap among FGCSs than that of males or of racial and ethnic minority students and led to the development of two programs geared toward creating access to study abroad among FGCSs: the Hutchison International Scholars Program and the First Abroad Program. This case study focuses specifically on the Hutchison program.

The Hutchison program is a five-year pilot program created, funded, and administered by UT Austin's study abroad unit. The program provides academically outstanding, first-generation, first-year students entering college the opportunity to study abroad by reducing the financial barrier that may prevent some students from considering study abroad during their undergraduate careers. Participants receive a one-time scholarship of $4,000 to help cover the cost of a study abroad program. Once awarded, scholars have four years to apply these funds toward the UT Austin program of their choice. Scholars are selected on admission to UT Austin and are notified of their award during the spring immediately preceding their first year. They are not required to accept the award to give them time to determine if study abroad is the best choice for them.

The program has three main goals: increase study abroad participation among FGCSs by reducing funding as a barrier to entry, influence student retention at UT Austin for the target population, and influence acceptance decisions to attend UT Austin among the target population.

Scholar Selection

To initiate the program, the study abroad team and the Office of Admissions developed selection criteria to identify academically outstanding FGCSs. In addition to neither parent having a four-year college degree, other criteria are that students graduated high school in Texas, meet a sliding SAT or ACT test score above their high school's average scores, were admitted to UT Austin with a strong application, and have a combined family income of $60,000 or less. Students do not apply to receive this award, thus removing a key barrier for possible candidates.

Program Support and Outreach Activities

Research has found that FGCSs face a knowledge deficit when adjusting to the culture of academia (Terenzini et al., 1996), which can become even more burdensome when navigating the study abroad process and overseas academic systems. Examining the academic and social needs of college students, studies have found that continuing-generation students benefit from involvement in student organizations and clubs, whereas FGCSs have a greater need for academic engagement (Lohfink & Paulsen, 2005; Pascarella et al., 2004). With this in mind, the program incorporates multiple layers of support that are intended to enable participation among a diverse group of students. Students and their parents are invited to a study abroad session at summer orientation detailing the individual support they can expect to receive throughout their years at the university. This includes help with identifying academically relevant programs with courses abroad that fulfill upper-division degree requirements, determining when to participate, applying for additional scholarships, receiving feedback on scholarship application essays, understanding financial aid, and receiving support with family or other concerns.

Scholars are encouraged to touch base with the program coordinator each semester to plan the study abroad experience that best meets individual academic, personal, and professional goals, making advising support a critical component of the program. Students are also given the opportunity to participate in the Hutchison Scholars First-Year Interest Group, a one-hour weekly class for incoming scholars led by the program coordinator and a senior Hutchison scholar. The class is tailored to the unique needs of FGCSs and provides scholars with the opportunity to take multiple classes with their scholar peers.

First-year Hutchison scholars are invited to a study abroad reception attended by hundreds of incoming FGCSs to encourage study abroad early before students decide against it. Many campus partners, including representatives from all the major academic success programs, also attend to endorse the idea of study abroad. Additionally, scholars are invited to a wide range of programming throughout the academic year, such as sessions hosted by visiting professionals and events featuring Hutchison scholars who have studied abroad.

Yield, Retention, and Study Abroad Participation Rates

Students are notified of their scholarship awards the spring preceding their first year at UT Austin with the goal of recruiting them to attend the university. With a target of 32 scholars annually, cohort size is dependent on

TABLE 4.4
Hutchison International Scholar Yield Rates

Entering Cohort	Awards Offered	Accepted	Hutchison Yield Rate	University Yield Rate
2011	62	36	58%	47%
2012	65	41	63%	49%
2013	63	31	49%	47%
2014	64	29	45%	47%
2015	66	40	61%	46%

Note. From University of Texas at Austin, Office of Institutional Reporting, Research, and Information Systems (2014, 2015).

the yield rate, averaging 35 scholars from 2011 to 2016. Because the 2010 Hutchison scholar cohort was not created until after the start of the fall semester, yield rates do not apply to this cohort. Table 4.4 demonstrates that the yield rates of those offered the Hutchison scholarship among the 2011, 2012, 2013 and 2015 cohorts are consistently above the university average, even though the 2014 yield rate dipped slightly. Although the average yield rate for FGCSs is not known, this suggests that the program may influence acceptance decisions for the target population.

Program administrators also sought to determine if a scholarship reduces the dropout rate among FCGSs. Comparing retention data, Hutchison scholars were consistently retained after their first and second years at higher rates than the overall university average (see Table 4.5). Considering that FGCSs tend to be retained at much lower rates than the university average (Greninger, 2011), the Hutchison program may have an impact. In 2010 UT Austin lost 15% of its FGCSs after the first year of attendance, compared to 10% of minority students and 12% of low-income students (Greninger, 2011). Comparatively, from 2011 to 2016 the Hutchison program had a maximum attrition rate of 5% after the first year of college, whereas the university attrition rate was higher than that of each scholar cohort. Although the scholars are retained at higher rates than their peers, they likely benefitted from a university-wide effort that was launched in 2012 to significantly increase four-year graduation rates overall.

Striving for parity in study abroad participation, a key goal has been for FGCS participation to be on par with the percentage of FGCSs in the student body. Figure 4.3 shows that 67% of the 2010 Hutchison cohort, 53% of the 2011 cohort, and 41% of the 2012 cohort ultimately studied abroad. More than half the students in each of these cohorts who remained at the university

TABLE 4.5

Retention of Hutchison International Scholars, 2011–2015 Cohorts

Entering Cohort	Students	Hutchison Year 1 (n)	University Year 1	Hutchison Year 2 (n)	University Year 2	Hutchison Year 3 (n)	University Year 3
2011	36	100% (36)	93.2%	94.4% (34)	89.4%	91.7% (33)	84.2%
2012	41	95.1% (39)	93.6%	87.8% (36)	89.5%	78% (32)	83.9%
2013	31	100% (31)	94.5%	96.7% (30)	90.5%	87.1% (27)	85.2%
2014	29	96.6% (28)	95.4%	96.6% (28)	91.9%		
2015	40	100% (40)	95.1%				

Note. From UT Austin, Office of Institutional Reporting, Research, and Information Systems (2016, p. 46).

Figure 4.3. Hutchison International scholar cohort data: Study abroad and retention.

Hutchison International Scholars 2010 Cohort: Finalized

67% studied abroad (14 of 21 scholars)
88% of scholars who remained at UT Austin for four years studied abroad

Hutchison International Scholarship 2011 Cohort: Finalized

53% studied abroad (19 of 36 scholars)
59% of scholars who remained at UT Austin for four years studied abroad

Hutchison International Scholarship 2012 Cohort: Finalized

41% have studied abroad (17 of 41 scholars)
55% of scholars who remained at UT Austin for four years studied abroad (17 of 31)

Hutchison International Scholarship 2013 Cohort: One Year Remaining

35% have studied abroad (11 of 31 scholars)

Hutchison International Scholarship 2014 Cohort: Two Years Remaining

21% have studied abroad (6 of 29 scholars)

Hutchison International Scholarship 2015 Cohort: Three Years Remaining

8% have studied abroad (3 of 40 scholars)

Note. Retention rates are calculated through spring 2016. Study abroad participation is calculated through summer 2016.

for four years participated in study abroad. Although the Hutchison program is reserved for high-achieving FGCSs, every cohort, apart from the latest one, has already shown a significantly higher percentage of students studying abroad than campus averages of 18% of the student body and 8% of FGCSs.

Survey and Focus Group Results

In addition to program data, a survey was developed and administered to Hutchison scholars in the 2010–2013 cohorts, and focus groups were conducted in April 2014 with approval from UT Austin's institutional review board. When the survey was administered, 116 Hutchison scholars were still at UT Austin or had just graduated, and 79 students completed the survey for a 68% participation rate. Questions were designed to gauge effectiveness of the program structure in achieving the three main program goals. Additionally, a total of 15 Hutchison scholars participated in the focus groups. Highlights from the data gathered are presented next.

Influencing Acceptance Decisions

Figure 4.4 demonstrates that 74% of survey respondents indicated that the award had at least a minimal impact on their decision to attend UT Austin. This finding, coupled with cohort yield rates, suggests that a major goal of the program, to influence acceptance of admission to UT Austin among the target population, is being achieved.

A majority of scholars indicated that they were not planning to study abroad before receiving the scholarship. "Study abroad was never on my radar. I never thought I'd be the kind of person that would go and live abroad. But the Hutchison scholarship changed that," explained one participant. Another student was skeptical, saying, "I have to get in and get out because I can't afford to stay any longer." These sentiments point to the reality that many students underrepresented in study abroad participation are deciding against the opportunity early and that an individual investment in the student, such as efforts to break down financial and academic barriers to study abroad, may be necessary to break through access barriers.

When asked if the scholarship influenced students' decision to attend the university, one participant said, "Absolutely. Money was a big deal coming out of high school. I couldn't get this award if I didn't come to UT." When asked if the scholarship should be offered later in their academic careers, students responded no, adding that it was important to know early so they could fit study abroad into their degree plans. Guiding students to programs that offer academically relevant coursework is a vital component of the program as Hutchison scholars tend to hesitate in taking a risk on studying abroad if it is likely to slow them down on their path to graduation.

Figure 4.4. Responses to "How influential was your Hutchison award in your decision to attend University of Texas?"

Removing Funding as a Barrier to Entry
Several survey questions were designed to gauge the impact the program has had on influencing attitudes toward study abroad among students, their families, and their networks. Other questions investigated funding, award timing, and program structure to determine if the program is structured appropriately to meet the needs of students and the goals of increasing access to study abroad for low-income FGCSs.

Nine percent of the scholars said they were very likely to study abroad, even if they had not been given the scholarship, which is consistent with the typical 8% of FGCSs that do end up studying abroad at UT Austin. Although nearly 75% of scholars indicated very high interest in study abroad after receiving the award, a majority reported they would not have studied abroad without the funding. This finding demonstrates the importance of early awards that do not require an application, thereby reaching a population that would likely have never pursued study abroad on its own.

The Program's Sphere of Influence
Although the Hutchison program is resource intensive, and only so many scholars can be admitted, a cultural change among the large FGCS campus population could have a significant impact on their perceptions of their ability to access study abroad at the university. More than 60% of survey respondents indicated that being a scholar significantly affected their discussions with friends about study abroad, and two-thirds reported the program had a great impact on their parents' perspectives on the value of study abroad.

Students cited the strength of peer influence regarding study abroad and about the students themselves becoming, as one student put it, "huge advocates" for studying abroad. One student said, "My friends don't think studying abroad is possible, but now that I have done it, they try." This discussion demonstrates the ripple effect taking place among friends of the scholars. Another student pointed to the impact on his family stating, "I am the oldest in my family and first to go to college. Now my brothers know it's a possibility and they are spreading the knowledge back at my high school." Nearly 80% of respondents indicated that the scholarship also helped in trying to convince their parents to support them in studying abroad.

Challenges of Studying Abroad
A deep understanding of the challenges students face in pursuing opportunities is critical for developing successful interventions like the Hutchison program. Figure 4.5 indicates that costs were the primary barrier for study abroad. Coursework abroad was a significant concern for two-thirds of the students. Nearly half the students struggled with program length and

Figure 4.5. Responses to "Which of these factors were most important or challenging to you in planning study abroad?"

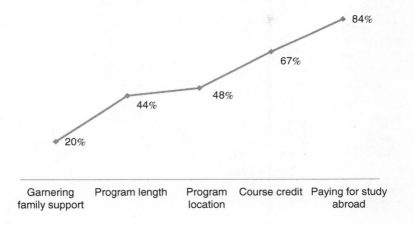

location. However, it should be pointed out that the challenges were interconnected; students typically faced multiple barriers, which can be overwhelming for those who are also new to higher education.

Program Structure, Components, and Effectiveness
Scholars receive hour-long advising sessions and tend to use this time to explore credit and finances in depth. Assistance is provided for identifying programs and classes abroad that match degree requirements and provide credit guarantees. The program is designed to mitigate the academic risks of participating in study abroad with support for academically integrating study abroad coursework into the four-year degree plan. One student said that the "biggest challenge was finding course credit, but [he or she] felt assured" in the advising session. As indicated in Figure 4.6, three components clearly rose to the top in terms of what students found most valuable: help with scholarships, assistance with determining how overseas courses will count for credit, and having access to a dedicated staff mentor to help students figure out how to navigate the entire process.

Survey Limitations and Implications
The focus group and survey research data clearly point to a successful program model. One limitation of the survey, however, is that the results are taken collectively from students at different stages of the study abroad process. Some have already studied abroad, whereas others are still planning their experience, which could affect the results. This may require delineating results based on who has already studied abroad or separating students into

Figure 4.6. Responses to "Please rate the value to you of the following components of the Hutchison International Scholars Program."

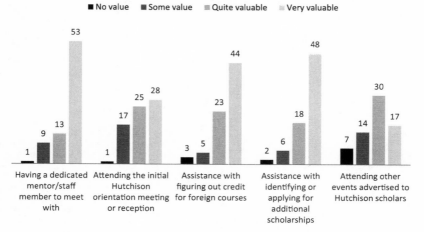

cohorts to see if those further along in their academic careers have different responses. Another factor is that participation was voluntary. Students unlikely to study abroad may be among the 32% of Hutchison scholars who did not participate in the survey.

The final focus group question challenged students to provide ideas on how to improve the program. Students suggested that more events should be offered for scholars to meet one another and that events should be mandatory; thus the idea of creating a mentor program matching younger and older scholars emerged. A final recommendation was to provide a predeparture orientation session specifically for Hutchison scholars, which could be arranged easily, although coordination would be necessary to ensure that the session does not duplicate any other required orientations.

Given the statistics provided in the tables, it is clear that the program is structured effectively to achieve its goal of increasing access to study abroad for FGCSs. Students are accepting their admission to the university at higher rates than their peers, and they are participating in study abroad at substantially higher rates than other FGCSs. Even if the scholarship funding was not available, elements of this program may serve as a model for other institutions seeking to influence matriculation, retention, and study abroad participation among this population.

Conclusion

Although the programs outlined here clearly improved access to study abroad, they are ever-changing works in progress attempting to meet FCGSs' multifaceted needs. With scant research on how FGCSs interact with study abroad specifically, administrators of both programs attempt to use direct feedback from the students themselves to better understand what works and, often more important, what does not.

FGCSs need comprehensive support, although they may not realize it. By providing up-front guidance to the systems involved in study abroad, students reflecting on their experiences in the UT Austin and IFSA-Butler programs reported a great appreciation for having dedicated staff and support services to guide them through what may not be an intuitive process. This timely support requires early and nonobstructive identification, either via shared campus information and outreach efforts or initial intake documents. The identification itself can help institutions track success of programming and use future partnerships and departmental collaboration.

Another important takeaway is that cost is not the only factor. In keeping with the principles of inclusive excellence itself, providing financial alleviants focuses narrowly on access rather than recalibrating to consider the type of diversity itself. FGCSs face multiple challenges like familial responsibilities, cultural differences, work hours, and often regimented major requirements. Creating systems that address all these very real obstacles may be the only way to provide scholarship support in a meaningful way, acknowledging that FGCSs need multipronged support before, during, and even after they have decided to pursue study abroad.

It is likewise necessary to recognize the importance of early investment in students' academic careers, ideally even before students arrive on campus. According to Hutchison scholar survey respondents, FGCSs decided early if the process, finances, or academic obligations were too great. Although advisers might be tempted to prepare students for the independence required of them abroad, leaving FGCSs to figure out the process themselves results in their failure to anticipate and mitigate their unique challenges. This may mean retooling practices and giving them time to plan.

Finally, it is useful to create a sphere of influence and reshape the value proposition. As FGCSs are a particularly risk-averse population, determining course options and using academically oriented language may be especially critical. Going beyond cost itself and explaining what students can gain from experiences abroad means reshaping how institutions conceive and market education abroad. Entrusting FGCSs themselves to advance that sphere of influence as participants provides not only peer-oriented content marketing but also an opportunity to learn from the study abroad pioneers it has successfully attracted. The Hutchison research and the IFSA-Butler student narratives are examples of institutions learning from students to improve long-term support.

Although FCGSs can seem like moving targets when it comes to engagement because of their inherent diversity and unique challenges, their participation in education abroad is advantageous to them and to the programs they attend. As a large constituency of undergraduate enrollment, study abroad programs benefit from the cultural acumen these students may already possess, and these students may benefit from the high-impact practice of international study. It is a complex challenge with multifaceted rewards—for institutions; students; their families; and, more broadly, their communities.

References

Barclay Hamir, H. (2011). *Go abroad and graduate on time: Study abroad participation, degree completion, and time to degree* (Doctoral dissertation). Available from ProQuest Dissertations and Theses database. (UMI No. 3450065)

Billson, J. M., & Terry, M. B. (1982). In search of the silken purse: Factors in attrition among first-generation students. *College and University, 58*(1), 57–75.

Causa, O., & Johansson, Å. (2011). Intergenerational social mobility in OECD countries. *OECD Journal: Economic Studies, 2010,* 1–44. doi:10.1787/eco_studies-2010-5km33scz5rjj

Chen, X., & Carroll, C. D. (2005). *First-generation students in postsecondary education: A look at their college transcripts* [NCES Report No. 2005171]. Washington, DC: National Center for Education Statistics.

Choy, S. (2001). *Findings from the condition of education 2001: Students whose parents did not go to college: Postsecondary access, persistence, and attainment.* Retrieved from nces.ed.gov/pubs2001/2001126.pdf

Greninger, S. A. (2011). *Documents of the general faculty: Annual reports of the standing committees of the general faculty for 2010–2011.* Retrieved from facultycouncil.utexas.edu/a3-faculty-committee-committees

Institute for Study Abroad. (2016a). [Percentage of semester participants who indicated FGCS status]. Unpublished raw data.

Institute for Study Abroad. (2016b). [Semester and summer enrollment by major]. Unpublished raw data.

Institute for Study Abroad. (2016c). [Participant grade point average by generational status: Upon application and completion of term abroad]. Unpublished raw data.

Institute for Study Abroad. (2016d). *Scholarships and funding opportunities* [Brochure]. Indianapolis, IN: Author.

Institute for Study Abroad. (2017). *Unpacked: A study abroad guide for students like me.* Retrieved from unpacked.ifsa-butler.org

Kuh, G. D. (2008). *High-impact educational practices: What they are, who has access to them, and why they matter.* Washington, DC: Association of American Colleges & Universities.

Lohfink, M. M., & Paulsen, M. B. (2005). Comparing the determinants of persistence for first-generation and continuing-generation students. *Journal of College Student Development, 46,* 409–248. doi:10.1353/csd.2005.0040

Milem, J. F., Chang, M. J., & Antonio, A. L. (2005). *Making diversity work on campus: A research-based perspective.* Washington, DC: Association American Colleges & Universities.

Murphy, M. C., Walton, G. M., & Stangor, C. (2013). From prejudiced people to prejudiced places: A social-contextual approach to prejudice. In C. Stangor, & C. Crandall, (Eds.), *Frontiers in social psychology series: Stereotyping and prejudice* (pp. 181–204). New York, NY: Psychology Press.

Orbe, M. P. (2004). Negotiating multiple identities within multiple frames: An analysis of first-generation college students. *Communication Education, 53,* 131–149. doi:10.1080/03634520410001682401

National Survey of Student Engagement. (2007). *Experiences that matter: Enhancing student learning and success annual report 2007.* Retrieved from nsse.indiana.edu/nsse_2007_annual_report/docs/withhold/nsse_2007_annual_report.pdf

Pascarella, E., Pierson, C., Wolniak, G., & Terenzini, P. (2004). First-generation college students: Additional evidence on college experiences and outcomes. *Journal of Higher Education, 75,* 249–284. doi:10.1353/jhe.2004.0016

Saenz, V.B., Hurtado, S., Barrera, D., Wolf, D., & Yeung, F. (2007). *First in my family: A profile of first-generation college students at four-year institutions since 1971.* Los Angeles, CA: Higher Education Research Institute, University of California.

Skomsvold. P. (2014). *Profile of undergraduate students: 2011–12* [NCES Report No. 2015167]. Washington, DC: National Center for Education Statistics.

Terenzini, P. T., Springer, L., Yaeger, P. M., Pascarella, E. T., & Nora, A. (1996). First-generation college students: Characteristics, experiences, and cognitive development. *Research in Higher Education, 37,* 1–22. doi:10.1007/BF01680039

University of Texas at Austin. (2012, September 19). The University of Texas at Austin releases preliminary enrollment data. *UT News.* Retrieved from news .utexas.edu/2012/09/19/2012-preliminary-enrollment-data

University of Texas at Austin, Office of Institutional Reporting, Research, and Information Systems. (2014). *Application/admission/enrollment management for first-time freshmen by ethnicity/race: Fall and summer entrants combined.* Retrieved from sps.austin.utexas.edu/sites/ut/IRRIS/StatHandbook/IMA_S_AppAdmitFTIC _2014_Fall.pdf

University of Texas at Austin, Office of Institutional Reporting, Research, and Information Systems. (2015). *Application/admission/enrollment management for first-time freshmen by ethnicity/race: Fall and summer entrants combined.* Retrieved from sps.austin.utexas.edu/sites/ut/IRRIS/StatHandbook/IMA_S_AppAdmitFTIC_2015_ Fall.pdf

University of Texas at Austin, Office of Institutional Reporting, Research, and Information Systems. (2016). *Statistical handbook: 2016–2017.* Retrieved from https://utexas.app.box.com/v/SHB16-17Complete

5

THERE AND BACK AGAIN

A Study Abroad Journey With Men

James M. Lucas

According to 10 years of data from the Institute for International Education, the female-to-male participation rate has consistently been about two to one for students studying abroad from U.S. institutions of higher education (Farrugia & Bhandari, 2015). Male participation rates remain flat despite a host of interventions on the part of education abroad professionals and organizations, including a trend toward short-term programs; more research and internship options; increased science, technology, engineering, and math (STEM) programming; and curricular integration efforts. Using results from a mixed-methods project conducted at a midwestern public university, this chapter explores the reasons males are underrepresented in education abroad and suggests practical intervention strategies based on the research findings.

Key Terminology

Many studies use *gender* to refer to differences between males and females, yet *sex* is more accurate. Sex refers to one's biological status as a man, woman, or intersex; gender is a complex concept, referring to one's internal sense of self (gender identity), external behavior (gender expression), or behavioral norms (gender role). Gender is a continuum of identities including female, male, transgendered, bigendered, gender fluid, and so on. The study described in this chapter looks at differences based on sex, men and women, and gender roles among men who identify as males, termed *cisgendered* (Porter, 2015). Males who identify as gay are participants in the research population, but neither sexuality nor gender identity were variables used in the analysis, which is a limitation that future studies should correct.

Males and Education Abroad

Although males are not underrepresented in most aspects of American society, their underrepresentation in education abroad is problematic for a variety of reasons. First, an imbalance of males and females makes logistical details (e.g., housing) difficult. Second, female-dominated programs lack a male perspective and create an isolating environment for males who do participate; males missing from the program environment pose the same pedagogical and climate challenges as any educational program lacking diversity.

Third, outcomes associated with participation correlate with beneficial growth for male college students. Participation improves personal and social growth, including students' confidence, maturity, and self-reliance; ability to work with diverse groups; ability to clarify values; and willingness to accept new ideas (Stebleton, Soria, & Cherney, 2013). This growth is especially helpful for males as it enhances skills needed to understand individuals from diverse backgrounds (Laker, 2005). One might argue that this is particularly critical in an era of revived nationalism and xenophobia in which "angry White men" (Kimmel, 2013) are seeking ways to reassert historic privileges.

When considering why males are underrepresented, gender studies suggest the influence of gender roles (Harper, Harris, & Kenechukwa, 2011). Although the meaning of *manhood* varies over time and culture, many young men are still socialized to follow traditional male norms (Harris, 2008; Kimmel, 2008). For this study, I used Brannon (1976) to define four hypermasculine norms: males are socialized to avoid feminine behaviors; to prioritize success, status, and power; to be reliable, steadfast, and self-sufficient; and to seek aggressive, risky, and independent behavior. Although individual students' beliefs vary, the presence of these norms in the collegiate context can help explain why males do not participate in education abroad: Many males view education abroad as a female-dominated activity that does not help them professionally, advance their financial stability, or allow them independence from an adult chaperone.

Participation Studies

This project contributes to the literature on participation studies in education abroad, begun in part by scholars such as Booker (2001) who surveyed students to determine why those who expressed interest never applied. He found that applicants were more likely to be "middle-class, non-minority, females" (p. iii), who start planning early and show more interest in cultural learning. Nonapplicants were more likely to be double majors, receive financial aid, and worry about the delay of graduation. Chieffo (2001) conducted a similar study, finding that most students chose to participate to have fun, have a cultural experience, and help their careers. Students who did not participate cited conflicts with other obligations and cost. Her study indicated that 20% of students first hear about education abroad and 66% seek information about it from peers.

Gore (2005) examined messages related to the Junior Year Abroad programs at the University of Delaware and Sweet Briar College. She believed that low male participation allows administrators to marginalize education abroad. If females dominate enrollment, then administrators "associate that recognition with the cultural assumption that women's search for education is not as serious as that of men" (pp. 43–44). Gore's work suggests current education abroad messaging might attract females more than males and that referrals from same-gendered professionals, peers, and parents might be different for males than for females. Redden (2009) supports this point, reporting that because most education abroad participants are female, most professionals in the field are female, and in turn most education abroad offices tend to create materials that target females. In short, there is a cyclical nature to the predominance of females in education abroad.

Several studies have critiqued the belief that males participate less because education abroad does not fit with their curriculum, particularly for those in STEM fields in which males tend to be overrepresented on college campuses. Shirley's (2006) study indicates that STEM programs accounted for 12.9% of education abroad in 2004, up from 7.7% in 1986, yet male participation decreased or remained constant. Similarly, Redden (2009) cites data that physical and life science participation rates increased about 14.5% and engineering rates about 13% in 2007. Given these increases, one would expect higher male participation; yet although 80% of engineers are males, 40% of engineers studying abroad are female according to the Global Engineering Education Exchange (Redden, 2009).

Shirley (2006) found several significant differences between males and females. First, parents and relatives were less likely to influence males than females. Second, females were more likely than males (65% to 49%) to view education abroad as conflicting with internships or work opportunities. Similarly, females expressed a significantly greater concern than males (87% to 68%) that cost was a barrier. For delaying graduation, the situation reversed, with males twice as likely (10% versus 5%) to report concern about delaying their graduation as an obstacle.

Salisbury, Umbach, Paulsen, and Pascarella (2009) conducted a large-scale analysis of the Wabash National Study on Liberal Arts Education about the decision to participate. This study found that men are 8% less likely than women to intend to study abroad. This statistic reflects findings by the American Council on Education and the College Board (2008), which found that females were 18% more likely to plan to participate, and Stroud (2010), whose study found that females were 2.4 times more interested in participation. Both studies also found that STEM majors had the same intent to participate as other students. In a follow-up analysis, Salisbury, Paulsen, and Pascarella (2010) focused on differences between the intent to participate of males and females, finding that active high school engagement negatively influenced males, experiences with influential peers positively influenced males, and an increased ability to integrate knowledge positively influenced males.

Although many studies have looked at students' decision to participate, few studies have focused on differences based on sex, and even fewer have employed a gender lens to interpret data. Even as these studies have provided a baseline for specific obstacles facing males, most have relied on quantitative research, which does not allow researchers to map the complexity of what male students are thinking and feeling as they consider whether to go abroad. To fill these critical gaps in the literature, this study employs a mixed-methods design to investigate male participants and nonparticipants, using a gendered lens to analyze the data.

Mixed-Methods Study

This study explored participation at a university that is a leader in education abroad, serving about 2,400 students per year and offering diverse program models. This setting was ideal because it offered a wide range of program opportunities relative to topics, experiences, and time frames; therefore, the setting was beneficial in that its size and scope addressed many of the common rationales for not going abroad (e.g., no time to go or no program related to the student's curriculum), which allowed this study to investigate why individual students did or did not participate. Other variables such as program availability, program reputation, and institutional commitment would most certainly play a larger role, or at least serve as an intervening factor, at other institutions.

For the study's first phase, data were analyzed from a 2007 survey of more than 2,000 education abroad participants and nonparticipants (65% response rate). During the second phase in 2009, I interviewed 24 male students; 12 were education abroad participants and 12 were nonparticipants. All respondents were recruited through e-mails sent to campus advisers targeting a similar demographic: college students, age 21 to 22; about to graduate; and pursuing majors with statistically high, average, or below average education abroad participation rates. Names used in this chapter are pseudonyms chosen by the students. This qualitative component delved deeper by investigating issues from previous studies that lacked sufficient context, such as the nature of family messaging. Finally, since 2009 this work has been road tested with male students, including two programs for fraternity males in 2015 and 2017. Efforts to get men to go abroad have led to questions about what to do with them once they are abroad; therefore, knowledge gained from applying this study's findings are integrated into the recommendations.

Quantitative Findings

In the first stage, survey analysis confirmed previous studies. Females were significantly more likely (*p*-value of .00) to go abroad; non-STEM majors and students with higher grade point averages (GPA) were more likely to go, with males more likely to be STEM majors and have a lower GPA. These variables all represented potential confounding issues to be addressed in the second phase. For example, why are STEM majors not participating? Is it the major or the large number of men in the population?

Table 5.1 presents the variables considered as influencers of participation and nonparticipation, with comparisons between male and female participants and nonparticipants measured on a 6-point Likert scale (1 = *no influence*, 6 = *strong influence*). Note that nonparticipants did not complete questions about obstacles to participation, which is a limitation of the survey design. Despite this issue, the survey suggests that males generally, participants and nonparticipants, find money to be less of an issue than females, yet male participants are more concerned about delaying their graduation or interfering with a campus athletic commitment. The study also indicates that male nonparticipants were significantly more likely to express no interest in education abroad than females.

To look at the decision-making process, I used a regression analysis to explore the factors in Table 5.1. As suggested by Salisbury and colleagues (2009) and Salisbury and colleagues (2010), obstacles factored higher in this process, supporting the idea that students dismiss education abroad before they investigate it. Coupled with the idea that male nonparticipants show significantly less interest, these findings suggest that some males do not consider education abroad or look at their options relative to the experience; they just assume it is not for them. Next, males reported less concern about opportunity costs or financing the program; however, they were more concerned about obligations at home (i.e., academic, family). Males prioritized

TABLE 5.1
Summary of Significant Quantitative Findings

Variables			Participants			Nonparticipants		
			Men	Women	Significance	Men	Women	Significance
Influences	1	Cost	3.27	3.59	.014			
	2	Location	5.16	5.44	.000			
	3	Duration	4.33	4.70	.000			
	4	Timing	4.63	4.92	.008			
	5	Coursework	4.43	4.61	.125			
	6	Language	3.21	3.31	.501			
	7	Home stay option	4.01	4.06	.727			
	8	Family support	3.32	3.71	.044			
	9	Peer messages	3.30	2.16	.015			
	10	Know faculty going	2.60	2.60	.968			
	11	Know peers going	2.30	2.16	.296			
	12	Supports future plans	4.82	4.97	.137			
	13	Fun	5.38	5.50	.088			
Obstacles	14	Finding time	2.72	2.75	.813	4.27	4.29	.875
	15	Finding money	3.82	4.11	.026	4.16	4.60	.004
	16	Lost wages	3.03	3.32	.034	3.50	3.88	.022
	17	Delay graduation	2.17	1.92	.032	3.19	3.07	.457
	18	Finding courses	2.77	2.62	2.82	3.25	3.34	.540
	19	Meet requirements	1.69	1.62	.405	1.88	1.87	.933
	20	Academic performance	1.92	1.87	.639	2.16	2.00	.213
	21	Health	1.69	2.14	.000	1.91	1.93	.854
	22	Safety	1.82	2.44	.000	2.04	2.13	.511
	23	Lease	1.89	2.08	.097	2.56	2.72	.252
	24	Leadership obligations	1.86	1.97	.303	2.44	2.41	.835
	25	Lack of family support	1.53	1.78	.015	2.08	2.18	.451
	26	Family obligations	1.75	1.82	.453	2.24	2.24	.988
	27	Homesickness	2.24	2.89	.000	2.76	2.90	.397
	28	Athletic obligations	1.33	1.25	.223	1.63	1.40	.023
	29	No interest				2.89	2.22	.000

Note. Significance level set at $p<.05$.

peer and marketing messages more highly than did females. Family concerns factored highly as an obstacle for all nonparticipants.

Qualitative Findings

The quantitative analyses confirmed previous studies, but the results were more complicated with the introduction of qualitative findings using student interviews. Students spoke a lot about the influence of their families, supporting earlier findings that the family's socioeconomic status alone did not seem to influence interest, but exposure to travel was significant. Having been raised in a family that traveled or interacted with diverse cultures increased motivation for the student and support from the parents. For example, participants whose parents had traveled overseas or who had traveled extensively with their families reported an easier time approaching their parents about going abroad and obtaining approval; males whose families had not traveled a lot had to do more convincing in the areas of safety and value.

Many males noted that they did not talk with their parents about education abroad because they believed that their obligations to school, work, and family made participation impossible. When they did discuss education abroad with their parents, they noted that the major discussion points were safety and purpose for attending, and a need to convince their parents about its value. Oscar, an international relations major, responded,

> With my dad, I had to sell it as a step in my career, that study abroad was a component of my education and my career that would take me places afterwards, and then I can show him how they've taken me places. . . . To my mom, I had to first convince her it was safe, and then there were several components like it was both the pragmatic, "This is my career. Look where I'm going to go with it."

In relation to cost, males stated that their parents seemed neutral, meaning that if their son could pay for it, he could do what he wanted. Several students compared this treatment to their sisters, to whom parents showed a more active interest in education abroad as an option. This finding supports research that parents, when it comes to their daughters, tend to be more engaged with educational decision-making (Frenette & Zeman, 2007), more proactive about safety (Sax, 2008), and less likely to push work and self-sufficiency (Dessoff, 2006; Gore, 2005).

Messages from peers and the institution also played a role in decision-making. The student interviews involved defining *education abroad* and reviewing promotional materials. Participants generally had a positive, yet limited, understanding of education abroad. Many males believed that education abroad was limited to taking classes at an overseas university; they were not aware of the full range of international programs offered through their home institution, including programs for first-year students, general education programs, and research or internship options. When Shaun, an international relations major, spoke about his second program in South Africa, he stated: "It was an internship. It would never be a study abroad program."

Related to campus messaging about education abroad, students agreed it was pervasive but limited in depth and value. They wanted more information from faculty and peers, particularly from other males. There was a belief that institutional claims were less authentic, offering more of a used-car salesman approach. At the same time, respondents wanted to know more about the substance of programs in terms of academics, noting that most of what they heard from peers was about drinking and fun. Jason, a STEM major, stated, "I guess from my experience, from what I picked up from students, they think a lotta [sic] study abroad is like a vacation during the summer." Danny, another STEM student, echoed his friend's sentiments: "You'll never have to study and pretty much get drunk every day, and like, you won't have to do any work."

Uniformly, the students interviewed stated that the dominant message about education abroad was that it is fun and an adventure—another theme—yet many added that they could just as easily have had fun on campus. They wanted to hear that the program was valuable and that they could gain something significant by studying in another country. Similarly, the males believed they could have just as much fun by traveling independently. Jack, a liberal arts major, stated,

> I'd rather—if I'm going to travel somewhere—go on my own accord and find cheap deals when I want to go. . . . I'd be more comfortable just kind of experiencing things and figuring out stuff on my own than having a preset program to what you're going to do.

Frank, a STEM major, also believed that males were more independent.

> Guys that I've talked to that went on study abroad say that like they had curfew and stuff like that and they were put off by that. They weren't allowed to really control the trip; they felt like they didn't have like a lot of input of like where they were going on the trip. It was kind of like "this is what you're doing at this time." . . . A lot of guys felt it was over-structured and then girls thought like it was perfectly structured.

Jack and Frank's comments suggest that if a male believed that education abroad was only about fun and visiting museums, he could plan that trip himself. Participants desired programs that not only were fun and exciting but also included value-added components that they could not achieve independently, such as access to businesses and multicountry travel.

The final theme is a strong preference for experiences that contribute to graduation and career success. The major difference between the participants and nonparticipants was that all participants had a strategic reason for going, often related to their major (e.g., language) or career (e.g., living abroad). In their decision-making, they considered the program's value and the cost of lost opportunities in other areas, such as not working for pay. Nonparticipants appreciated education abroad but found it less valuable than other opportunities. Greg, an international relations major and nonparticipant, exemplified this sentiment, saying,

> It's something that personally enriches you a lot, but I haven't seen—and my major is international relations, so obviously it would help my resume to get abroad—but as far as like academically, I haven't seen a whole lot of advantages to it.

Will, an engineering nonparticipant, added,

> I've got two internship experiences right now. Employers also like for engineering and, like if you are going to go to grad school, they want to see research, like not just necessarily study abroad. Unless if I could have found a study abroad program related to engineering, I would have done engineering research abroad, then that would have been something I would consider very carefully.

Figure 5.1 depicts a model of male decision-making. It suggests multiple layers of meaning that a male can ascribe to education abroad and the barriers between each layer are determined by each male's disposition (i.e., gender role) and situation (e.g., income, major). Participants who adhered to traditional notions of gender appeared to be harder to recruit, as were males with multiple situational factors that served as obstacles. Looking at the layers, the first layer, fun, was a common, pervasive message yet a weak motivator. The second layer, culture, was also a common narrative associated with education abroad. Again, this message did not motivate males relative to personal growth, but if a male associated culture with academic or professional value, then he often participated. This lack of interest in culture seems connected with the idea that arts and humanities are commonly associated with femininity in the United States, and that although males might want to seek risky physical activity, they seem reticent about cultural experiences in which they

Figure 5.1. Male education abroad participation model.

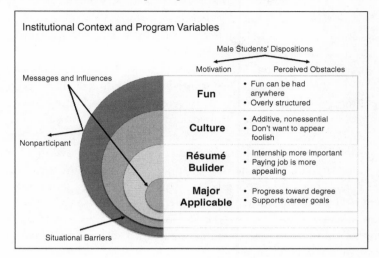

could appear foolish (i.e., weak) by having to live and learn in a new language and culture.

The third layer has to do with education abroad as a résumé builder. The professional connection is powerful and supported by the gender role norm of being successful, yet the male had to see education abroad as an integral method to be successful. Respondents viewed internships, summer work, and research as also productive, so if education abroad did not make sense in terms of the timing, cost, and focus, then it did not supersede other options. The fourth layer, the core of male decision-making, seems to be the student's ability to make a connection between education abroad and his goals. If the experience clearly connected with something the student saw as important for his major and career, then he went abroad, even if it meant overcoming some situational obstacles.

Applying Theory to Practice

This study's results suggest needed changes relative to engaging males in education abroad. These changes fell into three broad domains: messaging, recruitment, and educational interventions. Building off this work, I began to immediately alter my work in alignment with my findings, which included specialized marketing and recruitment and the creation of a program for male students. The recommendations presented in the following section represent ideas not only suggested by the research study but also honed during six years of implementing theory into practice.

Better Messaging

The research project's findings demonstrated that messaging used to promote education abroad is often ineffective with male students. Respondents found that group photos and selfies with famous sites looked too much like photos from a family vacation, and the quirky group shots (i.e., people jumping in the air) seemed childish. They wanted to see photos of students conducting field research, meeting with company executives, and doing service or community engagement. They wanted active, academic photos that helped them understand what education abroad entails. For the written narrative, they reported that common phrases used on websites such as "life changing" or "outside my comfort zone" are unappealing as well. These messages reflect the perspective of the converted, of a student who has gone abroad and has a new view of the world. This perspective does not relate to students who have not participated. Also, the ideas of cultural learning, stepping outside one's comfort zone, and learning about one's self did not square well with masculine gender norms.

Adapting to this orientation requires for one to be intentional about the images and language used for marketing. At the most basic level, materials should incorporate pictures of diverse males with images of students engaged in fieldwork, especially photos that can merge a global focus of the program with an academic setting, creating a stronger message relative to males' values. Education abroad literature must balance a straightforward, utilitarian message about the value of education abroad to one's profession and academic studies with the traditional cultural messages. Instead of uncoached testimonials from students' peers, education abroad office staff should seek responses to prepared questions (e.g., How did study abroad help you academically?) from graduating seniors, recent male alumni, graduate schools, and potential employers. Males want to hear from someone who made education abroad work for them, not just from someone who went abroad.

These findings also suggest changes to the way one typically responds to students' questions. In advising students, purposefully including more information about how to overcome various obstacles before focusing on the benefits helps them get beyond an initial can't-afford-to-go mentality. Then, one can frame benefits in terms of academic and professional impact, avoiding generic boilerplate program descriptions, to strengthen the value proposition of participation. This approach is particularly effective in tandem with information specifically connecting a selection of opportunities to students' stated major and explaining why each option might be a good fit for them. Such a tactic provides choice and highlights a range of formats that are often less obvious to students.

Following up with students' e-mails, calls, or questions is also an important factor; this study suggested that men might apply for a program later and be less prepared than females, so retaining correspondence and staying connected with students until they apply or decide against participation helps to compensate for behaviors that might otherwise winnow out students who would benefit from the experience. For example, following up on initial inquiries to check on male students has prompted action on their part, whereas something as simple as "How long should my essay be?" will cause a delay in an application. Additionally it can help to reserve spaces in programs for male students, especially for those with rolling admissions. With a limited-space program, the program could fill with female students before a male even applies.

A final messaging issue involves naming and describing the programs. Sometimes programs are designed for specific majors, and tailoring the description to that population makes a lot of sense; however, if the program is open to a wide range of students, the program title and description need to be written in such a way to attract students' attention. For example, the program title The Maori and the Kiwi: Environmental Values and Practice in New Zealand was changed to Hobbits versus Dwarves: Environmental Values, Issues, and Practice in New Zealand. The program not only garnered more applicants but also attracted a large number of males. Similar outcomes have been achieved by relating program descriptions to current events and popular culture. For example, it has been effective to use zombies and the popularity of dystopian movies to talk about climate change, science fiction and comics to talk about environmental values, and Wonder Woman to talk about feminism.

Some education abroad professionals believe these tactics pander to students and lower rigor; in fact, such strategies are not meant to alter the course content, outcomes, or difficulty. I am merely suggesting that academics sometimes create descriptors full of jargon that students do not understand. Meeting students where they are—using words, metaphors, and examples that make the program sound more appealing and accessible—by connecting academic ideas to students' lived experience is rather a best practice in integrative learning (Hanstedt, 2012).

Directed Recruitment

An important lesson learned from the research was a necessity to think about advertising education abroad versus marketing education abroad. This distinction separates generic messages emitted passively from directed, differentiated messages designed to recruit diverse students in active ways. One strategy is to use different messages for different student audiences by sex and by major. For example, in an e-mail to male engineering students, one might depict students engaged in engineering fieldwork; feature engineering-related sites or activities; and quote engineering returnees, preferably males. Another method involves using statistics and information about the importance of global education for students' future professions. Finally, because males are drawn to a program's unique experiences and opportunities, highlighting features such as company visits, might become the focus for a marketing message instead of academic content, credits, or location.

Professionals can employ the same tactics in face-to-face interactions with students. The first question to ask is, "What is your major?" followed by, "What interests you most in going abroad?" The discussion moving forward is based on the student's response, with emphasis on how the programs available can help the student advance his (or her) interests. Also, the goal should be to help a student to go abroad, not to go on a specific program. Often, returnees and faculty leaders promote their own programs. If using returnees and faculty leaders to recruit applicants, then education abroad staff should provide training and parameters about how to advise students. As the males in this study said, they want to hear from male peers, but the messages they get are the war stories associated with drinking, adventure, and sex, which are not compelling. They also do not want to hear from used car salesmen who want to push their program; they need to know about the full range of options that will benefit them as individuals.

Finally, education abroad leaders need to market education abroad in male-dominated spaces and work with male returnees to give presentations in their clubs, fraternities, and classrooms. Education abroad offices should also establish a network of advisers, administrators, and faculty to recruit in classes and via e-mail. Students are more likely to read an e-mail from someone they know, and male students expressed a desire to hear about education abroad from faculty, not the education abroad office. Approaching a well-respected academic adviser, faculty member, or program director has proven successful. Asking these individuals to nominate or recommend students for a program or to provide an introduction for a student are more likely to succeed than cold calling a student through phone, e-mail, or social media, which often does not work with today's students.

Males feel pressured to graduate quickly or find relevant work experience, and some academic advisers and faculty perpetuate that message. Experience suggests that this message can be strongest in male-dominated majors such as engineering and science. Education abroad leaders and offices must collaborate to dispel common myths and advance pro-academic messaging. Based on the findings of this study, if an education abroad office promotes going abroad, but the engineering faculty do not back up this message, many students and especially male students will listen more to their faculty. In these situations, educating and focusing marketing toward students is insufficient; offices must also target campus leaders.

Male-Friendly Programming

If offices want to highlight interesting programmatic features, then those features need to actually exist. Males value programs that offer experiences they cannot achieve through personal travel, so program designers should consider a series of pedagogical issues. Coursework and assignments should help students connect their experience to their major, even if the program's focus is outside their major. Allowing students to focus their assignments on broad themes or questions gives students the freedom to explore areas of interest. For example, in a class about sustainability, the assignment can be to write about water, so a business student writing about water might look at how water scarcity influences tourism operations, whereas an agriculture student might discuss crop production. Feedback from course evaluations suggests that students like this flexibility and rate programs better when this flexibility is present.

Next, instructors can reduce the lecture time to allow an increase in active learning. Davis (2002), Sax (2007), and Kimmel (2008) indicate that male students tend to be more tactile learners than females; they tend to have trouble sitting and listening for long periods of time and want to touch and manipulate objects while learning. Males seek real-world applications and practical uses for their learning, so when visiting a place like a museum, instead of a group tour, a leader might design a scavenger hunt or set of questions to get students to discover exhibits independently. This pedagogical approach allows students to explore at their own pace instead of leading them as a group. If a guest speaker is applicable, then leaders should ensure the guest talks with not at the students. In support of this effort, leaders can send the guest information about the group, the program's design, suggestions about how to work with the group, and the key ideas and outcomes desired for the interaction. Of course, some females are also tactile learners, and so these different approaches will help vary the pedagogical approaches used in programs for the benefit of all students.

Beyond academics, the literature suggests that male students are more likely to engage in risky behavior and have disciplinary problems (Harper et al., 2011; Laker, 2005), indicating that program designers should think carefully about how to prepare students during predeparture and on-site orientations. Moreover, it is useful to consider male program leaders. There are abundant studies about the importance of a male role model during students' formative years and how having a male teacher can be important developmentally for male students (Kimmel, 2008). Male students tend to test limits; therefore, the leader's reaction to the students is important. Laker (2005) states that educators tend to react to discipline problems by chastising students like bad dogs, when instead educators need to work with males where they are developmentally. Instead of acting like a ship's captain and leading from the bridge, a leader who gets on deck with male students gets a better response by establishing trust yet not being a pushover. Ideally, a program's leadership will include males and females because each male and female student will respond and relate differently to different types of leaders.

Conclusion

Masculinity, just like gender, is not monolithic. Male students come to education abroad with many different values, ideas, and needs. Although this study suggests that gender roles can partially account for differences in participation by sex, further research is needed to confirm this work, as well as look at issues related to gender identity and sexuality. Also, dispositional and situational factors influencing decisions at the individual level can be mediated by aspects of one's identity; therefore, the issues presented in this chapter relate to males generally but not all men specifically. Using an inclusive lens requires those in the field to start considering how the results of one population can inform work with other populations as well as how students who fall into multiple low-participation categories (e.g., White versus Black males) may face different additional obstacles.

Despite the fact that ongoing research is required, a core outcome from this study is that nonparticipants may not consider education abroad because of lack of interest, lack of knowledge, or a belief that they cannot participate because of time or costs. Educators need to continue research about obstacles to participation, but those in the field also need to integrate existing knowledge into practice. A first step is to review the current communication materials and switch from generic advertising to differentiated marketing. This tactic means not only improving visual and written messaging but also directly recruiting students in the spaces they inhabit. Underrepresented students often do not attend fairs or look at websites; educators need to go out to the places where these students live, work, and play with compelling messages about the variety of programs and reasons to participate.

More important, this study suggests that the use of active and experiential learning in the design of programs is important. It is not enough to sell the programs well; those in the field need to think carefully about who their students are and what they need or want from an international education experience.

References

American Council on Education Art & Science Group, & the College Board. (2008). *College-bound students' interests in study abroad and other international learning activities.* Retrieved from www.acenet.edu/news-room/Documents/2008-Student-Poll.pdf

Booker, R. W. (2001). *Differences between applicants and non-applicants relevant to the decision to apply to study abroad* (Doctoral dissertation). Available from ProQuest Dissertations and Theses database. (UMI No. 3012949)

Brannon, R. (1976). The male sex role: Our culture's blueprint for manhood and what it's done for us lately. In D. David & R. Brannon (Eds.), *The forty-nine percent majority: The male sex role* (pp. 1–48). Reading, MA: Addison-Wesley.

Chieffo, L. P. (2001). *Determinants of student participation in study abroad programs at the University of Delaware: A quantitative study* (Doctoral dissertation). Available from ProQuest Dissertations and Theses database. (UMI No. 9982678)

Davis, T. (2002). Voices of gender role conflict: The social construction of college men's identity. *Journal of College Student Development, 43*, 508–521.

Dessoff, A. (2006). Who's not going abroad? *International Educator, 15*(2), 20–27. Retrieved from www.nafsa.org/_/File/_/alandesssoffarticle.pdf

Farrugia, C., & Bhandari, R. (2015). *Open doors 2015: Report on international educational exchange.* New York, NY: Institute of International Education.

Frenette, M., & Zeman, K. (2007). *Why are most university students women? Evidence based on academic performance, study habits, and parental influences.* Ottawa, CA: Statistics Canada, Analytical Studies Branch.

Gore, J. E. (2005). *Dominant beliefs and alternative voices: Discourse, belief, and gender in American study abroad.* New York, NY: Routledge.

Hanstedt, P. (2012). *General education essentials: A guide for college faculty.* Hoboken, NJ: Wiley.

Harper, S. R., Harris, F., & Kenechukwa, M. (2011). A theoretical model to explain the overrepresentation of college men among campus judicial offenders: Implications for campus administration. In S. R. Harper & F. Harris III (Eds.), *College men and masculinities: Theory, research, and implications for practice* (pp. 221–238). San Francisco, CA: Jossey-Bass.

Harris, F. (2008). Deconstructing masculinity: A qualitative study of college men's masculine conceptualizations and gender performance. *NASPA Journal, 45*, 453–474.

Kimmel, M. S. (2008). *Guyland: The perilous world where boys become men.* New York, NY: HarperCollins.

Kimmel, M. S. (2013). *Angry White men: American masculinity at the end of an era*. New York, NY: National Books.

Laker, J. A. (2005). *Beyond bad dogs: Towards a pedagogy of engagement of male students* (Doctoral dissertation). Retrieved from arizona.openrepository.com/ arizona/bitstream/10150/193751/1/azu_etd_1073_sip1_m.pdf

Porter, T. (2015). *Breaking out of the "man box": The next generation of manhood*. New York, NY: Skyhorse.

Redden, E. (2009, May 22). Lost men on campus. *Inside Higher Ed*. Retrieved from www.insidehighered.com/news/2009/05/22/men

Salisbury, M. H., Paulsen, M. B., & Pascarella, E. T. (2010). To see the world or stay at home: Applying an integrated student choice model to explore the gender gap in the intent to study abroad. *Research in Higher Education, 51*, 615–640.

Salisbury, M. H., Umbach, P. D., Paulsen, M. B., & Pascarella, E. T. (2009). Going global: Understanding the choice process of the intent to study abroad. *Research in Higher Education, 50*, 119–143.

Sax, L. J. (2007). *Boys adrift: The five factors driving the growing epidemic of unmotivated boys and underachieving young men*. New York, NY: Basic Books.

Sax, L. J. (2008). *The gender gap in college: Maximizing the developmental potential of women and men*. San Francisco, CA: Jossey-Bass.

Shirley, S. (2006). *The gender gap in post-secondary study abroad: Understanding and marketing to male students* (Doctoral dissertation). Available from ProQuest Dissertations and Theses database. (UMI No. 3233968)

Stebleton, M. J., Soria, K. M., & Cherney, B. (2013). The high impact of education abroad: College students' engagement in international experiences and the development of intercultural competencies. *Frontiers, 22*, 1–24.

Stroud, A. H. (2010). Who plans (not) to study abroad? An examination of U.S. student intent. *Journal of Studies in International Education, 14*, 491–507.

6

COMMITMENTS THAT WORK

Removing Barriers for Students With Disabilities in
Education Abroad

Ashley Holben and Monica Malhotra

*Too often, there's this expectation that students with disabilities should just do the bare minimum
to get through college. Things like study abroad don't even come up.*

—Jay Ruckelshaus, study abroad alumnus, Rhodes Scholar, student with a disability

Although U.S. college and university students with disabilities are still
reported to be underrepresented in study abroad, their participation
rates have increased over time (Institute of International Education,
2016), indicating a desire by these students to have the same experiences as
their peers without disabilities. In response to this increase in participation,
international education practitioners have often looked to disability-related
nondiscrimination laws to determine their practice. However, because the
application of U.S. laws to international education programs overseas are
ambiguous at best, and nondiscrimination laws in host countries are often
unenforceable or nonexistent, they must explore other solutions.

To remove barriers for students with disabilities, forward-looking international education professionals and institutions must implement internal
practices and policies that ensure inclusion beyond the minimum requirements of the laws. With its growing focus on issues of equity and diversity,
and with the current ambiguity in the application of these laws overseas,
the field of international education is shifting from fulfilling only the minimum requirements of disability nondiscrimination laws to fostering an
institutional culture of inclusion to create greater access for students with
disabilities to participate in education abroad.

This chapter traces such recent shifts by briefly reviewing the laws
that affect students with disabilities in education abroad and then, more

importantly, discusses how institutions can uphold their own commitments to inclusion to increase the number of students with disabilities in education abroad and the quality of their experiences. To illustrate these points, we draw from the experience and research of Mobility International USA (MIUSA), a disability-led, nonprofit organization, as well as the insights of professionals in the international education field.

Americans with Disabilities Act and the Definition of *Disability*

It is difficult to have a discussion on disabilities and international education without first defining the terminology and considering the corresponding legislation that has been applicable in the U.S. higher education system. To begin, it is important to note that the same protections provided in the United States on the basis of race, sex, national origin, and religion also apply to disability. The Americans with Disabilities Act (ADA, 1990) is the comprehensive U.S. civil rights law protecting people with disabilities from discrimination in employment, public accommodation, transportation, telecommunications, and the activities of state and local governments. Furthermore, any program or activity receiving federal financial assistance is covered by Section 504 of the Rehabilitation Act of 1973, a law that has requirements similar to the ADA but follows a different enforcement process (Sygall & Scheib, 2005, p. 107).

The ADA (1990) defines a *person with a disability* as someone with a physical or mental impairment that substantially limits one or more major life activities, someone with a record of such an impairment, or someone who is regarded or perceived as having such an impairment. In 2008 Congress passed the ADA Amendments Act, which has made it easier for individuals with impairments such as cancer, diabetes, epilepsy, and bipolar disorder to be recognized as individuals with disabilities (Grossman, 2014). It should be noted that not all people who qualify for protections under the ADA identify as having a disability.

In the United States, the ADA's public accommodations requirement includes accessibility of facilities and programs open to the public; post-secondary institutions are subject to the ADA, Section 504, or both (Higher Education Compliance Alliance, n.d.), and policies apply to a broad scope of institutional activities, including facilities, programs, and employment. When an educational product or environment is not fully accessible, institutions must extend reasonable accommodations to those who disclose their disabilities and present appropriate documentation. Although most institutions have traditionally focused on this individual accommodation approach, other institutions have advocated for approaches that embrace the principles of "universal design" to create environments and products that are "usable by all people to the greatest extent possible" (Mace, Hardie, & Plaice, 1991, p. 155), and to shift the burden of implementing access from individual students to the institution (Ashmore & Kasnitz, 2014). An example would be to reduce the need for students with disabilities to submit disability documentation or request specialized accommodations because the design of the campus or a course is inherently accessible. Although progress with disability rights legislation in the United States has led to increased numbers of people with disabilities attending U.S. colleges and universities (Burgstahler, 2014; National Council on Disability, 2003), the higher education field continues to explore how to provide students with disabilities access not only to academic requirements but also to the experiences beyond the classroom that contribute to a holistic and well-rounded student life, including student clubs, social activities, Greek life, athletics, career services, internships, practicums, and study abroad.

Application of U.S. Disability Laws in International Education

All aspects of an international education program that takes place on U.S. soil are subject to the ADA, and in some cases, Section 504 of the Rehabilitation Act and other nondiscrimination laws (Yee, 2010). Examples might include ensuring that a program website and online application are accessible to a blind person who uses screen-reading technology to navigate the Internet or ensuring that captions are provided on a predeparture webinar for a person who is hard of hearing.

How these laws apply to the overseas component of international education programs is less obvious. In 2012 the National Association of College and University Attorneys addressed the state of federal disability discrimination law with respect to college and university study abroad programs for students, noting that very few federal courts have examined the applicability of federal disability discrimination laws to study abroad programs, and those that have do not provide absolute clarity on whether Section 504 and the ADA apply to study abroad programs. The National Association of College and University Attorneys article concluded that "because of the unsettled state of the law . . . institutions should strongly consider designing and administering study abroad programs as if the ADA and Section 504 apply to them" (Charney & Whitlock, 2012). Conducting study abroad programs as if the ADA and Section 504 apply mitigates potential legal risks and also results in greater access to study abroad programs for students with disabilities. Furthermore, a 2010 memo from the Disability Rights Education and Defense Fund suggested that U.S. institutions of higher education and education abroad providers must take some proactive steps to encourage their overseas program partners and organizations to provide physical and program modifications, auxiliary aids, and other accommodations (Yee, 2010).

The ADA "sets only minimal requirements" (Vance, Lipsitz, & Parks, 2014, p. x), and therefore in the face of uncertain applications of the law, international educators can choose to go beyond what is required by the laws in the United States and host countries. Risk of litigation aside, an ethical motivation for international educators to advocate for inclusion may be to uphold institutional or departmental missions, such as those designed to create equitable opportunities for all students to build skills, knowledge, and experiences to become global citizens, preparing them to navigate an increasingly global landscape.

Students With Disabilities in Education Abroad

Since 2009 the U.S.-based Institute of International Education (2015) has collected disability data on U.S. study abroad through its Open Doors survey, although the disability status for many education abroad students remains unknown. Among those institutions where disability status is known, the number of U.S. students with disabilities studying abroad rose to 3,194 in 2012–2013, an increase from 2,786 in the previous academic year, and represented 5.1% of total study abroad students. Meanwhile, 11% of undergraduates in 2011–2012 reported having a disability (National Center for Education Statistics, 2016). These data can be improved as more institutions accurately respond to the disability-related questions on the survey and as more students who identify as having a disability disclose that information.

Following an earlier study surveying college students with disabilities about their intent to study abroad, Groff, Hameister, Hosley, and Matthews (1999) listed four concepts for international education staff to consider when including students with disabilities in study abroad, ultimately concluding that

> university staff may yearn for a concise set of rules for what they must do to allow students with disabilities to study abroad, but such rules do not exist. Disability services, instead, is about applying common sense, goodwill, creativity, and knowledge about the intent of nondiscrimination legislation to the needs and interests of individual students. (p. 98)

Cordano and Soneson (2009) also acknowledged that legal cases have raised more questions than answers regarding the applicability of U.S. disability rights laws to study abroad programs and proposed that the application of universal design principles to overseas programming may be a smart approach to benefit students with diverse disabilities: "By moving away from understanding the needs of participants from a legalistic perspective towards understanding the types of access each program offers, study abroad offices can make more effective programming decisions" (pp. 271–272).

Other works in the literature have focused on the unique aspects of supporting students with a particular subset of disabilities. Alden and Shames (2005) offer recommendations for college study abroad personnel and administrators interested in making study abroad programs more responsive to students with learning disabilities or attention-deficit/hyperactivity disorder in the spirit of the universal design model, arguing that this model will stand up to the test of good pedagogy for all study abroad students, regardless of ability or disability. Lucas (2009) said that when properly managed, most students with mental health conditions such as depression and anxiety are fully capable of functioning on a study abroad program, but resident directors commonly face several challenges in providing the necessary supports. Although Lucas's work does not situate *mental health* under the larger umbrella term of *disability* or discuss the impact of disability-related legislation and policy on students with mental health conditions going abroad, it does emphasize the role of international educators to assume the responsibility of changing internal processes to meet students' individual needs.

It would be inaccurate to state that little has been written on the subject of students with disabilities participating (or not) in international education. Indeed, there is a diverse and growing body of literature and practical resources. There is, however, an ongoing need for examples of best practices that illustrate how institutions can instill and sustain a culture of inclusion that goes beyond compliance and individual-level support. We turn next to MIUSA and other organizations that have sought to close the gap between theory and practice.

The Role of MIUSA

The national nonprofit organization MIUSA remains one of the leading and most active contributors to the growing body of literature on the participation of students with disabilities in education abroad. Since 1981 it has conducted over 100 disability-focused international exchanges intended to build the leadership capacity of people with disabilities and nondisabled allies worldwide. By 2015 more than 2,000 individuals from more than 130 countries, the majority of whom have apparent or nonapparent disabilities, had participated in cross-disability MIUSA programs to and from the United States (MIUSA, 2016).

Drawing from these decades of fully inclusive program design for participants representing diverse disabilities and countries, MIUSA has positioned itself as a trusted resource to international education professionals seeking technical assistance for including people with disabilities in their own programs. In 1995 MIUSA was charged with administering the National Clearinghouse on Disability and Exchange (NCDE), a project sponsored by the U.S. Department of State's Bureau of Educational and Cultural Affairs, to increase the representation of people with disabilities in the broad range of public sector and private sector people-to-people programs between the United States and other countries. The State Department continues to sponsor the clearinghouse annually. MIUSA publications produced as part of the NCDE project include a manual on accommodating people with disabilities in international education programs, a guide to national and international disability-related laws for international education organizations and participants, a booklet on working with overseas partners to include students with disabilities, an online resource library of tip sheets and good practices from the field, and personal stories from exchange alumni with disabilities. Other core activities of the NCDE project include providing expert technical assistance, training, and free information related to disability adaptations abroad and budgeting for inclusion, logistical problem-solving, recruitment, and comprehensive resources to reduce the barriers that prevent people with disabilities from accessing international opportunities. In the first 20 years since the NCDE project was established, MIUSA staff have responded to more than 10,000 unique inquiries from higher education institutions; international education program providers; the Bureau of Educational and Cultural Affairs and its private-sector cooperating agency partners, colleges, and universities; U.S. and foreign disability organizations; volunteer entities; and individuals with disabilities from around the world.

It should be noted that MIUSA is not alone in its efforts. The University of Minnesota project Access Abroad and the No Barriers to Study consortium of Pennsylvania-area institutions are two initiatives that, although no longer active, have contributed valuable information and materials to influence institutional practices (Sygall & Scheib, 2005). Meanwhile, organizations such as Abroad With Disabilities, as well as many faculty, international educators, disability service professionals, and student researchers, have added to the body of expertise and research, investigating factors that influence the participation and quality of experiences of students with disabilities in education abroad.

Creating and Sustaining an Institutional Culture of Inclusion

In this section, we shift from looking at the literature to reviewing best practices in the field. All these examples have been collected from across the country by MIUSA to demonstrate models for building a foundation to implement inclusive strategies in campus collaboration, partnerships, on-site assessment, program design, and outreach. These practices expand on discussions about diversity that are already occurring in education abroad programs to include students with disabilities.

Campus Collaborations

To ensure that all students are given an equal opportunity to engage in education abroad programming, including those with disabilities, MIUSA has found it important for international educators to work with key players on campus, including faculty, staff, and students. In one successful case, the University of Wisconsin–Whitewater (UW–Whitewater) Center of Global Education has worked not only to increase but also exceed the participation of traditionally underrepresented students in its study abroad programs, including ethnic minorities; first-generation students; and lesbian, gay, bisexual, transgender, queer, and other students, and then applied those successful methods to also increase the participation of students with disabilities (MIUSA, n.d.-c).

UW–Whitewater connected with key centers on campus that directly worked with diverse students including the Office of Multicultural Affairs and Student Success. The next step was to recruit faculty to develop study abroad programs that would attract underrepresented students, provide academic fit, and create more familiarity to reduce fear of going abroad among students and their families. For instance, the director of the Center for Students with Disabilities and an Intercultural Communication faculty member at UW–Whitewater created a study program in Brazil to examine diversity issues in amateur and professional sports from the 1930s to the present day, which was designed to appeal to students with disabilities and lesbian, gay, bisexual, transgender, queer, and other students by addressing diversity barriers in sports and the need for and the rising significance of the Paralympic Games, Gay Games, and Special Olympics. This topic especially attracted applicants with disabilities because UW–Whitewater has a strong wheelchair basketball program, yet it also appealed to students from other sports and interdisciplinary academic fields. The program leaders did not intend to develop a program only for a select group of students but to learn more about access needs for all programs by starting with topics of inclusion. By joining other offices on campus, the education abroad office was able to more effectively communicate with diverse underrepresented students as well as advance the institution's commitment to broader inclusion.

In addition to developing new programming, some administrators of education abroad programs have found it useful to develop a campuswide disability working group, involving colleagues with expertise in technology, outreach, marketing, advising, and disability-related accessibility. These groups can provide a necessary space for sharing practices on campus that serve all involved. Others have found it instructive to involve education abroad alumni with disabilities, who add a critical voice to the table and challenge assumptions about students' needs and abilities.

Overseas Partnerships

In addition to on-campus collaborations, many institutions have reported to MIUSA staff through surveys, interviews, and inquiries that it is necessary to work with overseas partners to ensure they are prepared to receive students with disabilities. One specific strategy has been to incorporate a nondiscrimination policy in international partnership agreements, setting expectations for diversity. For example, in its *Handbook for International Agreements*, Eastern Michigan University states as part of its nondiscrimination policy that "each institution will conform with equal opportunity and will not discriminate based on race, color, national origin, or disability" (Narayanan & Palosaari, 2014). Other institutions like Wellesley College and Michigan Technological University use similar language, which not only communicates the sending institution's commitment to inclusion but also makes clear from the outset that partner institutions should anticipate receiving diverse students, including students with disabilities.

Additional measures for gaining support and cooperation have included urging institutional partners to set expectations for how programs can be modified for students with disabilities as needed and to agree on how financial responsibilities will be shared among the parties to fund any necessary accommodations (McLeod & Scheib, 2005). Before sending a Deaf student to study abroad at a partner institution in Scotland, for example, international educators at the University of California, Santa Cruz reached an agreement with staff at the Scottish university about how disability-related accommodations for that student would be provided. Staff at Santa Cruz agreed to arrange to send an American Sign Language interpreter with the student, and the host institution, the University of Edinburgh, agreed to provide note takers and contacts for local Deaf organizations and resources.

More investigation is needed to determine outcomes from cases in which sending institutions negotiated with overseas partner institutions to advocate on behalf of disabled students' participation in international programming.

Program Design

International education professionals who request technical assistance from MIUSA staff often find that MIUSA's practice of designing international programs with a wide range of disabilities in mind is applicable to their broad range of international education programs. Throughout its 35-plus years of operation, MIUSA has pioneered a variety of approaches, using a human rights framework, to provide over 100 short-term, cross-disability exchange programs between the United States and other countries, which it administers for people with diverse types of disabilities and nondisabled people alike. These approaches include researching the exchange program's host site's disability-related laws and policies and its cultural attitudes and perceptions toward disability, physical accessibility, and disability-related services and resources; building flexibility into the program design or schedule to accommodate a variety of individual needs; budgeting for disability-related accommodations such as sign language interpretation, specialized computer hardware and software, or supplementary health insurance coverage; encouraging interdependence among all participants; and requiring all participants and host families to sign an agreement to be respectful of diversity, including but not limited to people with disabilities.

Applying the sort of framework advocated by MIUSA, one teaching associate from the University of Illinois' Department of Human and Community Development designed a winter break trip to South Africa to include students with and without mobility disabilities and had favorable results. One of the students who participated and uses a wheelchair reflected on what made the program design inclusive in the following:

> [The faculty leader] knew that she wanted to make her Cape Town trip accessible, so she started to plan for it in advance. She made sure that our living accommodations, volunteer placements, and cultural activities and excursions were accessible. Our hostel had ramps, plus large bedrooms and bathrooms for easy access. Since she put in all that time, that took a lot of stress out of the experience for me, since I didn't have to worry about accommodations as much. (MIUSA, n.d.-d)

Education abroad professionals or leaders of education abroad programs who do not anticipate the participation of students with disabilities run the risk of designing the program without accessibility in mind, and therefore often find themselves having to retrofit an inaccessible program when a student with a disability registers, creating a lot more work and stress for all involved.

On-Site Assessment

Researching and providing information about accessibility overseas ahead of time can allow students to make informed decisions about which education abroad programs are most suitable for them and can help students and advisers plan for accommodations more accurately (Cordano & Soneson, 2009). Gathering the criteria necessary to survey the accessibility at their overseas sites is one step that some universities are taking toward greater transparency.

To illustrate, representatives from MIUSA interviewed staff at the University of North Carolina at Chapel Hill's study abroad office to document its approach to this practice. The office first funded a half-time position to evaluate and ensure accessibility for students with disabilities to participate in its programs. The adviser visited every host site to evaluate criteria for accessibility, which she gathered after collaborating with disability organizations such as MIUSA. The adviser took note of site information such as physical accessibility of classrooms, public transportation, restaurants, and restrooms. These findings were reported to the university's Accessibility Resource and Service Office, a liaison of the study abroad office. Once the information was collected, study abroad staff posted their findings and photos under an Accessibility tab on the office's website (MIUSA, n.d.-a). After students returned from an education abroad program, they received a program evaluation form to provide feedback on the resources they received and information for future applicants with disabilities.

The goal of this process is to empower students with disabilities to choose a program independently and confidently and to prepare for any necessary accommodations. As Bates, Smith, and Carr Allen (2014) noted,

> With this approach, [the adviser] hopes to be able to give students with disabilities the information that they need to make informed decisions about possible study abroad options; their educational experience is not limited by their disability, but by access to information about study abroad locations, programs, and options. (para.16)

The University of Minnesota likewise provides resources online through Access Abroad, a collaborative initiative between its Learning Abroad Center and its Disability Resource Center, which are intended for faculty, professionals, parents, and students. Access Abroad offers a checklist for students with disabilities as they prepare for a program as well as accessibility information for programs, including disability culture, classroom and excursion accessibility, housing and food, technology, and transportation. These resources are available to University of Minnesota students as well as those at other institutions (University of Minnesota, n.d.).

Outreach

Many higher education institutions and education abroad providers are already prioritizing diversity and underrepresented communities in their outreach efforts, and MIUSA has documented a number of U.S. institutions' strategies to ensure that people with disabilities are included among them (Sygall & Lewis, 2006). Texas A&M University's Study Abroad Programs Office includes disability-related resources on its website to demonstrate its expectation of disabled students' participation. These resources include, for example, instructions on how to disclose a disability and how to request disability-related accommodations in education abroad. Likewise, Western Michigan University incorporates disability-positive messages into its outreach materials. One of its study abroad brochures, designed to appeal to students with disabilities, includes the following comment from Juanita Lillie, founding director of Abroad with Disabilities:

> I went to Costa Rica as part of a three-month study abroad experience with many other exchange students from across the United States. Once I returned to Michigan, many individuals were surprised that I was able to successfully go abroad with my disability (vision impaired). I know my situation is not unique, and I am an avid believer that students of all abilities should travel abroad. (Western Michigan University, n.d.)

Another outreach strategy practiced at U.S. institutions is to create recruitment positions in the education abroad offices that prioritize diversity and inclusion. For instance, the University of California, Berkeley offered a study abroad program alumnus, who is blind, an internship with its study abroad office to speak at study abroad fairs and conduct outreach among students with disabilities. The alumnus spoke about the impact of his program, the process to get disability-related accommodations, and his personal tips to be successful abroad. Initiating and nurturing relationships with alumni with disabilities is a simple method to continue to learn about access needs for students with disabilities and to provide useful contacts to recruit, mentor, and support more students with disabilities (Sygall & Lewis, 2006).

Next Steps

In moving forward, scholars and practitioners can help improve the quality and depth of data on students with disabilities in education abroad by asking or responding to disability-related questions in surveys. As noted previously, the Institute of International Education's (2016) Open Doors survey tracks the disability status and disability type of students who go abroad. The National Survey of Student Engagement asks students each year if they have a disability, have studied abroad, or are an international student, along with many other campus experience questions (Scheib, 2016). Likewise, i-graduate's International Student Barometer likewise asks students if they use disability services at their host institution, and, if so, asks them to report their satisfaction level with those services (MIUSA, n.d.-b). Surveys should continue collecting disability demographics in the same way they gather data related to participants' gender, ethnicity, first-generation college student status, and other diversity factors. Analysis of students with disabilities, moreover, should not be left out of final reports and presentations, further marginalizing their issues and possibilities for institutions to create effective change.

At the institutional level, more can be done in terms of data collection and research. When conducting an international student learning outcomes survey or study abroad alumni research, program administrators may consider asking whether respondents have a disability, among other demographic questions. With follow-up analysis, correlations can be drawn to determine which practices and programs work best for students with disabilities, not only in terms of the number of students participating but also in supporting the quality of the students' experience.

It is important for international education professionals to gain a sense of the quality of students' experiences throughout the study abroad process, from initial advising to reentry. Many of the inquiries the NCDE receives are based on a reactive approach from study abroad programs for individual cases to support a student with a disability. Questions relate to the various types of accommodations that need to be made, how to arrange and pay for such accommodations, and how to work with overseas partners. It is time the trend shifts to a proactive approach of conducting research and broadly sharing strategies that work.

One proactive approach is to consider avenues for funding. This includes identifying on-campus resources, third-party provider resources, and services at host universities while also expanding the search, which may include reaching out to local Veterans Affairs offices for disability equipment, disabled people's organizations that advocate for the rights of people with disabilities, international organizations for the disabled, and overseas resources such as sign language interpreters. A number of organizations would like to contribute to the advancement of people with disabilities and have the resources to do so; taking time to connect with these organizations on this shared goal is the first step to achieving contributions.

As professionals continue to reimagine the field of international education, they should consider involving not only students with disabilities but also interns, advisers, and consultants with disabilities who do not necessarily have a background in education abroad. Inviting people with disabilities to lend their experiences and expertise will help shape and inform the future of the field into one that is inclusive by their standards.

Conclusions

Although the practices described in this chapter are not part of any formal disability-related laws, international education professionals can implement them immediately, even if no student with a disability has yet expressed interest in going abroad. Briefly, these practices include strengthening relationships with diverse offices and departments on campus that support students with disabilities, communicating a commitment to inclusion to overseas partners and negotiating how disability-related support will be provided, designing education abroad programs to be inclusive of and accessible to participants with disabilities from the outset, surveying the accessibility of the overseas sites, and conducting targeted outreach to students with disabilities in media and publicity strategies.

Regardless of where the evolving laws stand, it is imperative for institution administrators to strategize how they will fully include students with disabilities in international education, motivated not only by a desire to comply with basic legal requirements for nondiscrimination but also by a stronger desire to be thought of as leaders and innovators supporting the most underserved students so that all students are given an opportunity to reach their full potential. To challenge the expectation that students with disabilities should just do the bare minimum to get through college, international educators must expect the participation of students with disabilities in their programs and go beyond minimum compliance for the benefit of all involved.

References

Alden, P., & Shames, W. (2005). The impact of short-term study abroad on the identity development of college students with learning disabilities and/or AD/HD. *Frontiers, 11*, 1–31.

Americans with Disabilities Act, 42 U.S.C. § 12101 et seq. (1990).

Ashmore, J., & Kasnitz, D. (2014). Models of disability in higher education. In M. L. Vance, N. E. Lipsitz, & K. Parks (Eds.), *Beyond the Americans with Disabilities Act: Inclusive policy and practice for higher education* (pp. 21–34). Washington, DC: National Association of Student Personnel Administrators.

Bates, C., Smith, C., & Carr Allen, M. (2014, April 29). "*Basic information is the first barrier*": Lori Rezzouk's Story. Retrieved from disabilityrights.web.unc.edu/2014/04/29/lori-rezzouk

Burgstahler, S. (2014). Universal design in higher education. In M. L. Vance, N. E. Lipsitz, & K. Parks (Eds.), *Beyond the Americans with Disabilities Act: Inclusive policy and practice for higher education* (pp. 35–48). Washington, DC: National Association of Student Personnel Administrators.

Charney, A., & Whitlock, J. (2012, April 26). Federal disability laws: Do they translate to study abroad programs? *NACUANotes, 10*(7). Retrieved from www.higheredcompliance.org/resources/publications/ADAAbroad.pdf

Cordano, R., & Soneson, H. (2009). Universal design and study abroad: (Re-) designing programs for effectiveness and access. *Frontiers, 18,* 269–288.

Groff, M., Hameister, B., Hosley, N., & Matthews, P. (1999). College students with disabilities and study abroad: Implications for international education staff. *Frontiers, 5,* 81–100.

Grossman, P. (2014). The greatest change in disability law in 20 years. In M. L. Vance, N. E. Lipsitz, & K. Parks (Eds.), *Beyond the Americans with Disabilities Act: Inclusive policy and practice for higher education* (pp. 3–19). Washington, DC: National Association of Student Personnel Administrators.

Higher Education Compliance Alliance. (n.d.). *Disabilities and accommodations.* Retrieved from www.higheredcompliance.org/resources/disabilities-accommodations.html

Institute of International Education. (2016). *U.S. study abroad: Students with disabilities.* Retrieved from www.iie.org/Research-and-Insights/Open-Doors/Data/US-Study-Abroad/Students-with-Disabilities

Lucas, J. (2009). Over-stressed, overwhelmed, and over here: Resident directors and the challenges of student mental health abroad. *Frontiers, 18,* 187–215.

Mace, R., Hardie, G., & Plaice, J. (1991). Accessible environments: Toward universal design. In W. E. Preiser, J. C. Vischer, & E. T. White (Eds.), *Design interventions: Toward a more humane architecture* (pp. 155–176). New York, NY: Van Nostrand Reinhold.

McLeod, L., & Scheib, M. (Eds.). (2005). *A practice of yes: Working with overseas partners to include students with disabilities.* Mobility International USA and the National Clearinghouse on Disability and Exchange.

Mobility International USA. (2016). *Celebrating MIUSA's story.* Eugene, OR: Author.

Mobility International USA. (n.d.-a). *Scouting out accessibility overseas.* Retrieved from www.miusa.org/resource/bestpractice/scoutforaccess

Mobility International USA. (n.d.-b). *Students with disabilities in education abroad statistics.* Retrieved from www.miusa.org/resource/tipsheet/USstudentsatisfaction

Mobility International USA. (n.d.-c). *Using multicultural strategies to increase study abroad.* Retrieved from www.miusa.org/resource/bestpractice/uwisconsinwhitewater

Mobility International USA. (n.d.-d). *"We always found a way to make it work."* Retrieved from www.miusa.org/resource/story/shannon

National Center for Education Statistics. (2016). *Fast facts: Students with disabilities.* Retrieved from nces.ed.gov/fastfacts/display.asp?id=60

National Council on Disability. (2003). *People with disabilities and postsecondary education—position paper.* Retrieved from ncd.gov/publications/2003/people-disabilities-and-postsecondary-education-position-paper

Narayanan, K., & Palosaari, N. (2014). *Handbook for international agreements.* Ypsilanti, MI: Eastern Michigan University Office of International Initiatives.

Scheib, M. (2016). The case of missing data: Students with disabilities. *Forum,* 18–19.

Sygall, S., & Lewis, C. (Eds.). (2006). *Building bridges: A manual on including people with disabilities in international exchange programs.* Eugene, OR: Mobility International USA and the National Clearinghouse on Disability & Exchange.

Sygall, S., & Scheib, M. (Eds.). (2005). *Rights and responsibilities: A guide to national and international disability-related laws for international exchange organizations and participants.* Eugene, OR: Mobility International USA/National Clearinghouse on Disability and Exchange.

University of Minnesota. (n.d.). *Access abroad: Access abroad overview.* Retrieved from umabroad.umn.edu/professionals/accessabroad/

Vance, M. L., Lipsitz, N. E., & Parks, K. (2014). Introduction. In M. L. Vance, N. E. Lipsitz, & K. Parks (Eds.), *Beyond the Americans with Disabilities Act: Inclusive policy and practice for higher education* (pp. vii–x). Washington, DC: National Association of Student Personnel Administrators.

Western Michigan University. (n.d.). *WMU study abroad for students with disabilities.* Retrieved from wmich.edu/sites/default/files/attachments/u532/2015/Disabilities%20Abroad%20Flyer_0.pdf

Yee, S. (2010). *Update on U.S. federal disability rights laws and participation by students with disabilities in overseas exchange programs.* Retrieved from http://www.miusa.org/sites/default/files/documents/resource/DREDF%20Memo%202010%20Outbound.doc

7

PROMOTING EDUCATION ABROAD AMONG COMMUNITY COLLEGE STUDENTS

Overcoming Obstacles and Developing Inclusive Practices

Rosalind Latiner Raby and Gary M. Rhodes

Although many may associate education abroad with four-year institutions, linked to the traditional model of the junior year abroad program, the reality is that overseas opportunities for community college faculty, staff, and students have been available for more than 60 years. Such programming has been developed in large part with the explicit purpose of preparing students for a constantly evolving economy, one that requires graduates to be able to work with others from diverse backgrounds and cultures.

Despite this long history, the availability of education abroad programming in individual institutions has been sporadic, often changing from one year to the next and varying from one college to another. Much of the problem stems from the fact that education abroad is typically not viewed as an integral part of most colleges' missions, nor does it receive full leadership support, making it difficult to expand to its full potential. In a previous publication we concluded that for study abroad participation in community colleges to double, it would be necessary to understand the reasons for periphery status; conduct a critical examination of college policies, programs, and practices; and then enact new models that not only support the relevance of international education, but also create a context in which actions are supported and sustained over time. (Raby & Rhodes, 2014, p. 7)

Here we focus on education abroad offerings in California community colleges with the goal of presenting challenges in the field and sharing effective practices. A case study of California community colleges is valid because more than half of all U.S. community college faculty-led study abroad programs are offered by California community colleges. Of the 4,850 community college students nationwide who studied abroad in 2014–2015, 2,586 were California community college students (Institute of International Education [IIE], 2016).

Data from four research studies inform this chapter, including an analysis of the California Colleges for International Education (CCIE, n.d.) website; findings from the CCIE (2014) annual report detailing California community college stakeholder opinions on education abroad; results from the California Community College Student Outcomes Abroad Research Project (CCC SOAR) (Raby, Rhodes, & Biscarra, 2014), which provides demographic and student success measures from 14,216 California community college students who studied abroad from 2001 to 2010; and data from a June 2016 survey completed by 47 directors of California community college education abroad programs.

This chapter fills a gap in the community college education abroad literature by updating discussions of what works from the perspective of those who work in the field. Central to this discussion is an understanding of changing community college student characteristics, outreach efforts, and definitions of how to achieve student success.

Applying the Community College Mission to Education Abroad

Community colleges are designed to not only admit all students but also "offer a college-level curriculum to those who might otherwise not be able to take part in postsecondary education" (Cohen, Brawer, & Kisker, 2014, p. 1). The unique nature of the community college mission has opened opportunities for a far greater number of students to study abroad. Even a few decades ago, education abroad was considered to be only accessible by those attending traditional, often elite, four-year colleges and universities (Raby & Valeau, 2016).

Three factors in the community college mission help to expand access to education abroad. The first is the community college mandate to offer enrollment options for nontraditional students to achieve a higher education (some of whom may see community colleges as a second chance), to accommodate university overflow, and to serve the local community. The low cost and flexible programing reinforce these enrollment options. As a result, more than half of U.S. adults in higher education (13 million) take classes at one of the 1,600 community colleges and their branch campuses (American Association of Community Colleges, 2016). California community college education abroad programs are designed as open access opportunities for community members not enrolled as students, enrolled students, and other university students. In this way, no student can be denied an opportunity to study abroad.

Second, the community college mission supports students who intend to transfer to a four-year college or university or study to gain specific skills to advance in their careers. In line with this objective, accredited study abroad courses must fit the needs of students seeking an academic program or specific career path, as well as community members who simply want to enroll for the learning experience. California community college education abroad classes are designed to be the same in number and course objectives as those offered for credit on campus and as such provide the college with state funding based on the state-mandated established ratio of faculty-to-student contact hours per unit per semester (Raby, 2008). In addition, academic education abroad programs are preapproved to fulfill California State University and University of California transfer requirements.

Finally, the community college open access mandate allows enrollment of any person over the age of 18, concurrent enrollment for those in high school, and reentry enrollment of university students. The purpose of open access is to offer equal and fair treatment to all students, resulting in a highly diverse student body. As applied to education abroad, California community colleges allow students to enroll without limits, including those related to background or previous studies. Most programs also enroll students with a grade point average as low as 1.7 to 2.0 and do not set any barriers concerning age.

California Community College Programs

California community colleges offer programs of varying lengths, including a distribution of full-semester and short-term winter and summer programs of more than 3 weeks. Some 7- to 10-day classes abroad are integrated into home campus offerings, often with some on-campus or online instruction

TABLE 7.1
Enrollment Overview, California Community College
Education Abroad Programs

Academic Year	Number of Colleges With Programs Enrolling						
	No Students	Fewer Than 10 Students	11–20 Students	21–50 Students	51–99 Students	More Than 100 Students	More Than 200 Students
2013–2014	38	1	8	22	11	4	1
2014–2015	35	5	8	17	15	1	1

From California Colleges for International Education (n.d.).

(CCIE, n.d.). California allows students to attend multiple community colleges at the same time, permitting students to study in another college's program and transfer credits to their home campus.

Most community college education abroad classes are faculty led. Few community college students participate in direct enrollment at an overseas university or program designed by a third-party provider that is not organized through a community college study abroad office. At the same time, travel, living arrangements, and institutional liability insurance are typically arranged by a provider. Faculty-led programs offer a variety of benefits for community colleges. Faculty members design, lead, and market programs to their own students with whom they can develop special bonds and group affinity (Robertson, 2015). Community college students, moreover, often prefer being with other students from their community college, as is the case in a faculty-led program (Amani, 2011; Brenner, 2016). Finally, faculty-led programs often adhere to minimum enrollment numbers based on on-campus enrollment formulas that ensure adequate program size and support institutional budget planning (Raby, 2008). Table 7.1 shows current enrollment patterns in California.

Student Demographics

Community colleges and their education abroad students are highly diverse. That said, it is difficult to track trends because few community colleges maintain records on student study abroad demographics (Quezada & Cordeiro, 2016). Of the 124 CCIE member program offerings in 2015–2016, only 38 programs kept demographic records; 13 of these recorded only gender, and 25 recorded gender and race (CCIE, n.d.). Minimal data collection is explained in part by the fact that for some colleges, such designations go against the open access policy. From a logistical perspective, moreover, because most California community colleges do not have a dedicated education abroad office, there is no one to collect and analyze the data. Nor are faculty members expected to track demographic data, as this is not something they would ordinarily do in their regular courses on campus.

What we do know about the diversity in education abroad programs can be gathered through combining multiple sources of data. Table 7.2 compares community college student demographics from the following sources: AACC's (2016) national demographics of all students who attend community colleges; California Community College Chancellor's Office (2016) of all students who attend California community colleges; IIE's (2016) Open Doors report of community college students nationally who study abroad; CCC SOAR study (Raby, Rhodes, & Biscarra, 2014), which includes 14,216 students from 36 California districts who studied abroad, and of this group, 1,906 first-time, full-time students who studied abroad; and a survey of CCIE (n.d.) colleges who conducted a study abroad program that includes a sample of 647 California community college students who studied abroad.

One might assume that because the student body is inherently diverse, then those who participate in education abroad programs will also be diverse. In actual numbers, this assumption does bear out on some level. For example, a larger percentage of students of color study abroad through community colleges than through four-year universities (IIE, 2016). Moreover, the percentages of some racial and ethnic groups who study abroad are beginning to match their overall racial and ethnic percentages nationally and at the California state level.

Given that many community colleges reflect a homogenous local community, any discussion of a target number for outreach programs needs to take into consideration college, state, and national percentages. For example, the IIE (2016) shows that nationally 7.5% of all community college students who study abroad are African American. On the surface, this seems like an extremely low number, especially when compared to White, non-Hispanic students who represent 66% of that population (IIE, 2016). However, 7.5% as a percentage is almost half of all national community college students who are African American (14%) (AACC, 2016) and is greater than the percentage of African Americans who attend California community colleges (6.3%)(California Community Colleges Chancellor's Office, 2016). Likewise, the same report indicates that nationally 16.7% of all community college students who study abroad are Latino (IIE, 2016). Although much lower than those for White non-Hispanic students who study abroad, these numbers indicate that Latino study abroad students almost meet national

TABLE 7.2

Comparative Demographics: Community College Enrollment and Education Abroad Participation

	American Association of Community Colleges (2016) National (1200 colleges) 2015–2016	California Community Colleges Chancellor's Office (2016) Statewide (113 colleges) fall 2015	Institute of International Education (2016) National (106 community colleges) 2014–2015	All education abroad students represented in the California Community College Student Outcomes Abroad Research Project (Raby, Rhodes, & Biscarra, 2014) State (36 community colleges) 2001–2012	Sample of surveyed education abroad students represented in the California Community College Student Outcomes Abroad Research Project (Raby, Rhodes, & Biscarra, 2014) State (36 community colleges) 2001–2012	California Colleges for International Education (2016) State (47 community colleges) 2015–2016
Female	57%	50.5%	NA	69%	66%	62%
Male	43%	50.5%	NA	31%	34%	38%
White non-Hispanic	49%	21.19%	66.0%	59%	52%	25% 3% (Armenian) .25% (Iranian) .25% (Russian)
Latino or Hispanic	22%	43.99%	16.8%	16%	21%	40%
African American	14%	6.31%	7.5%	2%	3%	10.5%

(Continued)

Table 7.2 (*Continued*)

	American Association of Community Colleges (2016) National (1200 colleges) 2015–2016	California Community Colleges Chancellor's Office (2016) Statewide (113 colleges) fall 2015	Institute of International Education (2016) National (106 community colleges) 2014–2015	All education abroad students represented in the California Community College Student Outcomes Abroad Research Project (Raby, Rhodes, & Biscarra, 2014) State (36 community colleges) 2001–2012	Sample of surveyed education abroad students represented in the California Community College Student Outcomes Abroad Research Project (Raby, Rhodes, & Biscarra, 2014) State (36 community colleges) 2001–2012	California Colleges for International Education (2016) State (47 community colleges) 2015–2016
Asian or Pacific Islander	6%	11.11% (Asian) 2.84% (Filipino) .43% (Pacific Islander)	5.1%	7 % (Asian) 1.6% (Filipino) .4 % (Pacific Islander)	9 % (Asian) 1 % (Filipino) 1 % (Pacific Islander)	14% .25% (Japanese) .25% (Korean) .5% (Chinese) .25% (Indian) .25% (Hawaiian)
Native American or Alaskan Native	1%	.44%	.4%	1%	1%	.5%
Multiethnic	3%	3.7%	3.5%	.5%	.5%	2.7%
Unknown	4%	4.12%	NA	13%	13%	1.2%

percentages (22%) (AACC, 2016) but are low for California percentages (44%) (California Community Colleges Chancellor's Office, 2016).

Obstacles to Expanding Education Abroad

Many of the same obstacles that create barriers to studying abroad at universities also exist for community colleges, including program costs, inadequate staffing, and gaps in office support. At the same time, some obstacles are particularly critical in community colleges, such as a lack of inclusion of study abroad in college policies, a shortage of institutional funding for a designated office and staff, the insularity of education abroad programs vis-à-vis other academic and student support programs, and limited program availability. It remains important to identify obstacles before addressing how one might go about changing the system.

Student Program Cost

The increasingly expensive nature of an education abroad program is a critical issue for community colleges that serve communities that are often economically challenged. Policies related to the use of financial aid for education abroad vary and are contingent on staff who understand that such aid can be used for study abroad. For students not eligible for financial aid, concerted efforts to ensure alternate funding options are necessary. In 2015–2016 the average cost of a California community college education abroad program, including airfare, was about $3,500 for a four- to five-week summer program and $7,500 for a semester program (CCIE, n.d.). Although considered low cost for the field, these fees are high when compared to an annual California community college tuition of about $1,200. Innovative college-directed student funding models exist (Giammarella, 2011) but are rarely implemented.

Inclusion in Strategic Plans at College, State, and National levels

National, accreditation agency, and nonprofit policies that define community college retention, success, and completion objectives have largely ignored internationalization efforts. Echoing national community college policy, some community college mission statements have recently eliminated the global or international language that once marked a pivotal reform strategy and whose loss will have long-reaching consequences (Raby & Valeau, 2016). In California 45.5% of community colleges do not mention the word *international* in any policy and only 3% specifically mention the words *education abroad* or *study abroad* (CCIE, 2014).

Line Item in Budget to Support Full-Time Positions and Office

Few California community colleges have a line item in their budget for physical office and affiliated education abroad office costs. It remains common to
have faculty who volunteer services, faculty on release time, or administrators who are given education abroad as a small part of their duties. This lack
of a comprehensive support office and staff creates a situation in which few
community college professionals know about or understand how to apply
guiding principles and theories in the field (Raby & Rhodes, 2014). A recent
leadership study by Valeau and Raby (2016) shows a national change in that
61% of 91 community college respondents work full-time and have professional titles that include the words *global, international,* or *intercultural,* only
7% of which have positions specifically devoted to education abroad. The
rest are split between positions in international student offices and positions
administering all international-related programs, including internationalizing curricula and overseas partnership development programs.

Institutional Program Costs

No literature to date has determined the precise costs related to minimal
levels of staffing or administration needed to sustain a community college education abroad program. Necessary expenditures typically include
administrative salaries, salaries or replacement costs for faculty who teach
abroad, site visits, marketing costs, the administrative costs of running an
office, counseling and career integration services, and predeparture and reentry programming. Although exact amounts have not been identified by the
research, it is clear that limited funding on community college campuses is
an important issue, especially when services and overhead must be absorbed
by students as part of program fees.

Programmatic Insularity and Individual Rivalry

In California, community colleges' education abroad programs are often iso-
lated from other units on campus as they are rooted in specific academic
departments, often supported only by a single faculty member. This mini-
mizes opportunities to conduct institution-wide student outreach or work
effectively with other units on campus on counseling, financial aid, and student success. Insularity is most problematic when faculty retire, move elsewhere, or opt not to run an abroad program any longer, as the continuity,
experience, and expertise related to implementing the program are lost (Raby
& Valeau, 2016). When another faculty member does offer his or her services
to fill the void, the challenge of ensuring that he or she can gain access to the

professional development and training necessary for running the program effectively is significant.

Availability of Programs

In 2015–2016 community colleges in California offered a total of 28 semester programs, 12 winter or spring break programs, and 75 summer programs. Often faculty-led programs can accommodate only a limited number of students. Thus, any effort to increase options to study abroad must include an increase in the number of programs offered. For example, from 2013–2014 to 2014–2015, CCIE colleges increased their offerings by four fall semester, four winter term, three spring semester, and five summer programs that increased student enrollment from 2,391 in 2013–2014 to 2,586 in 2014–2015. These additions allowed only 195 more students to study abroad (CCIE, n.d.). Despite the range of offerings, it is likely that few California community college students know about existing study abroad options, even on their own campus. Because California has more than 2 million community college students, the number of available programs would need to increase greatly to provide for significant growth.

New Opportunities to Counter Obstacles

In June 2016 we conducted an online survey of 47 California community college study abroad leaders to learn (a) current practices, (b) specific practices that target defined student populations, and (c) specific needs in terms of increasing student diversity in education abroad classes. The following is a compilation of data from this survey, which provides insights into new opportunities for enhancing education abroad, all of which could be factors in changing student characteristics, outreach efforts, and definitions of how to achieve student success.

Changing Student Characteristics

Student diversity in community colleges creates spaces for internationally oriented conversations in the classroom or through specifically planned events (Raby, Budd, Serban, & Van Hook, 2016). Yet, a discussion is still needed about target goals to achieve equity in diversity for education abroad that purposefully reflects the community that is served by the community college. One California community college dean who participated in the survey said,

> We have a large number of Asian and Latino students on campus and they enroll in study abroad in large numbers. [Our efforts have not been] as

successful with African Americans who comprise a significantly smaller student population on campus and study abroad in low numbers.

When the goal is to match overall racial and ethnic percentages, the point of equity changes depending on whether statewide or national percentages are the point of comparison.

Changing Outreach Efforts by California Community Colleges

The literature suggests it is important to define specific outreach activities for students of color, and yet for community colleges that serve a naturally diverse student population, different forms of outreach already take place (Quezada & Cordeiro, 2016). The following subsections present responses from our June 2016 survey of 47 California community college education abroad leaders.

Outreach Responsibility
All respondents agreed that the faculty member leading the study abroad program was also the person with primary responsibility for recruitment. Recruitment begins with the class taught by that faculty member. Eighteen participants reported they do not purposefully target any particular student group because their intent is to serve all students, and because their student population is already diverse, those who choose to study abroad mirror that diversity.

Intersection of Program Design With Effective Outreach
All respondents agreed that program design is the most important factor in reaching nontraditional students, and, above all, it remains critical to keep costs low.

Personal Connections
All respondents noted that word of mouth is an effective and critical strategy and is mostly done in the classroom or at other events on campus, such as club day, welcome day, and student appreciation day. One respondent pointed out that "when faculty conduct classroom visits, it is the personal invitation that makes all the difference." Faculty and student relationships, sometimes over multiple semesters, also build trust and support outreach. One respondent noted that "for the last 10 years, 98% of our study abroad students are African American and word-of-mouth was the only strategy used." Fifteen respondents conduct on-the-spot conversations with students during class breaks, lunch, and at student meetings. Most said that they have no strategy on which group of students to target; one said that "the only

intent is to go where there are the most students." Only two respondents recounted that they go to places where ethnic minority students gather with the intent to increase the number of participants from these populations.

Intentional In-Person Marketing
All respondents said they plan classroom presentations based on the discipline of the study abroad course, and eight plan a series of informational meetings that are listed on the master calendar. Four respondents visit department meetings of the same discipline at nearby colleges. One respondent is on the program of a local university study abroad informational session and draws heavily from university students as participants for the community college study abroad program.

Traditional Marketing
All respondents said that traditional methods of marketing, including posters and flyers and answering phone and e-mail requests, are the most effective methods for reaching students. Ten respondents gain permission from other local community colleges to place posters and flyers of noncompeting programs on their campuses. Traditional marketing practices also include use of an electronic message board that is centrally located on the campus and that provides information about upcoming education abroad programs for deadlines, placement of ads in college newspapers, web banners on college website home pages, and updated web pages. Ten respondents create lists of potential students based on their major and e-mail them or send blast e-mails to all students at the college. None of these practices noted outreach to specific racial or ethnic groups. The evidence of only one California community college hosting a study abroad fair demonstrates either the lack of importance to this known marketing strategy or that resources available at study abroad offices are limited. Study abroad fairs are used most often by California universities, and program leaders find that these fairs contribute to large numbers of study abroad student participants.

Collaboration With Campus Offices
Fourteen respondents said they routinely hand out posters and provide information to designees at various campus offices to remind students about options to study abroad. They specifically target counselors for incoming students and financial aid counselors. Three respondents also target campus offices that serve nontraditional students such as State Student Support Services and Federal TRiO Program offices. One respondent receives a list of students who are eligible for Pell Grants from the financial aid office and then targets them for study abroad recruitment.

Targeted Support to Help Students With Paperwork
Eight respondents said they have a program to help students complete the study abroad program application, the Free Application for Federal Student Aid (FAFSA), and the U.S. Department of State's Benjamin A. Gilman International Scholarship application essays. These respondents maintain that the process of completing an application enhances the chance that the student will actually enroll in a study abroad program. Fourteen respondents said that preparing to study abroad at least one year in advance is also important for most community college students.

Online Marketing
Thirteen respondents said they list their programs on the CCIE web page, and although they do not depend on enrollment from other campuses, they often reach their own students through this website. Seven respondents said they update their campus web page more than once a year. Only four respondents use Facebook to share information on financial aid and scholarships. Other forms of outreach seen as contributing to enrollment success include three respondents who invite parents to orientation meetings, one respondent who produces brochures in multiple languages, one respondent who offers local community grants only to ethnic minority students, and one respondent that oversees an outreach program to local high schools (a strategy that is affiliated with multiyear planning).

Changing Definitions of How to Achieve Student Success

Research has found that student engagement leads to positive college outcomes. Harper and Quaye (2009) note that the "participation in educationally effective practices, both inside and outside the classroom, leads to a range of measurable outcomes" (p. 3) and can be used to create specific programs. Many community college programs that promote positive outcomes involve close interaction with faculty and culturally diverse groups of people in hands-on situations (McCormick, Kinzie, & Gonyea, 2013). Similarly, community college education abroad involves close interaction with faculty, focuses on student cohorts, uses reflection as a learning activity, and when managed properly can be a way to help students develop in line with institutional goals and learning outcomes (Raby et al., 2014).

The student engagement literature found a link between student background in terms of age, ability, and effort toward college persistence and completion (McCormick et al., 2013). Yet, for community college education abroad, a student's background is not a factor because interest rather than age or ability is a criterion for enrollment. Community college students can study abroad at any point of their education, including in their first semester. A lack of prerequisites allows greater open access to study abroad, and, indeed, it may be the lack of constraints in student backgrounds that allows study abroad students to skip tracked remedial studies at rates higher than students who did not study abroad (Raby et al., 2014). The engagement literature also suggests that community college students are less active in college-sponsored extracurricular activities because of family and work obligations as well as their commuter status, making learning communities fostered in classroom activities critical to advancing engagement (McClenney, Marti, & Adkins, 2012). There is evidence that intentionally designed learning communities in community college education abroad contribute to higher student engagement (Brenner, 2016), enhance career readiness (Zamani-Gallaher, Lang, & Leon, 2016), and build stronger self-belief in students of color (Willis, 2016).

As further proof of such gains, the CCC SOAR study compared a cohort of first-time, full-time California community college students who studied abroad with those who did not (Raby et al., 2014). Statistical controls were conducted for possible variables that are known to limit student success such as differences including ability indicators, prior college achievement, and socioeconomic status markers. Findings showed that study abroad participants showed complex academic gains such as higher rates of transfer and higher rates of earning a degree or certificate. Table 7.3 illustrates a variation of the CCC SOAR methodology that was applied to two additional community colleges in New Jersey— Bergen Community College and Brookdale Community College—and that resulted in similar conclusions (Rhodes et al., 2016). It is important to note that although gains occurred for all students who studied abroad, in the CCC SOAR study in California, Latino students who study abroad showed higher gains, and at Brookdale College, gains were higher for African American students who studied abroad. These studies indicate a positive impact of study abroad on retention and success for nontraditional students and suggest that it may be possible that studying abroad can help narrow the achievement gap among racial and ethnic groups with similar historical patterns.

Conclusions

In alignment with the philosophy of open access at community colleges, it is necessary for all programming, including education abroad, to be available to all students. As we have seen in this case study of community colleges in the state of California, access is especially important because research shows that participation in education abroad extends opportunities to nontraditional

TABLE 7.3

Comparative Success Markers Among Education Abroad Participants

Outcome Within Three Years	Bergen Community College		Brookdale Community College		California Community College Student Outcomes Abroad Research			
	Education Abroad	Noneducation Abroad	Education Abroad	Noneducation Abroad	Education Abroad	Noneducation Abroad	Latino Education Abroad	Latino Noneducation Abroad
Completion of English level	–	–	88.2%	58.1%	16.6%	15.4%	34.7%	32.2%
Completion of math level	–	–	67.9%	32.6%	7.6%	6.4%	19.9%	16.9%
One-year retention	61%	–	91%	57.7%	62.4%	55.9%	–	–
Transfer completion	61.4 %	–	51.6%	23.7%	11.8%	8.0%	16.8%	11.4%
Earned degree or certificate	55%	14%	47.1%	15.4%	3.6%	2.7%	7.8%	5.8%

Note. California Community College Student Outcomes Abroad Research measures marginal means using regression analysis. Bergen and Brookdale use unadjusted means not using regression analysis. Adapted from Rhodes and colleagues, 2016.

students in terms of international literacy acquisition (Raby, 2008), positively affects retention and success (Raby et al., 2014), and enables students to compete more effectively and fairly for careers in a globalized economy (Zamani-Gallaher et al., 2016). However, with limited program options, it is difficult to argue that study abroad is truly viewed as a possibility for all students. Moreover, when education abroad becomes a component of the strategic planning initiatives and is integrated into programs designed to have an impact on student learning, retention, and success, rather than as an optional add-on for a few, it will become available to a larger number of students.

In transforming education abroad into an integral college program, three myths need to be dispelled. First, contrary to common perceptions, students of color and nontraditional students do study abroad. Although there is significant room for racial and ethnic diversity equity, the philosophy of serving all students means that community colleges maintain the highest levels of diversity of any type of postsecondary institution. In turn, it remains important to increase community college access to study abroad as a critical goal in increasing diversity at the national level. Second, it is not true that community college students do not want to study abroad. Research shows that with sufficient support, community college students will study abroad despite family or work responsibilities (Amani, 2011). In the CCC SOAR project, some student respondents had previous international experiences, including prior study abroad, travel or living abroad, and military deployment (Raby et al., 2014). Some of these students also had close family and friends who previously studied abroad or who received positive encouragement from friends and family to study abroad (Raby et al., 2014). Third, it is also not accurate that community college students do not have the academic ability to study abroad. Depending on the type of program, neither academic standing nor grade point average interferes with successful study abroad experiences. Additional training of faculty and staff may need to occur to help them overcome their existing preconceptions of students' limitations (Amani, 2011; Willis, 2016). To counter these three myths, new program options need to be based on impact surveys of the current generation of students rather than relying on stereotypes (Raby & Rhodes, 2005).

Education abroad will remain on the periphery of available opportunities for community college students as long as individualized international programs stay independent, with few, if any, ties to the broader on-campus community. The holistic nature of change intensifies when internationalized classes feed interest in education abroad, as international students provide a context for understanding diverse opinions, and as education abroad returnees reinforce enrollment in internationalized classes. In terms of program development, study abroad providers and those working in community colleges need to work together to implement new designs that include traditional faculty-led programs and nontraditional statewide consortia modeling. Although each new faculty-led program increases overall numbers, fewer than 40 new faculty-led programs have been added to California community colleges in the past five years.

Other options may allow more students to study abroad. Of the many models that might be proposed, for example, we propose options for short-term, one-week add-on thematic programs that could be linked to courses at many different home institutions. For example, a business-focused study abroad program could be added to any in-class or online course offered in the business department where international business could be seen to enhance the content. With appropriate predeparture and reentry advisement, these courses would be integrated into student learning during a regular term; for example, the program could take place during spring break.

Whatever the exact approach, philosophical and structural changes need to be made to community college study abroad programs. Change begins with a policy to eliminate existing obstacles that inhibit expansion of programs and limit opportunities for student participants, beginning with making international learning and education abroad an integral part of the community college mission and finding new funding sources for institutional offices, staff, and marketing. Evolving definitions of how to achieve student success should acknowledge the role of studying abroad as an academic and career program. Finally, new constructs need to be created to include study abroad as part of a combination of strategies that colleges adopt to counter historic achievement gaps in student success.

References

Amani, M. (2011). *Study abroad decision and participation at community colleges: Influential factors and challenges from the voices of students and coordinators* (Doctoral dissertation). Available from ProQuest Dissertations and Theses database. (UMI No. 3438831)

American Association of Community Colleges. (2016). *Fast facts from our fact sheet.* Retrieved from www.aacc.nche.edu/AboutCC/Pages/fastfactsfactsheet.aspx

Brenner, A. (2016). Transformative learning through education abroad: A case study of a community college program. In R. R. Latiner & E. J. Valeau (Eds.), *International education at community colleges: Themes, practices, research, and case studies* (pp. 370–390). New York, NY: Palgrave.

California Colleges for International Education (n.d.). *Study abroad.* Retrieved from ccieworld.org/saprograms.php

California Colleges for International Education. (2014). *State of the field report.* Unpublished manuscript, California Colleges for International Education, Los Angeles, CA.

California Community Colleges Chancellor's Office. (2016). *Management information systems data mart.* Retrieved from datamart.cccco.edu

Cohen, A. M., Brawer, F. B., & Kisker, C. B. (2014). *The American community college* (6th ed.). San Francisco, CA: Jossey-Bass.

Giammarella, M. (2011). *Using student fees to support education abroad.* In S. E. Sutin, D. Derrico, R. L. Raby, & E. J. Valeau (Eds.), *Increasing effectiveness of the community college financial model: A global perspective for the global economy* (pp. 215–223). New York, NY: Palgrave Macmillan.

Harper, S. R., & Quaye, S. J. (2009). Beyond sameness, with engagement and outcomes for all: An introduction. In S. R. Harper & S. J. Quaye (Eds.), *Student engagement in higher education: Theoretical perspectives and practical approaches for diverse populations* (pp. 1–15). New York, NY: Routledge.

Institute of International Education. (2016). *Open Doors 2015 data tables: Community college demographics.* Retrieved from www.iie.org/en/Research-and-Insights/ Open-Doors/Data/Community-College-Data-Resource

McClenney, K., Marti, C. N., & Adkins, C. (2012). *Student engagement and student outcomes: Key findings from CCSSE validation research.* Retrieved from www.ccsse .org/aboutsurvey/docs/CCSSE%20Validation%20Summary.pdf

McCormick, A. C., Kinzie, J., & Gonyea, R. M. (2013). Student engagement: Bridging research and practice to improve the quality of undergraduate education. In M. B. Paulsen (Ed.), *Higher education: Handbook of theory and research* (pp. 47–91). New York, NY: Springer.

Quezada, R. L., & Cordeiro, P. A. (2016). Creating and enhancing a global consciousness among students of color in our community colleges. In R. L. Latiner & E. J. Valeau (Eds.), *International education at community colleges: Themes, practices, research, and case studies* (pp. 335–355). New York, NY: Palgrave.

Raby, R. L. (2008). *Meeting America's global education challenge: Expanding education abroad at U.S. community colleges.* New York, NY: Institute for International Education.

Raby, R. L., Budd, D., Serban, A., & Van Hook, D. (2016). International Student Mobility at California community colleges. In K. Bista & C. Foster (Eds.), *International student mobility, services, and policy in higher education* (pp. 1–15). New York, NY: IGI.

Raby, R. L., & Rhodes, G. M. (2005). *Barriers for underrepresented students' participation in California community college study abroad programs.* Sacramento, CA: Chancellor's Office of California Community Colleges, Fund for Instructional Improvement Publications.

Raby, R. L., & Rhodes, G. M. (2014). What will it take to double community college enrollment in education abroad? *IIENetwork*, 20–22.

Raby, R. L., Rhodes, G. M., & Biscarra, A. (2014). Community college study abroad: Implications for student success. *Community College Journal of Research and Practice, 38*, 174–183.

Raby, R. L., & Valeau, E. J. (Eds.). (2016). *International education at community colleges: Themes, practices, research, and case studies.* New York, NY: Palgrave.

Rhodes, G. M., Raby, R. L., Thomas, J. M., Codding, A., & Lynch, A. (2016). Community college study abroad and implications for student success: Comparing California and New Jersey community colleges. In R. L. Raby & E. J. Valeau (Eds.), *International education at community colleges: Themes, practices, research, and case studies* (pp. 356–369). New York, NY: Palgrave.

Robertson, J. J. (2015). Student interest in international education at the community college. *Community College Journal of Research and Practice, 39*, 473–484.

Valeau, E. J., & Raby, R. L. (2016). Building the pipeline for community college international education leadership. In R. L. Raby & E. J. Valeau (Eds.), *International education at community colleges: Themes, practices, research, and case studies* (pp. 212–223). New York, NY: Palgrave.

Willis, T. Y. (2016). Microaggressions and intersectionality in the experiences of Black women studying abroad through community colleges: Implications for practice. In R. L. Raby & E. J. Valeau (Eds.), *International education at community colleges: Themes, practices, research, and case studies* (pp. 167–186). New York, NY: Palgrave.

Zamani-Gallaher, E. M., Leon, R. A., & Lang, J. (2016). Self-authorship beyond borders: Reconceptualizing college and career readiness. In R. L. Raby & E. J. Valeau (Eds.), *International education at community colleges: Themes, practices, research, and case studies* (pp. 146–166). New York, NY: Palgrave.

8

STRATEGIES FOR MOBILIZING STUDENTS IN THE SCIENCES

A Case Study

Lynda Gonzales, Benjamin Flores, and Sarah Simmons

In an era when administrators of colleges and universities have sought to internationalize their curricula, there is a consistent disconnect between the broad goal of providing a world-class education and the actual preparation of students. In particular, science students are less likely to study abroad, participating in percentages significantly below their domestic undergraduate enrollment (Blumenthal & Laughlin, 2009; Boggs, Berry, & Davidson, 2003; Farrugia & Bhandari, 2015). Successful efforts to increase and diversify study abroad participation by students in science, technology, engineering, and mathematics (STEM) require a careful examination of barriers endemic to STEM and creative approaches to address them. This chapter presents a case study of the journey toward curricular internationalization at the College of Natural Sciences at the University of Texas at Austin (UT Austin), one of the largest U.S. state universities, and three key innovations implemented there that resulted in significant increases in science student participation in study abroad. Although this chapter is primarily focused on efforts to diversify study abroad along disciplinary lines, the narrative of STEM study abroad efforts is closely intertwined with the national imperative to improve the persistence of underrepresented minorities in STEM.

Benefits of Study Abroad for STEM Students

Much work has been done to identify general barriers to study abroad participation among STEM students, which include highly structured degree plans, difficulty transferring credits, lack of awareness of the benefits among students and STEM faculty, lack of a science background among study abroad advisers, and financial barriers (Boggs et al., 2003). However, there is evidence that students who study abroad have higher retention rates at the university, shorter graduation times, and higher grade point averages following study abroad participation, even when differences in background and ability are taken into account (Barclay Hamir, 2011; Ingraham & Peterson, 2004; Posey, 2003; Sutton & Rubin, 2004; Young, 2008).

Experiences abroad also benefit students in ways that directly address the objective of preparing students for graduate work and careers in STEM, which has long been recognized by many scientific professional societies, such as the American Chemical Society and the American Physical Society. Particularly relevant is the evidence that students who participate in study abroad have improved their ability to work well under pressure; analyze, evaluate, and interpret well; work effectively outside their comfort zone; listen and observe well (Trooboff, Vande Berg, & Rayman, 2007); interact with people from diverse backgrounds; understand cultural differences in the workplace; adapt to changing situations; gain new knowledge from experiences (Gardner, Gross, & Steglitz, 2008); be flexible, change oriented, and adaptable; communicate well; and innovate, lead, and think critically (Foundation for Asia Pacific Education, 2010).

Although these skills are all relevant to a student's development as a scientist, many are becoming more important as science becomes an increasingly global endeavor; to be competitive, students must be aware of and engaged in scientific discourse at an international level and able to interact with scientists all over the world (Blumenthal & Laughlin, 2009; Braskamp, Braskamp, & Merrill, 2009; Leggett, 2011). In fact, some of the greatest challenges facing society will only be solved through global scientific collaboration, including but not limited to the global demand for energy, emerging infectious diseases and pandemics, water resources, food security and agriculture, and population growth.

Case Study: College of Natural Sciences at UT Austin

The College of Natural Sciences (CNS) at UT Austin is one of the largest colleges of science in the United States, with a community of more than 10,000 undergraduate students, and graduates about 1,800 students each year with baccalaureate degrees from 11 academic departments. The CNS has a long commitment to educational innovation, student persistence, and diversity, and has a history of data and evidence-driven reform. These efforts expanded to include study abroad in 2005 when a campuswide analysis of study abroad participation found that although science students ranked fourth in participation in study abroad programs across campus, this ranking obscured the real story: Science students were participating at rates less than 20% of those of liberal arts students in a college of comparable size. In response, the CNS underwent a self-study of student participation in study abroad with the intention of identifying barriers that could be addressed programmatically. This effort included student focus groups conducted informally across the college during seminar courses and student group meetings, survey questions added to existing student experience surveys, and a comprehensive analysis of the previous five years of data on courses taken abroad by CNS students and the credit they received for those courses. This first stage was designed to be an informal formative assessment to guide policy and program development to improve undergraduate science student participation in study abroad at our institution.

In general, analyses revealed barriers very similar to those outlined in Boggs and colleagues (2003) as mentioned previously, although two main themes stood out as major opportunities for program improvement. First, there was a severe underuse of available study abroad information and programming by science students and faculty. In general, students reported a lack of awareness of opportunities, a lack of understanding about how a study abroad experience might benefit them in a science career, concern about language barriers, and challenges in finding time in already crowded degree plans to take even a semester abroad. Science faculty felt their ideas were too unconventional for established study abroad mechanisms, or that proposals for faculty-led science programs were not reviewed well compared to other disciplines when competing for support from the central Study Abroad Office (SAO). Second, and most pervasive, there was a systemic issue with the lack of integration of study abroad courses into students' degrees. An unpublished analysis showed that students who studied abroad with approved exchange partners received credit that counted most commonly as a university elective; fulfilled a generic degree requirement, such as an upper-division biology elective; or only rarely replaced a specific degree requirement, such as organic chemistry. In some academic departments, the percentage of courses students took abroad at approved exchange partners that counted toward their degree was as low as 4% (Simmons, 2004).

Following the self-study, CNS leadership embarked on a comprehensive effort to improve the access to, relevance of, and participation in study abroad for science students. The college focused on three main strategies: the creation and fortification of bridges among CNS students, faculty and staff, and the campuswide SAO; facilitation and sponsorship of scientific research abroad to increase opportunities abroad that had a clear benefit and connection to a future career in science; and a curriculum integration effort aimed at creating space in every CNS degree for study abroad, with preapproved course equivalencies at specific partner schools.

Innovation 1: The Science Liaison, a Bridge to Study Abroad

The UT Austin SAO serves the entire campus, including its nearly 40,000 undergraduate students, and is separated physically from the main campus. A robust portfolio of exchange partners is maintained by this office, and dedicated advisers offer student consultation and assistance with exchange planning. However, CNS student and faculty focus group data made apparent that the considerable resources available to students and faculty through the campuswide SAO had little penetration into the college and its culture. CNS students lacked awareness of the opportunities that existed and did not see the benefits of a study abroad experience for their future scientific careers.

It became evident that having a liaison to faculty and students in the sciences and colleagues in the SAO would be key to increasing participation by science students, building strong and sustainable working relationships with science faculty, and ensuring that the CNS was positioned to take advantage of the new initiatives and existing structures in place at the university level. It was important for the individual in this role of liaison to be a credible intermediary firmly rooted in the sciences, who understood the scientific culture, and could develop trust and deep relationships with individual science faculty and departments. Appointing someone for the science liaison role in the CNS also signaled to colleagues in the SAO that there was genuine and serious interest in improving study abroad access in the sciences.

The liaison was designed first and foremost to serve as a sort of translator. The message of study abroad needed to be presented to science students in a way that highlighted the benefits specific to their needs and interests. New science-focused publicity materials were created, and information sessions for academic advisers and students were tailored to address specific concerns of science students, especially in regard to science degree plans, such as course sequencing, prehealth course requirements, and course equivalencies. Increased study abroad promotion occurred at all levels, including at new-student orientation, presentations to small freshman cohort groups, information sessions, and in academic advising. The liaison organized and sponsored a new science-focused study abroad student group, which provided a venue for peer-to-peer mentoring on study abroad and connected interested students with study abroad alumni.

The science liaison had a thorough understanding of the unique challenges faced by science students studying abroad (e.g., prehealth curriculum, Spanish language skills, course sequencing) and the unique teaching styles important to the sciences (e.g., research-based, field courses), communicated the needs and interests of science faculty to colleagues in the SAO, and was able to take advantage of new university-level initiatives and existing structures in place to support study abroad broadly. The science liaison also helped science faculty adapt their program activities to fit better within the structure of the SAO's programming.

One concrete example of the critical role the science liaison played in the expansion of study abroad participation was the development of science-specific faculty-led programming. Beginning in the early years of the twenty-first century, efforts to increase study abroad participation were being supported at the highest levels at UT Austin, with a focus on faculty-led programs as a mechanism to improve participation. These faculty-led programs were offered typically as part of a short-term experience, often during intersession, where students would travel with a UT Austin faculty member and take one or two courses approved in the UT Austin course catalog. The SAO established a centralized system that allowed faculty to propose courses, and if approved, the SAO staff would assist with the setup and management of the course.

Although faculty-led offerings were effective in several disciplines, they were not attracting science students in numbers relative to their peers in colleges of comparable size, and participating science students did not receive course credit that could be applied to their degree plan. When one version of these faculty-led programs, "Maymester" courses, were first offered in 2003, no science students participated, and only 7 of 139 participants were science majors the following year, despite the inclusion of the university's first CNS faculty-led program, Plants, Environment and Human Affairs in Spain. Most of the students were nonscience majors, likely because it was a lower division course aimed at a broad audience, which seemed to have little appeal for CNS students. As the faculty-led model continued to expand on campus, the majority of the courses developed under this model were not in science, and particular barriers existed to offering more science courses. Faculty focus groups revealed that the science faculty were not engaged in the application process, and there was a perception that the centrally organized application, budgeting, implementation, and management process run by the SAO, although efficient, was not flexible enough to accommodate the kinds of science-specific courses faculty were interested in offering. Most of these courses involved unique scientific field sites or opportunities to conduct large-scale research projects with students and often involved a level of risk common in domestic science courses that seemed excessive when compared to courses proposed by other disciplines (e.g., research site visits, working with research-grade equipment, interaction with flora and fauna, hiking, and snorkeling).

In response to these challenges, and in collaboration with the SAO, the CNS moved to design and implement programs that met the specific needs of science faculty and students. The courses run by the CNS focused on the needs and objectives of science faculty, with the SAO model adapted to suit these needs. By offering these courses, the CNS provided opportunities for science students to earn course credit that applied to their major, take science courses taught by science faculty, conduct original laboratory and field-based research, and benefit from course offerings that were timed so that students in highly sequenced degree plans, such as chemistry and biology, could participate. The science liaison played a critical role in the development of these courses by translating the existing university program model to align with CNS goals and take advantage of CNS resources.

As a result, the CNS offered a number of faculty-led programs that greatly expanded student participation in a relatively short time span, including field study courses in Mexico (Marine Botany) and Australia (Coral Reef Ecology), and a program in Spain targeting rising sophomores. As an example, the latter program began offering Organic Chemistry II in Spain starting in 2009, primarily to serve premedical and predental science majors. Many of the students in these majors had a strong desire to study abroad yet faced challenges because of degree requirements and scheduling considerations. It was also difficult for them to study abroad during their junior or senior year, the years when most students go abroad, because they were required to take the Medical College Admission Test and participate in medical school interviews during that time. The program was developed to enable participants to go abroad in the summer after their freshman year and take a required sophomore-level course, resulting in a slight advancement rather than delay of their degree progress. Spain was selected as a destination because of the added benefit of Spanish language proficiency for health science workers, especially in Texas. Although there was hope that for some this would be a precursor to additional time abroad, the program was designed to provide a study abroad experience with minimum impact on the students' prepro-fessional trajectory, thus avoiding the necessity of choosing between study abroad and their career aspirations.

As a whole, these CNS-supported courses were highly successful, exponentially increasing science student participation in faculty-led courses in particular and study abroad in general during the years they were offered. Enrollment for Marine Botany totaled 85 students over 5 years, Coral Reef

Ecology had 62 students over 5 years, and Organic Chemistry had 152 students over 6 years. These courses served as proof to the faculty that the SAO faculty-led model could be adapted to accommodate their specific needs and that faculty-led courses could be aligned with students' degree plans and career goals. In light of the changes that specifically addressed the original CNS challenges, it was determined that the programs could be managed more efficiently for the long term as part of the campuswide initiative and, in 2014 management and coordination of science courses was returned to the SAO.

Innovation 2: Multicampus Research Abroad

The CNS student and faculty focus group data also emphasized a real and perceived lack of a connection between traditional study abroad experiences and preparation for scientific careers, particularly those anchored in research. The CNS has a strong tradition of providing undergraduate research experiences in the sciences and sponsoring international research experiences for graduate students through strong research collaborations with peer institutions abroad. Administrators began to explore a hybrid option that would make use of the college's international research network to create a summer scientific research experience abroad. Such an experience not only would be directly applicable to scientific careers but also could address other perceived barriers such as degree progression, because research was conducted in the summer; language, because the research was often conducted in English, regardless of the host country; and faculty mentor acceptance and support, because it involved scientific faculty abroad and at the home institution.

Initial efforts began in 2005 as part of a grant supporting undergraduate research from the Howard Hughes Medical Institute and focused on semester or summer full-time undergraduate research abroad. Over a period of 10 years, 40 students conducted research at premier institutions abroad. Courses or credit were rarely involved. Some students, although not all, received a fellowship to fund their work abroad. The impact of this program was measured primarily by the quality of students' research, which was exhibited, presented, or published. All students presented posters at local research conferences after returning to the United States, some presented at national or international conferences, and several were coauthors on peer-reviewed publications.

As the program developed, the CNS was also drastically expanding its domestic research opportunities, with a focus on early research experiences and their impact on diversity and retention. Such a shift allowed real innovation related to undergraduate research abroad as part of the institution's membership in the National Science Foundation's UT System Louis Stokes

Alliance for Minority Participation (LSAMP). The UT System LSAMP project is a collaborative effort among all eight academic campuses in the UT system and community colleges that play pivotal roles in the education of underrepresented groups in Texas. Since its inception in 1992, the primary goal of the alliance has been twofold: to increase the number and quality of underrepresented minority students who earn bachelor of science degrees and to encourage these students to pursue graduate education in a STEM discipline. The bedrock of the grant is undergraduate research (Flores, Darnell, & Renner, 2009).

In 2012 the alliance expanded its efforts in undergraduate research by creating the Summer Research Academy (SRA) Abroad, a community of undergraduate researchers and faculty mentors who represent each of the partner institutions in the STEM disciplines. Selected students prepare to go abroad together in the spring after they are selected and then participate in individual, independent research experiences as part of an international research team for a full summer. Although the SRA Abroad is a collaborative statewide effort, it is administered by UT Austin to simplify and streamline requirements and regulations such as travel guidelines for students, mandatory health insurance, contacts abroad, and fellowship disbursements. The goals of the LSAMP SRA Abroad are to provide STEM students, especially those from underrepresented groups, with an authentic research activity as part of the global STEM community. In the process, students are expected to gain confidence in new, unfamiliar, and multicultural environments; gain a global perspective to increase competitiveness in graduate or professional markets; achieve early membership and credibility in the global science community; and deepen their interest in STEM fields in the context of a global STEM community (Arciero-Pino et al., 2015).

Students with undergraduate research experience at any of the alliance campuses are encouraged to apply to the SRA Abroad in the fall before the summer they plan to travel. It was found that research abroad is most successful with students who have had some prior research experience as their research competency becomes their anchor in the new culture. The application reflects this preference and requires the students' home campus to evaluate their prior research experiences, academic records, the potential for impact on their scientific trajectories, and the potential for placement in a lab abroad.

Students select their potential research destination by indicating their top three choices from a list of approved countries, with other destinations possible by petition. Many participating science and engineering labs welcome English-speaking students even if they have limited capacity with the host language. The scientific community communicates primarily in English, which allows accessibility to scientific work, such as training, protocols, and relevant readings, regardless of the host country's language. However, the degree to which a student's language proficiency affects her or his life in the host country outside the laboratory depends on the student's comfort level, previous language experience, and the country itself.

Once accepted, the student begins the predeparture process by securing a research placement abroad that fits her or his area of interest and country or language preference. There is no list of prearranged placements or mentors; however, students are encouraged to take advantage of previously formed connections made by prior SRA Abroad students and in their current scientific community. For example, a student might work with her or his current home institution research supervisor to negotiate placement with a research collaborator abroad. Alternatively, the student can search online for groups and labs conducting research in line with the student's interests and make initial contact. The staff coordinator can also use LSAMP campus directors, faculty members at the home university, and faculty supervisors abroad who have hosted SRA Abroad students in prior summers as resources to assist with placements. The first approach, working with the student's own scientific network to make a connection, has proven to be the most efficient means of securing a placement that is a good fit for the student, although students have been successful in finding excellent placements by searching for and contacting potential supervisors on their own without a previous connection.

Throughout the predeparture phase, students attend a one-hour per week seminar that meets via video conference. This seminar facilitates the development of a student community, provides the support students need to feel empowered, and guides them toward solidifying their lab placements, housing, travel, and visas. It also prepares students more broadly for the experience abroad. Students are coached on how to function with the local language even if they lack proficiency, how to prepare for their trip by becoming familiar with their host country's culture, and how to establish day-to-day expectations in advance. Part of this seminar also investigates aspects of online research and maximizing study skills for academic success.

Student and host faculty expectations are articulated and documented before travel. A preliminary proposal or scope of work is written by the student or host faculty, and preparatory readings are identified. In some cases, students must secure letters of invitation or sign a visiting student contract. Students depart in late May or early June, and over the course of the summer document their experiences using social media, such as Facebook, by weekly postings about any aspect of their time abroad. These posts allow them to interact with their administrative institution as well as other students who visit the UT System LSAMP Facebook page. Students return in August and present their work at the annual UT System LSAMP Conference. As part of a continuous quality improvement plan, the SRA Abroad undergoes an annual evaluation.

Since the summer of 2014, 23 students have participated in the SRA Abroad program, representing 11 alliance institutions (Arciero-Pino et al., 2015). A total of 21 institutions abroad have hosted SRA Abroad students. A 32-question survey was administered to students asking about their level of satisfaction with the just-completed SRA Abroad experience and their perceived gains in predetermined categories. Most participants (80%) reported that the research experience abroad exceeded their expectations and indicated advancement of their research and professional skills. Students indicated that as a result of their experience abroad, they were more determined to stay in school and graduate, think and work more independently, express their own ideas, and felt more motivated to learn. Survey results also indicated that the experience and information the students collected have strongly influenced their decisions to go to graduate school. After returning, students participated in focus groups at the annual conference (Arciero-Pino, Flores, & Knaust, 2012). The students were very open regarding their impressions, experiences, and recommendations for future academies, and they placed particular importance on sharing these thoughts. The feedback from these conversations focused on ways to improve the program, which were considered subsequently in the revision of program policies and procedures. Students' main concerns were related to cost of living and their ability to successfully complete their projects given their academic backgrounds. All concluded that they would go through the experience again. In response to student feedback, stipends were increased to account for cost of living, and travel insurance was provided. In addition, steps were taken to better align disciplinary training with assigned research projects.

Innovation 3: A Year Abroad for Every Degree Through Collegewide Curriculum Integration

Another focus area identified by the original CNS self-study was a critical misalignment of student and faculty expectations regarding credit earned abroad. Students were extremely unlikely to be able to earn credit in their majors abroad, even at institutions with which UT Austin had negotiated exchange agreements. In response, the final, and arguably the most significant, of our strategies was curricular integration. This effort was loosely based on the Minnesota model of study abroad curriculum integration (Anderson, 2005), which emphasizes collaboration among study abroad and academic units to meet institutional goals of internationalizing curricula. Doing so spreads ownership for international education throughout the institution. Although labor intensive on the front end, curricular integration efforts are sustainable and scalable in ways that faculty-led programs and research abroad are not.

When closely examined, the very small numbers of course equivalencies granted to science students represent a complex and frustrating system that cannot be fixed piecemeal and instead requires a comprehensive solution. Prior to intervention, CNS students planning to go abroad were expected to propose a course of study and have the courses approved for credit in advance. However, this process was often not clear and differed vastly from department to department; in some cases, students received inconsistent and contradictory advice from faculty and advisers. The course equivalency approval process resided in the departments, and the materials required for course evaluation such as forms, syllabi, and supplementary materials varied across units. To approve a semester abroad, a student might have to attain consent from four different departments.

Faculty members in the department of study evaluated the materials, and each had a different philosophy about how and why a course should count. Many had strict requirements for a course abroad to count in lieu of a CNS course; they had high expectations for the institution and the instructor and often required a large percentage of the syllabus to be identical to the equivalent course on the home campus. The standards for courses taken abroad often were higher than the tolerance for variations among courses taught in house, and at times the student's current academic standing was considered as a factor in the decision. Students might be required to show the faculty their syllabi or textbooks, and some faculty went so far as to require notes, work samples, or exams to evaluate the course. Students sometimes waited months to hear a decision, and often only a few courses would be approved out of a long list provided to faculty reviewers because courses either did not align sufficiently with the departmental curriculum, or the student was unable to secure sufficient documentation in advance. Once students arrived in the host country, they were often registering last and were seldom able to get the specific approved courses. Alternatively, students were able to register for courses that might count but would have to wait until they returned to campus to seek course approval retroactively. All these factors had an impact on students' participation in overseas experiences.

Curriculum integration was a longer term effort, conducted in close collaboration with the SAO, which involved a full-time CNS staff member and a faculty committee from each of the departments in the college. The curriculum integration committee met four times over the course of a year, with the entire process taking close to two and a half years. The staff coordinator led all aspects of the project, including organizing and documenting the committee's efforts, maintaining communication among the committee and key partners, researching and collecting course materials from institutions abroad for course matching, and producing and disseminating advising materials. The goals of the committee were to simplify the study abroad planning process, identify partner institutions abroad and preapprove courses, and provide maps for students in each degree plan to illustrate how and when to study abroad. A key objective was to identify and acknowledge faculty members' reservations about science courses abroad while also removing barriers for students.

To address concerns about quality of instruction, UT Austin faculty initially identified 15 partner institutions around the world with strong science programs and respected curricula. Additional selection factors included whether UT Austin had an existing exchange agreement in place—that is, institutions that students naturally gravitated to; which institutions had courses available for all CNS majors; which institutions taught science courses in English; and whether the institution's inclusion contributed to development of a portfolio that included a wide range of regions (i.e., Europe, Oceania, Africa, Latin America, Asia). In addition, the committee identified a list of possible institutions with no existing exchange agreement in place that might otherwise be good candidates. For each degree, committee members then determined where study abroad would fit in the degree plan and which courses on a typical trajectory students might be required to take in those semesters.

Critical to the success of this effort, the faculty agreed to allow approved equivalencies to be valid for at least five years and have course-based rather than student-based approval, resulting in a database of course equivalencies available to every CNS student that could be used to plan study abroad experiences far in advance, even as early as the freshman year. Students and their advisers can check the database to see which course approvals are available to all students, which approvals are current, and when approvals are scheduled to expire.

The committee also agreed on standard requirements necessary to ensure the rigor and content of a course for substitution and a percentage fidelity, similar to the discretion UT Austin faculty on the home campus would have in designing their own course. To streamline the evaluation process, staff prepared course profiles with the following information: course name and number, institution, department, and location; where the course fits in the host's degree plans; course prerequisites, textbooks, or readings; and breakdown of instructional time (e.g., 33 hours of lecture, 16 hours of lab, 6 hours of field trips, and the name of the course instructor if available).

The committee evaluated as many courses as possible from each of the identified peer institutions. Committee members worked together across disciplines to approve suites of courses that could be combined to create a productive semester for students. The staff coordinator worked as a liaison with departments outside the CNS to identify nonscience courses that could also be used to form a full course load for science students. The final products were developed with input and review from the SAO, ensuring alignment with the exchange partner's course offerings and calendar, departmental academic advisers to allow student progression toward the degree, and faculty committee members to verify alignment with academic expectations of the major and academic legitimacy. In the end, the committee came up with 400 new course equivalency approvals at 15 partner institutions. Nine total degree maps were produced for biology, chemistry-biochemistry, computer science, human development and family sciences, marine and freshwater biology, mathematics, nutrition, physics, and textiles and apparel.

The final stage of the project involved a marketing initiative. Efforts were undertaken to reach incoming freshmen with banners containing statements such as "Thinking about studying abroad as a chemistry major? Here are 15 institutions you could attend, and here's how it would map onto your 4-year degree, approved in advance." Additionally, advising materials, brochures, and maps were produced for each major, with input from the SAO and departmental academic advisers, using photos and comments from students.

Figure 8.1. College of Natural Sciences student participation in exchange programs 2002–2016, comparing participation of all science students (total College of Natural Sciences) to that of underrepresented science students.

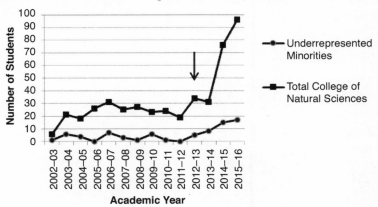

Note. Arrow indicates first year (2012–2013) of curriculum integration.

In the 10 years prior to implementation of the project, the CNS had minimal participation in exchange programs abroad, averaging only 22 students per year in a college of close to 10,000 majors. In the years following curriculum integration, the numbers have increased each year, reaching close to 100 in 2015–2016 with a 4-year average of 59 students per year (see Figure 8.1).

Although relative percentages of male and female participants have remained about the same, hovering around 40% for males and 60% for females, the CNS has seen improvement in participation among underrepresented racial and ethnic groups, such as African American, American Indian, and Hispanic in percentages and in raw numbers (see Figure 8.2).

From 2002 to 2012, underrepresented minority participation ranged from zero students in 2 of the years to 7 per year, with an annual average participation of 2.9 students (13%). In the 4 years since implementation, participation among these groups has increased to an average of 11 students per year (19%), with an all-time high in 2015–2016 of 17 students of color. The CNS has seen substantial increases in exchange participation at institutions that were included in the integration project and those that were not. This may be because degree maps address perceived as well as actual barriers to study abroad, and because the course database now includes additional courses from nonpartner institutions.

Figure 8.2. Average annual College of Natural Sciences student participation in exchange programs, before and after curriculum integration.

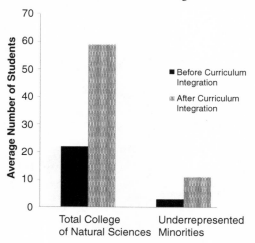

Conclusion

The case study described here represents efforts that originated with the singular purpose of increasing the participation of science students in study abroad experiences. The plan of action evolved from a concentrated exploration of the reasons science faculty, staff, and students were disenfranchised from the robust and successful study abroad activities centrally organized on our campus. Although our findings paralleled the literature in many ways (Blumenthal & Laughlin, 2009; Boggs et al., 2003), understanding the context of our individual institution and how our policy, practice, and culture played a role in the existence of these barriers to study abroad was critical. Armed with this information, we then identified several approaches to the problem, implementing evidence-based practice when possible and innovating when necessary. Our key innovations of a science faculty liaison, multicampus research abroad, and comprehensive science curriculum integration may be transferrable separately or as a whole to other institutions whose administrators wish to address similar challenges, but the process of discovery and action toward a common goal in context is absolutely necessary. For example, UT Austin, because of the size of its student population, required an approach to scaling curricular integration that might not be justified at a smaller institution where reform of faculty course evaluation processes might be more efficient. In addition, we might ask whether various study abroad models are being used by science students at different rates and whether these models have a differential impact on science students with different demographics, as they do for undergraduates in general. In conclusion, we believe the evidence and action cycle should be ongoing and adapted to the needs, resources, and culture of individual institutions to ensure that all STEM students have the opportunity to access study abroad experiences and their benefits.

References

Anderson, L. C. (2005). *Internationalizing undergraduate education: Integrating study abroad into the curriculum.* Minneapolis, MN: Learning Abroad Center, Office for International Programs, University of Minnesota.

Arciero-Pino, A., Flores, B., & Knaust, H. (2012, October). Work in progress: The University of Texas System Louis Stokes Alliance for Minority Participation: A state-wide initiative to promote STEM undergraduate research. *2012 Frontiers in Education Conference Proceedings.* doi:10.1109/fie.2012.6462343

Arciero-Pino, A., Flores, B., Knaust, H., Gonzales, L., & Quintana-Baker, M. (2015, October). Qualitative assessment of the University of Texas System Louis Stokes Alliance for Minority Participation Summer Research Academy Abroad:

An international experience in research and culture. *2015 IEEE Frontiers in Education Conference.* doi:10.1109/FIE.2015.7344038

Barclay Hamir, H. (2011). *Go abroad and graduate on-time: Study abroad participation, degree completion, and time-to-degree* (Doctoral dissertation). Available from ProQuest Dissertations and Theses database. (UMI No. 3450065)

Blumenthal, P., & Laughlin, S. (Eds.). (2009). *Promoting study abroad in science and technology fields.* New York, NY: Institute of International Education.

Boggs, J., Berry, P., & Davidson, L. (2003). *Study abroad for science and engineering students: Barriers to students and strategies for change.* Portland, ME: Council on International Educational Exchange.

Braskamp, L., Braskamp, D., & Merrill, K. (2009). Assessing progress in global learning and development of students with education abroad experiences. *Frontiers, 18,* 101–118.

Farrugia, C., & Bhandari, R. (2015). *Open doors 2015: Report on international educational exchange.* New York, NY: Institute of International Education.

Flores, B., Darnell, A., & Renner, J. (2009). The emergence of undergraduate research in the course of institutional change. In M. K. Boyd & J. L. Wesemann (Eds.), *Broadening participation in undergraduate research: Fostering excellence and enhancing the impact,* (pp. 295–306). Washington, DC: Council on Undergraduate Research.

Foundation for Asia Pacific Education. (2010). *The value of education abroad.* Denver, CO: Author.

Gardner, P., Gross, L., & Steglitz, I. (2008). *Unpacking your study abroad experience: Critical reflection for workplace competencies* (CERI Research Brief 1-2008). Retrieved from http://studyabroad.isp.msu.edu/unpacking_brief.pdf

Ingraham, E. C., & Peterson, D. L. (2004). Assessing the impact of study abroad on student learning at Michigan State University. *Frontiers, 10,* 83–100.

Leggett, K. (2011). Encouraging STEM students to study abroad. *International Educator, 20*(4), 44–48.

Posey, J. T. (2003). *Study abroad: Educational and employment outcomes of participants versus non participants* (Doctoral dissertation). Available from ProQuest Dissertations and Theses database. (UMI No. 3137474)

Simmons, S. L. (2004). [An analysis of student study abroad exchange in the College of Natural Sciences]. Unpublished raw data.

Sutton, R. C., & Rubin, D. L. (2004). The GLOSSARI project: Initial findings from a system-wide research initiative on study abroad learning outcomes. *Frontier, 10,* 65–82.

Trooboff, S., Vande Berg, M., & Rayman, J. (2007). Employer attitudes toward study abroad. *Frontiers, 15,* 17–33.

Young, D. Y. (2008). Persistence at a liberal arts university and participation in a study abroad program. *Frontiers, 15,* 93–110.

9

ENGINEERS ABROAD

Opportunities for Sophomores in International Education

Amalia Pérez-Juez and Solomon R. Eisenberg

I n an increasingly global economy in which engineering and technical innovation play fundamental roles, it has become ever more important for engineers to be knowledgeable about and comfortable with other cultures. Although it is generally accepted that engineering professionals will require a greater understanding of global issues and an ability to work collaboratively with international colleagues, developing opportunities for engineers to study abroad and advance in their required technical coursework has been challenging. Thus, at a time of the increasing need for global skills—fluency in a foreign language, intercultural understanding and communication, and a global perspective—study abroad programs where engineering students can develop these skills have not always been readily available (DeWinter, 1997; Gerhardt, Blumenthal, & Spodek, 2002; Klahr & Ratti, 2000).

A variety of formats and approaches have been developed to create coherent study abroad opportunities for engineers, and many of the advantages and challenges of each have been compared and contrasted (Parkinson, 2007). Such efforts have led to a dramatic increase in the percentage of engineering students studying overseas over the past two decades. This chapter explores the rationale, implementation, and development of one successful semester-long engineering study abroad program at Boston University (BU). The challenges, opportunities, and benefits of creating seamlessly integrated pathways for engineering students to study abroad are discussed, incorporating experiences from the development of the newest foreign language site in Madrid, Spain. Although each institution must develop programs that meet its students' needs, the case described here is offered as an example of how other colleges and universities might develop initiatives abroad designed specifically for engineering students.

Great Strides in Education Abroad Among Engineering Students

Before continuing, it is useful to trace the evolution of engineering students' enrollments in education abroad programs. Science and engineering bachelor's degrees have consistently accounted for roughly one-third of all bachelor's degrees awarded in the United States for the past 15 years (National Science Board [NSB], 2016). Over the same period, engineering bachelor's degrees have been awarded at an average of 4.6% of all degrees, with remarkably small variations (standard deviation = 0.12%). It is important to recognize that these roughly constant proportions play out against a backdrop of an almost 50% growth in the total number of bachelor's degrees awarded in the United States, from 1.25 million in 2000 to 1.86 million in 2013. Hence, the number of engineering bachelor's degrees awarded has increased by 48% between 2000 and 2013, from 59,487 to 87,812 (NSB, 2016).

It is helpful to consider the proportion of engineering students participating in study abroad programs in this context. The Institute of International Education (Farrugia & Bhandari, 2015) noted in its 2015 annual report that the total number of U.S. students participating in study abroad programs in 2012–2013 reached 289,408, up about 66% since 2002–2003. In that same academic year, engineering majors accounted for 4.1% of these students (11,866), up from 2.9% (5,064) in 2002–2003, a 2.3-fold increase; by 2013–2014 engineering majors accounted for 4.6% of the 304,467 students who studied abroad, and by 2014–2015, the percentage was 5.0% (Farrugia & Bhandari, 2016).

Engineering students studying abroad in 2002–2003 were underrepresented at 2.9% (Farrugia & Bhandari, 2015), compared to the proportion of engineering degrees awarded that year, which was 4.7% (NSB, 2016). However, by 2012–2013, these data indicate that the proportion of engineering students studying abroad, 4.1% (Farrugia & Bhandari, 2015), had almost reached parity with the proportion of engineering degrees awarded that year, which was 4.7% (NSB, 2016), with continued growth in 2013–2014 and 2014–2015. In short, it appears that engineering students have largely caught up with their peers in other disciplines such as the social sciences and humanities. This is not to say there is not more room to expand for engineering students to go abroad; rather, this group is not as underrepresented as was the case only a few years ago, marking a significant achievement in the field.

This rapid and disproportionate growth in the number of engineering students who study abroad reflects an emerging realization in the engineering community about the desirability of including a study abroad experience as a more normative part of an undergraduate engineering education. This is likely in part a response to increased industrial globalization and the changing nature of work in the worldwide economy. It is also possible that the modifications in engineering accreditation criteria that occurred around 2000 facilitated this growth. The introduction by the Accreditation Board for Engineering and Technology of *Engineering Criteria 2000*, its criteria for accrediting engineering programs, radically altered the evaluation of undergraduate engineering programs, shifting the emphasis from proscriptive curricular specifications to student learning outcomes and accountability (Lattuca, Terenzini, Volkwein, & Peterson, 2006).

The Case of BU: Background

To help understand how such successes in engineering abroad have been achieved, we turn to the case of BU, a large private urban research university, comprising 17 schools and colleges that serve about 16,500 undergraduate students and 14,000 graduate and professional students. BU was among the first universities in the United States to send students abroad, and it currently coordinates a broad array of study abroad programs at sites on six continents, serving about 2,100 undergraduates each year.

As one of 17 schools and colleges at BU, the College of Engineering enrolls about 1,600 undergraduates in four degree programs accredited by the Accreditation Board for Engineering and Technology: biomedical engineering, computer engineering, electrical engineering, and mechanical engineering. These undergraduate degree programs share a substantially common curriculum through the end of the sophomore year and then become highly specialized and differentiated in the junior and senior years. The BU undergraduate engineering community includes about 30% women and 20% international students.

In the years prior to developing specialized study abroad programs for engineers, virtually no engineering undergraduates at BU studied abroad. This was true even though BU had a well-established study abroad office (formerly called the Office of International Programs). To study abroad at that time, engineers needed to bunch their social science and humanities course requirements into a single semester and use coursework available in existing BU study abroad programs to fulfill these requirements. Alternatively, participation in a study abroad experience meant extending the length of time required to complete the degree, often while taking courses abroad that did not count toward degree requirements. Although shorter duration summer programs were available, they added cost and interfered with internships and other summer work opportunities.

When BU assessed the opportunity to develop a study abroad program for engineering undergraduates, a number of obstacles were identified that made it difficult for engineering students to consider an overseas experience, including a lack of flexibility in the engineering curricula, a lack of fluency in a language other than English in most domestic engineering students, difficulty in finding appropriate courses abroad that could be used to meet technical degree requirements, and a reluctance of engineering students to extend the time needed to earn a degree or to add to their costs. BU sites abroad at that time were primarily offering language and liberal arts curricula or providing internships in a myriad of fields, although not specifically for engineers because of the language barrier. Both realities needed to find a meeting point.

The lack of flexibility in engineering curricula creates several problems. There is little time in student schedules for nontechnical elective coursework that might be more easily taken in more traditional study abroad programs. It is very difficult for engineering students to study abroad in their junior year, the normative year for students to study abroad, because of the specificity of individual degree program requirements and the advanced technical nature of the required coursework. Additionally, engineers often lack foreign language training, whether from the need to acquire an extensive background in math and science in high school or from disinclination. It is generally exceedingly difficult to incorporate such training into their schedules in a four-year engineering degree program. Hence, engineering students are generally unable to acquire the fluency in a foreign language necessary to participate in regular technical coursework at foreign institutions where the language of instruction is not English.

An understanding of these obstacles led to the design of a study abroad experience specifically for engineering students. A collaboration between the BU College of Engineering and the Study Abroad office was forged to create a semester-long academic program that would enable participants to make normal progress on the technical aspects of their degree programs while enjoying all the cultural and linguistic opportunities associated with a traditional study abroad experience.

After evaluating a number of potential international partner institutions, the Technical University of Dresden (TUD) was chosen as the site for a pilot program, primarily because BU already operated a small language and liberal arts program there and had the necessary infrastructure in place to support a new initiative. The TUD had faculty available who were willing and able to teach the requisite technical courses in English. These instructors had prior experience as students or as visiting faculty at U.S. institutions and thus were familiar with the U.S. educational system and student expectations. The TUD administration was equally supportive of the initiative as it aligned with its own strategic vision. From this collaboration, a new study abroad program designed specifically for engineering students was inaugurated in spring 2001 (Eisenberg, DeWinter, & Murray, 2007; Murray, DeWinter, & Eisenberg, 2003).

Program Structure

BU's overseas programs for engineering students are offered in the spring semester and intended for second-semester sophomores. The second semester of the sophomore year was initially targeted because this is the last semester in which engineering students at the university share a substantially common curriculum. Therefore, it was possible to design a program with a limited number of courses for all engineering majors. This was an important pragmatic consideration that allowed a necessary critical mass of students to participate early in the program's evolution.

As part of the program, students are not required to have foreign language proficiency but must take a course in the local language if studying in a non-English-speaking country. This was another practical decision because it was found that engineering students generally did not enter the university with the requisite language ability and could not include language instruction in addition to the introductory engineering curriculum in a four-year program. It was viewed that requiring language ability as a prerequisite to studying abroad would be a significant obstacle to participation.

The program consists of an intensive language course (if applicable), a social science course focused on the host country, and three technical courses taught in English, for a total of five courses of four credits each. The technical courses are designed to be functionally equivalent to the technical courses students would have taken had they remained in Boston for the semester, often following the same syllabi and providing comparable laboratory experiences. All operate as official BU courses and appear directly on students' BU transcripts, thereby circumventing transfer credit issues. Thus, students are able to integrate the study abroad experience seamlessly into the regular academic program.

The initial model developed in Dresden in 2001 incorporated a set of stand-alone technical courses taught in English according to BU specifications by TUD faculty and using TUD laboratory resources. However, as these courses were not regular TUD courses, TUD students were not able to enroll in them. As this eliminated the possibility of classroom interactions with local students, other mechanisms were developed to ensure that visiting students had adequate opportunities to interact with local students in other settings.

Foundational math, science, and engineering courses around the world cover an essential set of standard topics and have substantial similarity even in more advanced coursework. This greatly facilitated program development and expansion to new sites over the years. It is also the case that specific course sequences and how particular topics are packaged into course modules can vary substantially, which has the potential to be the source of incongruities and friction in program development and expansion to other sites.

One design goal was for the program to be scalable so that it could increase to capacity with little additional faculty and staff effort and in turn be replicated easily at other sites. Twelve students participated in spring 2001, and four years later, the program had reached its capacity, set mostly by the availability of laboratory facilities. In spring 2006 a second site was established at the Guadalajara, Mexico, campus of Tecnológico de Monterrey, and a third site was established in spring 2007 at Tel Aviv University in Israel. The program in Guadalajara ran four years, through spring 2010, and the program in Tel Aviv ran five years, through spring 2012. Both sites were suspended because of underenrollment and security concerns. New sites were added at Grenoble University in France in spring 2012; the Universidad Autónoma de Madrid (UAM), Spain, in spring 2013; and the University of Sydney, Australia, in spring 2016. The partner institution in Madrid was changed to the ICAI School of Engineering at the Universidad Pontificia de Comillas in spring 2017. All program sites employ the same basic model, although the constraints and opportunities at each site account for minor differences, the most important being the total length of each program and dates that are dictated by the academic calendar of the host institutions.

The emergence at a number of foreign universities of international tracks in which a selection of courses is taught in English has presented additional opportunities for program development. At the same time, these opportunities have posed new challenges as courses need to satisfy BU's curricular needs as well as the curricular needs of the host institution. This has required addressing differences in the particular scope of topics covered, depth of coverage, and associated rigor to ensure that functional equivalence to the courses taught in Boston is maintained. The programs in Grenoble and in Madrid were structured to use courses in such international tracks. As a result, most of the courses in these programs also have local students enrolled, although not in large numbers. Mixed classrooms should provide substantially enhanced and natural opportunities for visiting and local students to interact, although incorporation of local students into these tracks has been slower than expected.

In all programs, support services are provided by the BU resident director and other administrative staff and faculty. Housing in Dresden and Sydney is in residence halls, whereas housing in Grenoble and Madrid is in home stays. It has been found that the form of housing is an important differentiator among programs. Some students avoid sites with home stays, others are attracted to them, and for others they are a source of initial anxiety. The total cost of participation includes tuition, room, board, round-trip transportation, field trips and excursions, and on-the-ground support, and is generally no more or less than a student would pay for tuition, room, and board for the semester in Boston. Extracurricular travel is not included. Financial aid is administered as though students had remained in Boston and is applied in full to the study abroad semester, thus reducing financial barriers to student participation.

BU in Madrid

The program in Madrid is the newest of the programs in a non-English-speaking country and serves as an ideal example in the portfolio of programs for several reasons. The Madrid site presents the challenges that arise in a non-English-speaking country, particularly for engineering students. Spain is also a popular destination for study abroad, in large part because of the prevalence of Spanish speakers in the United States, as well as the fact that many students are attracted to studying in Western Europe with its many opportunities for travel. In fact, engineering participants in Spain increased substantially from 2013 through 2016, rising from 16 students in 2013 to 35 in 2016. The data that follow derive from four years of running the BU program for engineers in Madrid, including observations, evaluations, student and faculty interviews, formal and informal workshops, and conversations with students.

Spain has traditionally been a destination for language and humanities students. In the past 20 years, it has evolved to include other fields that require a good knowledge of Spanish language such as international relations, education, and premed. It has not been very popular among engineering students until recently. Although all these students seemed different a few decades ago, major changes have taken place that affect all groups and make them more similar. In the past decade, students across disciplines have become less interested in pursuing language and culture while abroad and are more focused on building their résumés, developing networks, interning, traveling, and broadening their connections abroad to prepare for future careers. In many ways, students are less willing to adapt, and they seek replicas of their own academic and educational system abroad. The customer-service-oriented U.S. society and educational system is difficult to replicate in Europe, and finding ways of helping students deal with these differences has become a critical challenge for study abroad programs. Moreover, the lack of language proficiency among students has required overseas programs, including those offered by BU, to teach more classes in English. Compliance with the home campus, with the introduction of more technology in the classroom, more frequent feedback, and other requirements, has also required adapting course syllabi and teaching styles. Although less than ideal from a cultural immersion standpoint, these changes laid the groundwork for engineering programs.

The implementation of the engineering study abroad program in Madrid followed the structure of the previous European programs in Dresden and Grenoble, but, like them, it has its own specificities and personality. BU Madrid was already a large program before the introduction of the engineering track, with a consolidated portfolio of classes, long-term relationships with host families, and a well-organized set of extracurricular activities. The challenge was to incorporate engineering students into a preexisting structure, which required helping them meet all their academic requirements while also taking language and social science classes with the rest of the program participants. This introduced a novelty in the general dynamic of the semester while also providing an opportunity to teach students about language, culture, and Spain as a whole in a broader context and with a mixed audience.

When the program was developed, engineering classes were taken at UAM, where BU already had an exchange agreement. When possible, technical courses were selected from existing UAM courses but were taught in English with other small modifications. UAM students have been encouraged to enroll in the adapted courses, but this has been no easy task. Although most Spanish university students could follow classes in English, the novelty of this kind of education was intimidating.

When functionally equivalent courses did not exist, new courses were developed using BU syllabi as models. UAM students have also been able to enroll in these classes, but because the content differed from their own required courses, they only count as electives. To ensure opportunities for immersion, the program has provided other forms of interaction with locals such as informal meetings with former and prospective exchange students at BU as well as a semester fútbol (soccer) competition.

Nontechnical classes are taken with the rest of the BU study abroad students at the Instituto Internacional, located in the center of Madrid, where BU has its main offices and classroom space. Students are expected to take two courses at the center, one on Spanish language and the other on local culture. Heritage speakers and advanced Spanish students can take a cinema course in lieu of the language course. The interaction with other BU students in the program has worked well, allowing the two groups to learn from each other. Faculty have found some differences in the ways the two cohorts approach the social science and humanities courses and in the amount of time and willingness that the groups have been able or are ready to devote to immersion in the local culture. To ensure that engineering students are ready to make the most of their time in Spain, the BU Madrid staff have recognized that adjustments needed to be made to the program.

For a long time, the program scheduled field trips, including visits to museums, outings to theaters, and other events, as a way of introducing students to their surroundings. Instructors and staff found, however, that engineering students do not have the same level of knowledge of Spanish language and culture as their nonengineering counterparts, who in many cases have studied these topics for much longer and are devoting most of their time in Spain to learning about the host culture. For extracurricular activities, instructors have been required to provide more background material and information to fill in knowledge gaps and ensure that all participants can benefit from the experiences. The program administrators also have had to juggle schedules so that outings do not overlap with engineering courses. To address all these concerns, it has been most effective to incorporate the activities into required courses. Evaluations demonstrate that these interventions have helped students gain a greater knowledge of Spain, as one engineering student stated in the following: "The Spanish Civilization class gave me insight into Spain and its wealth of history and the field trips we took during the class allowed me to travel to places I may not have gone on my own."

Finally, the housing situation has played a major role in the design of the program in Spain. The program in Madrid places students only in home stays, which is, according to the students' evaluations, one of the high points of their experience. One student said,

> My host mom makes sure that I have everything I need and more, and is genuinely interested in my life. Any member of the family is willing to listen and answer any question that I may have. I think the highlight of my experience in Spain is this family because of how great they are.

Families can provide a nurturing and learning environment that engineering students need while also giving them a chance to practice their Spanish without fear or embarrassment. The families also introduce students to certain aspects of life in Spain including foods, traditions, and schedules. Program leaders work closely with families to review some key aspects that can be discussed with students and have incorporated family members into the orientation sessions; for example, families are responsible for some of the student's tours of the city. Students' evaluations demonstrate the great experience they have and the major improvement in their understanding of Spain and the Spanish language and culture. A majority of the evaluations agree with one student who wrote, "Living with my host family provided me with the cultural knowledge during the trip. I loved living with them and hearing about their culture." Data from evaluations are consistent with the small number of students (none to two) who request to change families every semester and leave a very clear picture of how important host families have become in the integration of engineering students. As another student reported,

> The family makes sure I know that I'm welcomed to any family events and treats me like I'm a part of their family. . . We always eat together and exclusively only speak in Spanish during these meals. They always listen to me and try to help me practice my Spanish.

Developing Skills for Adapting and Cultural Understanding

Culture shock is one of the biggest challenges of studying abroad. Tools to overcome cultural differences, understand one another, and internalize change have long been researched and tested (Kohls, 2001; Lewis, 2006; Paige et al., 2006). Although all students in the BU in Madrid program deal with some level of culture shock, it has become apparent that the engineering students require a slightly different approach. Most of the engineering students arrive in Spain with very little or no Spanish, and for some, English was already their second language. They are also shaped by their first three semesters at BU, which has influenced the way they work and learn through teamwork, structured lessons, feedback, and right or wrong answers to exercises. They have needed some additional coping skills to better adapt to living and learning in Madrid.

Culture shock can happen in the classroom, as well as in daily life. Although the syllabi taught at the UAM are functionally equivalent to those at BU, teaching styles, grading criteria, and the interaction with students in the classroom differ greatly. For instance, students at BU are used to immediate and frequent feedback, which allows them to track their progress in the class. In Spain, on the other hand, immediate feedback is not as common, and certainly there is a longer period of time between a test and the date when students receive their grade. Another example is the way professors follow the syllabus or use textbooks and manuals. In Spain the pedagogical approach is more teacher centered than learner centered, and therefore there is less emphasis on interaction, participation, and even cooperation between instructor and learner (Eland, Smithee, & Greenblatt, 2009).

Some of these differences are minor and even beneficial for students to gain skills such as flexibility, resilience, and adaptability. However, if students are not prepared well enough to cope, cultural variations can lead to frustration, loss of interest, and a decrease in motivation. As reflected in the evaluations, a few students have found it interesting, as one student put it, to "see how students from different countries approach subjects." For the most part, they have been frustrated by differences in teaching styles; for example, one student said that "grading [is] not clear," "it [is] difficult to find office hours," and there is, "not one text book but too many manuals." To help students understand and adapt to classroom life in Spain, the program has held frequent question-and-answer sessions, workshops, and role-playing activities. The program also pairs participants with Spanish students who have been abroad and act as tutors, exchanging experiences of culture shock in the class that both cohorts have undergone.

Outside the classroom, students equally have needed to adapt to a wide array of cultural variations with respect to time, space, cultural customs, and verbal and nonverbal communication styles. Most students have experienced culture shock, yet those in the general social science and humanities track have had more opportunities to discuss such challenges in their classes compared to engineering students. To address this deficit, it became clear that faculty and staff needed to offer time for a range of classroom discussions, extracurricular activities, and training sessions with the goal of creating a space for engineering students to express any difficulties they might be having.

Program Outcomes

Since the program's inception in 2001 through spring 2016, a total of 767 students have participated in the BU programs designed specifically for engineering students, including 453 males and 314 females. Of this total, almost 400 have studied abroad in the past 5 years. Although virtually no engineering students studied abroad prior to 2001, student interest, program scope, and participation rates have all increased substantially since that time; the participation rate of BU engineering undergraduates reached about 25% in spring 2016. Figure 9.1 shows the growth and distribution of students since the study abroad program's inception.

One explanation for the robust growth of these programs is directly related to the model, which was designed to mitigate elements that had been identified as barriers to participation. Specifically, all engineering majors at BU are able to participate because required technical coursework normally taken in Boston can be completed while abroad, knowledge of a foreign language is not required for admission, there are no additional costs, participation does not add time to complete degree requirements, and sites

Figure 9.1. BU sophomore study abroad participation.

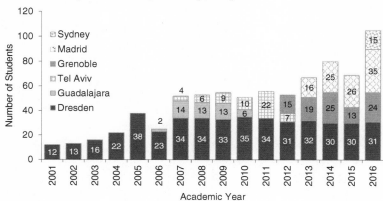

abroad offer appealing nontechnical courses that attract students beyond the engineering courses. The numbers suggest that engineering students will embrace the opportunity to study abroad when appropriate structures are implemented to reduce the barriers to participation and pathways are created to make the experience a normative, virtually seamless part of the undergraduate engineering program.

Follow-up focus groups for each site are held for each returning cohort in early fall. Feedback from these sessions, together with students' evaluations on site, numerous conversations with the staff and faculty at the host institution, and periodic visits from representatives of the BU College of Engineering have been invaluable in gauging students' experiences at each of the participating sites. The opportunity for students to reflect on their experiences abroad as a group after reintegration into campus life has also helped them put their experience into a broader context and develop a more multifaceted appreciation for the global community. Returning students have become enthusiastic ambassadors for the programs, promoting their value and participating in information sessions for prospective students.

The students' feedback shows that they have found the experience enriching academically, personally, and culturally. They have been enthusiastic about their exposure to another culture and different social practices; traveled locally and abroad; and, more important, studied diligently for their classes. Moreover, they have been impressed by the individual attention they received in most instances from faculty and staff abroad, and many have commented on their return that they feel even better prepared than their peers for their junior-level courses. However, students have had to face the reality that faculty teaching styles and expectations differ, as does the student culture and the amount of hand holding expected by U.S. students. Finally, most host faculty have enjoyed teaching U.S. students. They report that they particularly like the degree of classroom interaction and discussion characteristic of the educational style in the United States, which in turn has given students the opportunity to become ambassadors of their own culture.

As with any developing program, a number of challenges have been encountered. Grades have continued to be a concern for students. In general, grades are less important at partner institutions than they are in the United States. European students focus on passing exams, not earning grades in individual courses and certainly not on assessments on weekly problem sets. Faculty at partner institutions often have had a very hard time understanding the particular obsession that U.S. students have with their grades. U.S. students for their part have felt that the foreign faculty don't understand the students' need to demonstrate academic success by receiving high grades, nor have they felt that foreign faculty understand their need for tangible and frequent feedback. One might argue that this obsession with grades is a particularly unfortunate aspect of modern U.S. academic life. Nonetheless, it was an instance of cultural dissonance between the foreign faculty and the U.S. students. Student and faculty angst surrounding this issue notwithstanding, examination of students' preparticipation grade point averages and grades obtained in these programs has shown no systemic differences; some students' grades abroad are marginally better, and others are marginally worse than on their home campus.

Much of the study abroad program's success has been based on managing students' expectations prior to their participation, such as through information sessions, predeparture meetings, and written materials. At the same time, it has been necessary to prepare faculty on-site so that they have a better sense of what to expect from students and how best to accommodate their needs. The main differences are related to providing feedback, grading and evaluation, teaching styles, use of technology, and interaction in the class. Communication among all stakeholders is key for the program to run smoothly as well as for making sure that students have enough flexibility and tools to thrive.

Conclusions

In this chapter we explore the case of BU's semester-long study abroad programs for engineering students with a focus on the Madrid site. Developed in existing BU overseas locations, these programs were designed to provide access to a group of students who have not traditionally studied abroad for a variety of reasons, including inflexible degree requirements. By adding engineering courses that tie into curricula on the home campus as well as by making accommodations to help engineering students integrate into local life and adapt to cultural differences the university has been able to increase dramatically the percentage of engineering students going abroad.

Beyond the numbers alone, BU's engineering offerings overseas have met their primary goal of enabling a meaningful subset of engineering students to experience the benefits of study abroad without interrupting progress toward their degree or lengthening the time necessary to complete their engineering degree requirements. Although learning a language has not been the primary goal of studying abroad, students have walked away with basic knowledge that will enable them to pursue more language classes in the future. More important, they have learned a set of skills from studying in another culture, which includes their ability to overcome frustration, culture shock, and struggles with adapting.

It is hoped the BU model will help administrators of other colleges and universities as they seek to increase access for their engineering students. Of course, each institution is unique, and not all institutions already have their own centers abroad or the ability to collaborate with partner institutions to develop engineering tracks overseas. Still, other aspects that contributed to the success at BU can be scaled up or down as needed, such as curriculum mapping and collaborating with faculty.

At the same time, lessons learned at BU and in other engineering programs, which on a national level have made great strides over the past decade, may be instructive in increasing participation among other students who have been traditionally underrepresented in study abroad. Different groups of students have their own set of needs; yet if there is anything that we have learned, it is that it is necessary to assess barriers to study abroad, listen to and collaborate with all key stakeholders, and find ways of creating or adapting existing programs as possible to meet students where they are in their personal and academic stages of life.

References

DeWinter, U. J. (1997). Science and engineering education abroad: An overview. *Frontiers, 3*, 181–197.

Eisenberg, S. R., Murray, J., & DeWinter, U. J. (2007, June). *Assessment of an engineering study abroad program: Reflections from the first 124 students (2001–2006).* Paper presented at the annual conference of the American Society for Engineering Education, Honolulu, HI.

Eland, A., Smithee, M., & Greenblatt, S. L. (2009). *U.S. classroom culture.* Washington, DC: NAFSA: Association of International Educators.

Farrugia, C. A., & Bhandari, R. (2015). *Open doors report on international educational exchange.* New York, NY: Institute of International Education.

Farrugia, C. A., & Bhandari, R. (2016). *Open doors report on international educational exchange.* New York, NY: Institute of International Education.

Gerhardt, L. A., Blumenthal, P., & Spodek, S. (2002, June). *Educating the global engineer: A program to promote study abroad, international exchanges and diversity in undergraduate engineering.* Paper presented at the annual conference of the American Society for Engineering Education, Montréal, Québec, Canada.

Klahr, S. C., & Ratti, U. (2000). Increasing student participation abroad: A study of U.S. and European programs. *Journal of Studies in International Education, 4,* 79–102. doi:10.1177/102831530000400106

Kohls, L. R. (2001). *Survival kit for overseas living: For Americans planning to live and work abroad.* Boston, MA: Nicholas Brealey.

Lattuca, L. R, Terenzini, P. T., Volkwein, J. F., & Peterson, G. D. (2006). The changing face of engineering education. *The Bridge, 36*(2), 5–13.

Lewis, R. D. (2006). *When cultures collide: Leading across cultures* (3rd ed.). Boston, MA: Nicholas Brealey.

Murray, J., & DeWinter, U. J., & Eisenberg, S. R. (2003, June). *Developing a study abroad opportunity for engineering Undergraduates.* Paper presented at the annual conference of the American Society for Engineering Education, Nashville, TN.

National Science Board. (2016). *Science and engineering indicators 2016: Undergraduate education, enrollment, and degrees in the United States.* Retrieved from www.nsf.gov/statistics/2016/nsb20161/#/report/chapter-2/undergraduate-education-enrollment-and-degrees-in-the-united-states

Paige, R. M., Cohen, A., Kappler, B., Chi, J. C., & Lassegard, J. P. (2006). *Maximizing study abroad.* Minneapolis, MN: University of Minnesota Center for Advanced Research on Language Acquisition.

Parkinson, A. (2007) Engineering study abroad programs: Formats, challenges, best practices. *Online Journal for Global Engineering Education, 2*(2), Article 2. Retrieved from http://digitalcommons.uri.edu/ojgee/vol2/iss2/2

UNDOCUMENTED STUDENTS AND ACCESS TO EDUCATION ABROAD

Teri Albrecht, Arelis Palacios, and Daniel Siefken

A s of 2017 an estimated 11 million undocumented immigrants reside in the United States. Of that estimate, roughly 1 million are under the age of 18, and 4.4 million are under the age of 30. Many individuals and families come to the United States seeking humanitarian refuge, employment, or family reunification, and have crossed the border illegally or overstayed a legal work visa (American Psychological Association, 2017).

Within this context, Deferred Action for Childhood Arrivals (DACA, as the official memorandum from the Department of Homeland Security came to be known) (Napolitano, 2012) currently allows undocumented youths to obtain a temporary work permit, and grants an opportunity for temporary labor residency to a large population of America's undocumented youths. DACA is an executive order issued by President Barack Obama on June 15, 2012, that requires biennial renewal and is not a path to citizenship for undocumented youths but rather the opportunity to work and financially provide for themselves and their families. In referring to the thousands of undocumented youths who work and study in the United States, Obama said, "They are Americans in their heart, in their minds, in every single way but one: on paper" (Preston & Cushman, 2012). Across the nation, students and institutions alike have struggled to adjust to this new opportunity, facing challenges from admissions processes and financial aid and registration to on-campus issues such as social inclusion, academic support, and access to study abroad.

The results of the 2016 U.S. presidential election have raised questions about the future of DACA (2012) and overall immigration reform. Multiple grassroots organizations and higher education institutions have worked fervently to find appropriate guidance and legal counsel for DACA beneficiaries, as the future of the program and its corresponding work permits are uncertain. In the meantime, advisers recognize a need to be cautious in guiding undocumented students. Although multiple fears remain, the international education community continues to be a space for civil discourse. Educators should feel empowered to ensure that varying viewpoints, including those of undocumented students, are brought into the national spotlight.

We recognize that in a volume on inclusion in education abroad, the political landscape as it relates to undocumented students may be different tomorrow, much less next year. The information provided here is based on an assumption—and for that matter, hope—that future immigration directives and regulations, whether DACA (2012) or in the form of more formal legislation, allows students access to higher education and study abroad. Accordingly, this chapter seeks to address the challenges of undocumented immigrant youths, and particularly college-age students in the United States, in seeking temporary labor status; primary, secondary and tertiary education; and more specifically, international education opportunities such as study abroad, international internships, or international service-learning.

Legal History

Legislation as it pertains to undocumented immigrants has long been a challenge in the United States at the state and federal levels. More specifically, undocumented students have had to navigate varying state laws and deal with the absence of comprehensive federal immigration reform to gain access to higher education. To understand the current circumstances of undocumented students, it is necessary to consider the history of immigration legislation.

The Immigration and Nationality Act (INA, 1965), passed with the intention of supporting the civil rights of immigrants, continues to be the backbone of current legislation on immigration. One of the resulting actions of the INA was that annual quotas were set on the number of immigrants who could establish legal residency in the United States. These quotas continue to be in effect today, with limits of 170,000 immigrants from Eastern Hemisphere countries and 120,000 immigrants from the Western Hemisphere, including the Americas. The hemispherical divisions were defined as and continue to be remnants of early nineteenth-century policies that began to curb the influx of migrant workers from specific countries related to labor needs. Since the mid-1960s, the INA quotas have not been able to handle the massive number of immigrants seeking residency in the United States, leading to a backlog of applications. In 2015 the U.S. State Department's annual report stated that more than 1.3 million Mexican citizens alone were in the queue for residency applications, and more than 4.5 million individuals worldwide were waiting to apply for legal residency in the United States.

In part to ease such bottlenecks, the Immigration Reform and Control Act (1986) was passed under the Reagan administration. One component of the legislation was an amnesty program that sought to reduce the number of undocumented immigrants in the United States, estimated at that time to be 3 to 4 million. Although the amnesty program reduced the undocumented immigration population to some extent, the numbers again began to rise after the postamnesty period from 1986 to 1996.

The Clinton administration adopted a different approach. The Illegal Immigration Reform and Immigrant Responsibility Act (IIRIRA) (U.S. Congress, 1996) contained provisions that imposed stricter measures on undocumented immigrants. Section 505 of the IIRIRA focused on higher education institutions and deemed undocumented individuals ineligible for postsecondary benefits unless a U.S. citizen or resident was also eligible for the identical benefits. Although regulations were never drafted to provide legal guidance, Section 505 has been the pivotal question states have had to wrestle with in developing policies relating to undocumented students' admissions and subsequent benefits at public higher education institutions.

During the years of federal immigration reforms, the U.S. Supreme Court addressed the question of educational rights for undocumented students in several key cases. A landmark decision in the case of *Plyler v. Doe* (1982) guaranteed the rights of undocumented students to a K–12 education. Attaining a high school degree then prompted the question of access to higher education. Varying policies across the United States created mixed results on whether public universities could admit undocumented students, with lawsuits ensuing. The most prominent cases were fought in California between 1984 and 1995. Then, Texas legislation (HB1403) set the stage for state recognition of access to higher education for undocumented students. The legislation was drafted to adhere to Section 505 of the IIRIRA, and higher education access for undocumented students in Texas was opened. The main benefits of Texas's legislation granted in-state tuition to qualified students as well as eligibility for nonfederal financial aid. As of April 2017, 19 states and the District of Columbia (National Immigration Law Center, 2017) have followed suit to grant in-state tuition for undocumented students. At the same time, other states continue to deny in-state tuition and, in some cases, admission to public universities.

The solution to varying state practices has hinged on the need for comprehensive immigration reform packaged in the Development, Relief, and Education for Alien Minors (DREAM, 2001) Act to provide federal protection for securing benefits to undocumented students pursuing higher education. Since the federal DREAM Act was first introduced, it has met various challenges in being passed into legislation, and ultimately never passed. By way of finding a temporary solution, DACA provided the opportunity for certain undocumented immigrants to apply for a Social Security number, obtain legal employment with health benefits, acquire a driver's license, and even apply for credit in some states (Preston & Cushman, 2012).

Through DACA (2012), many undocumented college students have been able to apply for legal work authorization and approval to travel temporarily outside the United States. Work authorization benefits have opened the door for DACA students to hold internships, pursue professional jobs after graduation, and qualify for graduate or teaching assistantships at the graduate level, all of which had previously been unavailable. *Advance parole*, the official term for the immigration benefit that provides preapproval to travel and reenter the United States for educational, employment, and humanitarian purposes, was a significant development. With this permission, DACA beneficiaries can now consider a range of activities abroad including studying, visiting an ailing family member, or participating in work-associated travel with the appropriate supplemental documentation.

Although it is not a bid for general amnesty or a means for accessing the educational benefits granted to their citizen counterparts, DACA (2012) addresses what many previous attempts had failed to do: provide a legal, albeit temporary, means for broader participation in the country these students consider home. Obama's executive action did not occur in a vacuum—it was the result of years of policies, bills, and acts that have demarcated the capacity for social and legal integration of undocumented youths into the United States. DACA also serves as an indication of the growing national attention on undocumented students and their historic efforts to access higher education. International migration and the educational pursuit of undocumented students is not unique to the United States; rather it is a global trend that affects a large number of sending and receiving countries and higher education institutions in innumerable ways. Incorporation of undocumented students into educational communities forces governments and citizens worldwide to reconcile the effects of a changing demographic with more traditional notions of national identity, belief systems, practices, and ways of life that inform their collective sense of "we." International education is not exempt from this process, nor can international educators ignore the potentially positive and negative effects of their field on this demographic.

Why Educate Undocumented Students?

Many agree that higher education is a necessity for upward economic mobility, increased labor market opportunities, and general economic security (Baum & Flores, 2011). However, in an era of budgetary cutbacks and diminished institutional resources, the value of including undocumented students in higher education, and particularly in international education, requires additional discussion. As gatekeepers to global opportunities, international educators must embrace why as well as how to fully support and advocate for these students.

Educating and supporting undocumented students in higher education has a significant potential impact on the American populace and individual students alike. Regardless of whether there is an individual desire to provide academic access for undocumented students, first and foremost there is no federal restriction on undocumented students participating in higher education. For the moment at least, they also have legal access to study abroad through DACA (2012). The onus lies on the educator to provide an academic space for all students interested in and eligible for participation in higher education, regardless of personal belief or student status. Second, undocumented students demonstrate high levels of university retention and graduation rates, particularly when coupled with in-state tuition reductions (Lolovich, 2015) and increased social capital through social networks in the university space (Hallett, 2013). Educators must understand that many undocumented students who are enrolled in higher education institutions perceive themselves as the only hope a family has in breaking the cycle of poverty. They take their roles as students very seriously, to help set examples for siblings, and to validate to themselves and to their parents that their familial sacrifices are not in vain.

Third, undocumented students who graduate from universities contribute to economic stability by increasing tax revenues, adding to the job pool, using fewer social services, and preventing state expenditures on issues related to students dropping out of education, such as criminal justice costs, unemployment, job training, and welfare (Belanger, 2001). Fourth, higher education provides a platform for increased democratic, civic, and social integration for undocumented students. The U.S. education system acts as a mechanism of instilling political socialization and integration (Bedolla, 2012); in doing so, it can be considered the "center of democratic governance" (p. 23), where curricular and extracurricular activity is a primary catalyst for engaging undocumented students in the political, social, and cultural norms associated with U.S. society. Finally, postsecondary education for undocumented students maximizes the financial and educational investment in this population over their previous 12 years of engagement in the U.S. educational system (Eusebio & Mendoza, 2015).

Beyond the broader benefits of supporting undocumented students in higher education, international education opportunities are integral to the holistic experience of the undocumented student. Relative to their documented counterparts, undocumented students achieve lower educational attainment rates (Covarrubias & Lara, 2014) for many reasons, including but not limited to minimal academic language comprehension (Francis et al., 2006); inequitable and racially divided educational systems (Gandara & Contreras, 2009; Huber, 2009); and placement in underperforming schools, classes, and instruction (Gildersleeve, 2010). Because of issues of legal status, language difficulties, and comparative disadvantages developed and reproduced by an educational system directed by dominant cultural values, undocumented students have few opportunities to establish networks in secondary schooling, leaving them excluded from the informational resources often provided to other students in U.S. public schools (Garcia & Tierney, 2011). This can result in undocumented students entering higher education with fewer resources, smaller networks, and lesser access to social and cultural capital than their documented counterparts.

As undocumented students are already entering institutions with limited access to resources because of reduced social and cultural capital, their ability to access international education has a significant impact on their level of educational outcomes from their university experience. Considering the lower educational achievement rates of undocumented students, studying abroad can result in positive effects on their graduation rates and, presumably, on academic performance. Undocumented students may return to their U.S. campus with renewed and enhanced educational interest, pushing them toward degree completion and potentially improving their grade point average. The social and professional networks developed abroad could produce significant increases in the undocumented student's access to résumé-building experiences that open doors to future study opportunities and better jobs as he or she enters the labor market, including internships, research opportunities, mentorship and professional relationships, and graduate school connections.

Promoting study abroad among this population has the potential to engage undocumented students at a similar pace as their documented counterparts, providing them with the networks, intercultural capacities, and broad understanding of the globalized and culturally diverse world in which they live. If institutions and educators do not encourage and create proportionate and equitable access to international education, the educational achievement gap between documented and undocumented students may continue to widen, essentially leaving this already vulnerable student population behind. It is the responsibility of the international educator to acknowledge this growing disparity, promote international opportunities among undocumented students, and support these students as they seek to use their legal access to international education through DACA (2012).

Identities and Intersections in International Education

Undocumented students, even in the era of DACA (2012) and advance parole, face considerable barriers to accessing international education at the university level. Similar to the anti-immigrant public sentiment and campaigns occurring nearly 100 years ago during the peak of immigration primarily from Europe to the United States, undocumented students receive the brunt of societal apprehension concerning their assimilability and Americanization as newcomers (Stepick & Stepick, 2002). As the United States continues to become more diverse, American culture can no longer be considered a singular concept defined by an increasingly reduced White majority. Immigrants arrive to a culturally complex society with multiple ethnic and cultural identities and not some unified, homogenous construct of what it means to be American (Stepick & Stepick, 2002). Immigrants can fully assimilate into society yet define their place and interaction within it and retain elements of their own cultural heritage and familial histories. However, with such large numbers of immigrants and the ever increasing population of immigrant youths, the level of these youths' acculturation and integration will likely define the social and cultural landscape of U.S. civil society for generations to come.

Unfortunately, the futures of many youths are legally determined by their undocumented status. Citizenship is out of reach for the majority of undocumented students. However, legal citizenship isn't the only thing that bars most undocumented youths from full assimilation. Discrimination and social marginalization because of legal and immigrant status compound their self-perceived and socially perceived assimilability. Throughout their childhood, many immigrants form habits, actions, and attitudes representative of mainstream culture, such as language, music preferences, dress, and hobbies. As they reach their teens, most immigrant youths must confront their limited citizenship and the subsequent discrimination and exclusion because of their status. Although mainstream culture has become less homogenous, Golas-Boza (2006) contends that true citizenship is associated with Whiteness, forcing undocumented youths into an ethnically segmented assimilation. Even as these youths continue to act very American, they develop intersectional and hyphenated identities (e.g., Mexican-American, Iraqi-American). To drop the hyphenation one must essentially act and appear American (White). In other words, U.S. society doesn't want to grant full citizenship to those who are culturally different (Stepick & Stepick, 2002). It is in this sense that undocumented youths are forced to create intersected identities, culturally distinct yet still part of American society. In the face of being labeled as different and noncitizens, legally or socially, youths may respond in sharp defense of their cultural heritage and identity. Stepick and Stepick (2002) describe this as the development of an "ethnic consciousness" (p. 249) throughout the maturation process. Rejection and discrimination incite nationalistic pride, whereas loyalty to and association with American culture endures.

The effects of intersectional and hyphenated identities for undocumented youths only further complicate the transition from high school to college. Many students express intense feelings of neglect, discrimination, and social exclusion as their documented classmates apply to college and are accepted and proceed to enroll while they fail to move forward because of the many barriers restricting their postsecondary aspirations (Perez, 2009). Forming positive attitudes toward U.S. society becomes more difficult as they experience these sentiments of social, cultural, and legal rejection, essentially creating a self-perception as the other. Although this experience of otherness is developed throughout the entirety of the schooling process, it is poignantly felt and its effects are most detrimental as the student exits the semifamiliar and socially acceptable confines of primary and secondary school and confronts barriers in accessing higher education, considered the next logical step in education and social mobility.

At the institutional level, undocumented students also face multiple barriers in seeking international education opportunities. Considering that most states limit financial aid and in-state tuition rates to U.S. citizens only, undocumented students face a high financial burden, virtually precluding them from higher education. Beyond the already restrictive state policies, many institutions that allow enrollment to undocumented students do so under the status of international student. Although allowing students presumably full participation in the higher education system, this designation, as well as the broader immigration status, often conflicts at two points: issues of the student's self-assumed identity as American and institutional and departmental barriers in regard to international education opportunities. Although the former could foreseeably cause undocumented students to feel resistant toward engagement with institutional systems such as study abroad, the latter can create perceived and real barriers to accessing international education. Federal, state, and institutional financial aid and scholarships most often include citizenship as an eligibility requirement. Although administrators of an institution can do little about federal and state eligibility requirements, they can advocate for and create systems in which citizenship is not a factor in awarding institutional or departmental scholarships. Additionally, many institutions use the Free Application for Federal Student Aid (FAFSA) or comparable state financial aid applications as a method of determining need-based scholarships and other financial aid mechanisms. Undocumented students cannot apply for federal student aid, and each state determines their ability to apply for aid through state processes, meaning these students often appear in the financial aid system as low-need students because of their inability to access federal financial aid. Researching and adapting institutional policies regarding need-based aid processes can allow undocumented students to gain access to institutional aid like their documented counterparts. Developing a method of assessing need for these students allows them to be accurately recognized when awarding need-based aid.

Tuition rates for credit-bearing study abroad programs may also become prohibitive for undocumented students if an institution considers them as international students. As previously discussed, many institutions do not provide in-state tuition equity for undocumented students, often putting even short-term programming with concomitant institutional tuition out of reach financially for students who may have grown up within miles of a campus and identify as residents of their state. Again, analysis of institutional policy and tuition equity advocacy for undocumented students may have a positive impact on a student's ability to participate in international education.

Finally, universities often create policies and processes in study abroad programming that may become prohibitive to an undocumented student's engagement in international education. Federal law requires undocumented students to follow set guidelines and application processes for approval to travel abroad through advance parole, which often comes shortly before a student's departure. Program deposits, airfares, program fees, financial responsibility policies, and other such financially driven institutional deadlines often conflict with these federal requirements and time lines, putting students in a tenuous financial position. Aside from the added stress and costs directly incurred throughout these federal applications and processes, students often confront institutional deadlines that create high financial risk if a student was denied federal approval and thus is forced to withdraw from participation. For example, many universities require students to pay non-refundable deposits for study abroad programs. Already limited by federal, state, and institutional financial aid access, and facing unknown outcomes in their ability to travel abroad at the federal level, an undocumented student may be reluctant to persist to the point of paying a deposit. To promote access and inclusion of this student group, an institution might create accommodations in these circumstances, such as waived deposits, deadline extensions, or adjusted refund policies that would encourage students to continue in the process and reduce the financial risk assumed by the student. As an additional example, international flights present added barriers as many institutions require tickets to be purchased by a certain date. Institutions may accommodate undocumented students by postponing the deadline until after federal approval, encouraging students to purchase flight insurance, and creating internal policies or demarcating funds to assist in financial reimbursement if a student finds himself or herself in a difficult situation. These and other such examples show the responsibility and capacity of an institution to create inclusive policies and procedures for the increased international mobility of undocumented students.

Advising at the Campus and International Education Levels

Advising undocumented students for an international experience can be better understood by examining the interrelationship of five facets of the education abroad process to help advisers conceptualize and actualize effective advising processes. In this section we analyze (a) institutional acclimation and barrier reduction, (b) program selection and academic integration, (c) federal immigration policies and country-specific information, (d) deconstruction of program cost structures and financing options, and (e) reentry. International education professionals are tasked with understanding various facets of this process for undocumented students or where to find appropriate legal resources. The advising counsel provided here is subject to immigration changes at the federal level and requires institutions to reassess and realign when policy changes take place.

Institutional Acclimation and Barrier Reduction

"Each institution is larger than the sum of its individual units" (Theodorson & Theodorson, 1969, p. 395). More often than not, individual units such as departments, offices, schools and colleges, programs, and centers operate independently rather than interpedently. Units may have created their own internal policies for admissions, onboarding, and financial aid disbursement for specific student populations that do not always align with those in other units. For undocumented students, the correlation between educational attainment and resource availability is critical, and the transition for many students from secondary to tertiary education is precarious enough already. International education professionals must pay close attention to the policies created at the national, state, and, even more important, institutional levels as they could unintentionally create more barriers for undocumented students.

Collaborations with admissions, financial aid and bursar offices, multicultural units, and diverse-student retention programs can help determine factors that impede persistence to graduation and allow development of strategies that reduce or eliminate barriers altogether. Common barriers include admissions and student classifications, extraneous fees related to student services, and tuition prices related to in- and out-of-state classifications. A multitude of universities now have dedicated staff and offices to help support undocumented students, complete with legal and financial resources, as well as various student support services.

Program Selection and Academic Integration

An international experience should have academic relevance or increase a student's employment viability. To ensure compliance with advance parole requirements, options for study, interning, or service-learning should have specific academic relevance in the student's degree plan.

This is especially important as the necessary institutional program participation letter that confirms a student's participation in a program will be required to authenticate the academic rationale required for a successful advance parole application for the U.S. Citizenship and Immigration Services requirements. Long-term versus short-term opportunities both have their merits, and the portfolio of programs available at each institution can have a wide range in structure, cost, and academic foci. However, international education professionals should work closely with students to help them choose the program of best academic fit.

Federal Immigration Policies and Country-Specific Information

It is imperative to state that any advising is never intended to replace legal counsel. DACA (2012) continues to be an executive action and not a law, and although advisers should pay close attention to any shifts in immigration policy, it is just as important to know local legal resources that can assist students or inform and support those who choose to work with an attorney. Because of the uncertainties regarding reentry, many lawyers have advised students against overseas travel, yet the ability to apply for advance parole continues to be available to individuals through DACA. The I-131 Application for Travel Document, commonly known as advance parole, is complex, multilayered, and takes up to 90 days to process. To expedite the application, students may want to consult the original legal counsel who assisted the student with his or her original DACA application. What is more, student advisers should stress any specific visa requirements or transit visa requirements for specific airports, as these may pose challenges and additional costs for undocumented students. Ultimately, although the students are responsible for researching the appropriate visa requirements, an adviser can draw their attention to potential challenges.

Deconstruction of Program Cost Structures and Financing Options

The financial barriers for undocumented students can be insurmountable. Although they cannot apply for federal financial aid, a number of questions apply, including: What policies limit access to state and institutional aid? Can funds be diverted or set aside for this subset of students? Are there merit-based or high-financial-need study abroad scholarships available? Change at the institutional level may take longer, but can any of the costs related to deposits or program fees be structured differently or placed on a payment plan for the student to help alleviate the burdens of initial costs? The advance parole process often runs concurrently with the program application process, and fees related to both can add up quickly. In an initial advising appointment, conveying this information transparently will help students understand upfront costs and subsequent participation fees related to tuition, airfare, insurance, and personal expenses. Creating a sample budget can provide concrete information for students to use in discussing options with their families.

Reentry

The conversation related to students' possible concerns with reentry into the United States is a delicate one, and an adviser must be prepared to hear the full details of the student's history with impartiality as well as empathy. The reality is that an approved advance parole document, known as the I-512, does not guarantee reentry to the United States. It is important to reiterate a student's need to consult legal counsel so that they fully understand the grounds for inadmissibility and the ramifications if they are denied reentry. In an advising appointment, students may feel uncomfortable revealing facts about their personal situation because of fear, feeling ashamed, or risk of being further marginalized. Students may feel more comfortable speaking to an attorney who can provide a sense of the risks involved based on the student's individual case. There could be multiple reasons for inadmissibility related to prior misdemeanor charges, removal orders that were ignored, or an error in the original advance parole application. Students should also list all the countries of expected travel in their application so that this does not raise any concerns at the point of reentry into the United States.

When deferring students to legal counsel, it is also important to outline the types of legal counsel that can access U.S. Citizenship and Immigration Services information, specifically board certified attorneys or a Board of Immigration Appeals (BIA) representative. One thing for advisers to be aware of in counseling students is that there are predatory *notario* fraud schemes that often victimize vulnerable communities. According to the American Bar Association (2017), "the term 'notario publico' is particularly problematic in that it creates a unique opportunity for deception. The literal translation of 'notario publico' is 'notary public'" (para. 3). Although

> a notary public in the United States is authorized only to witness the signature of forms, a notary public in many Latin American (and European) countries refers to an individual who has received the equivalent of a law license and who is authorized to represent others before the government. (American Bar Association, 2017, para. 3)

Notarios represent themselves as lawyers or professionals who are qualified to offer legal advice concerning matters of law, have no such recognized qualification in the United States, and routinely victimize members of immigration communities. Often, families and individuals pay fees to notarios, and paperwork is never submitted on behalf of the applicants, or passports are illegally withheld in exchange for payment, which can result in devastating consequences, such as falsified documents, missed appointments with immigration officials, or lapses in immigration statuses.

The most important aspect of advising is to ensure that students have as much accurate and comprehensive information as possible to make an informed decision. Students take on full financial and personal risk, with the additional stress of facing scrutiny returning across the U.S. border. A student must weigh the pros and cons as they relate to the students, their futures, and their families. Although the institution cannot assume risk on behalf of the student, leaders and staff can do their best by informing but also ensuring that limitations aren't imposed on students with DACA (2012), either verbally or in writing. Given the current political climate, staff at many universities and legal sources have warned against travel, as the reentry process could be mired in even more complications.

Campus Programs

The University of California, Berkeley's (2017) Undocumented Student Program (USP) most illustratively represents a comprehensive institutional support model. Its mission conveys the following:

> USP practices a holistic, multicultural and solution-focused approach that delivers individualized service for each student. The academic counseling, legal support, financial aid resources and extensive campus referral network provided by USP helps students develop the unique gifts and talents they each bring to the university, while empowering a sense of belonging. The program's mission is to support the advancement of undocumented students within higher education and promote pathways for engaged scholarship. (para. 2)

Language and words matter. In the case of the USP and many other institutions, the visibility of specific terms of support, such as the educational campaigns created for National Educator's Coming Out Day by United We Dream that use Educator for Undocumented Students or Unafraid Educator, are critical in reframing the advising space. When creating a supportive culture for undocumented students it is important to display terms or posters that foster an environment of support at the onset of any advising appointment and encourage students to feel more comfortable and less stigmatized, as normalizing the identity on a college campus is instrumental. Students would likely be more inclined to come out of the shadows and be forthcoming with advisers throughout compliance and predeparture processes as there are various times of contact during the advance parole application phases.

Another example is the University of Texas (UT) at Austin, which has led the way in creating online content for DACA (2012) and studying abroad. The International Office and its departments of International Student and Scholar Services, English as a Second Language, and Study Abroad began by coordinating departmental support for undocumented students. The joint initiative, led by the International Office, developed a university-level website content that deconstructed the transition into the higher education process. One of the web pages outlined the steps necessary for studying abroad, thus placing this content within a larger set of resources for undocumented students (world.utexas.edu/undocumented/about).

Similarly, Georgetown University did much to vocalize support for undocumented students well before the inception of DACA (2012). The institution not only continues to support students' right to education but also connects this support to inclusion and Georgetown's Jesuit mission, noting that as a university located in our nation's capital and animated by our Catholic and Jesuit identity, we are called to support all of our students, including our undocumented students. These young women and men demonstrate an extraordinary passion to make America, and our increasingly interconnected world, a better place. Here at Georgetown, we are dedicated to creating a context where they can succeed, free from constraint or limitation. (DeGioia, 2013)

In each of these cases, it has been instrumental to have institution-wide support for undocumented students, which cannot be taken as a given (Palacios, 2017).

Although many institutions lack the financial resources to create centers or hire dedicated staff for undocumented student support, using specific terms in a mission or vision statement can also be the first step in shifting paradigms at the institution and possibly act as the catalyst for continued dialogue and change. More important, this change cannot take place in isolation, and working with various campus offices such as multicultural and institutional equity offices, community engagement partners, financial aid, and the registrar's offices creates strength in numbers.

Conclusion

Depending on one's state of residence, the dialogue surrounding undocumented youth and educational attainment can vary greatly. According to the National Conference of State Legislatures (2015),

> currently, at least 18 states have provisions allowing in-state tuition rates for undocumented students. Sixteen states provide these provisions through state legislation—California, Colorado, Connecticut, Florida, Illinois, Kansas, Maryland, Minnesota, Nebraska, New Mexico, New Jersey, New York, Oregon, Texas, Utah, and Washington. Two states—Oklahoma and Rhode Island—allow in-state tuition rates to undocumented students through Board of Regents decisions. California and Texas were the first states to enact legislation in 2001. (para. 2)

The provisions that grant in-state tuition waivers are not protected and are challenged annually by state legislators and the constituents they represent. It is important to note the ever evolving nature of this legislation as it relates to political influences, so we encourage advisers and institutions to review the most up-to-date information in their states. DACA (2012) hinges on the outcome of subsequent presidential elections, as it is an executive order and not a law. The results of the 2016 presidential election brought the uncertainty of DACA yet again into the national spotlight, and called into question the future of close to 790,000 DACA beneficiaries, many of whom are enrolled in colleges or universities as undergraduate or graduate students, gainfully employed in various professional industries across the nation, or in various military branches of service in the United States and overseas. Presently, there are legislative vehicles to put a program based on DACA onto solid legal footing. In December 2016, Senators Richard Durbin from Illinois and Lindsey Graham from South Carolina introduced the Bar Removal of Individuals Who Dream and Grow Our Economy Act (Bridge Act) into Congress, highlighting the remarkable economic impact of the program in its five-year history. In addition, newly revised bills of the DREAM Act were introduced in 2017 by congressional staff members who were original architects of the DREAM Act in 2001. While the program continues to be under intense scrutiny, there is a revitalized sense of urgency to resolve this legislatively rather than administratively.

Undocumented youth, advocacy organizations, and higher education institutions have played an integral role in giving unprecedented visibility to issues surrounding undocumented youth and families, yet the support or vilification of undocumented immigrants in the United States continues to be highly politicized. As the policies related to undocumented student support at all educational levels evolve, the need to champion the holistic development of *all* students, regardless of their immigration status, will become a critical need and a defining moment in an institution's values. This dialogue will undoubtedly continue to play a significant role in undocumented students' access to study abroad, which will need to be monitored and advocated for in the coming years.

References

American Bar Association. (2017). *About notario fraud.* Retrieved from www .americanbar.org/groups/public_services/immigration/projects_initiatives/ fightnotariofraud/about_notario_fraud.html

American Psychological Association. (2016). *Undocumented Americans.* Retrieved from www.apa.org/topics/immigration/undocumented-video.aspx

Bar Removal of Individuals Who Dream and Grow Our Economy Act of 2016, S.128, 115th Cong. (2017–2018).

Baum, S., & Flores, S. (2011). Higher education and children in immigrant families. *The Future of Children, 21*(1), 171–193.

Bedolla, L. (2012). Latino education, civic engagement and the public good. *Review of Research in Education, 36*(1), 23–42.

Belanger, K. (2001). Social justice in education for undocumented families. *Journal of Family and Social Work, 6*(4), 61–73.

Covarrubias, L., & Lara, A. (2014). The undocumented (im)migrant educational pipeline: The influence of citizenship status on educational attainment for people of Mexican origin. *Urban Education, 49*(1), 75–110.

DeGioia, J. (2013). *Undocumented student support.* Retrieved from undocumented.georgetown.edu

Development, Relief, and Education for Alien Minors Act, S. 952, 112th Cong. (2011).

Eusebio, C., & Mendoza, F. (2015). *The case for undocumented students in higher education.* Retrieved from www.e4fc.org/images/E4FC_TheCase.pdf

Francis, D., Kieffer, M., Lesaux, N., Rivera, H., & Rivera, M. (2006). *Practical guidelines for the education of English language learners: Research-based recommendations for instruction and academic intervention.* Washington, DC: U.S. Department of Education, Center on Instruction. Retrieved from www2.ed.gov/about/inits/ed/lep-partnership/interventions.pdf

Gandara, P., & Contreras, F. (2009). *The Latino education crisis: The consequences of failed social policies.* Cambridge, MA: Harvard University Press.

Garcia, L., & Tierney, W. (2011). Undocumented immigrants in higher education: A preliminary analysis. *Teachers College Record, 113*, 2739–2776.

Gildersleeve, R. (2010). Access between and beyond borders. *Journal of College Admission, 206*(4), 1–10.

Golas-Boza, T. (2006). Dropping the hyphen? Becoming Latino(a)-American through racialized assimilation. *Social Forces, 85*(1), 27–55.

Hallett, R. (2013). Undocumented student success: Navigating constraints related to retention. *Journal of Latino/Latin American Studies, 5*, 99–112.

HB1403, Texas Legislature, 77th Sess. (2001).

Huber, L. (2009). Disrupting apartheid of knowledge: Testimonio as methodology in Latina/o critical race research in education. *International Journal of Qualitative Studies in Education, 22*, 639–654.

Immigration and Nationality Act of 1965, 8 U.S.C . § 1151a-1156 (1965).

Lolovich, M. (2015). *The effect of in-state-resident-tuition on California undocumented immigrant postsecondary students.* Retrieved from gradworks.umi.com/37/45/3745382.html

National Conference of State Legislatures. (2015). *Undocumented student tuition: Overview.* Retrieved from www.ncsl.org/research/education/undocumented-student-tuition-overview.aspx

National Immigration Law Center. (2017). *Laws & policies improving access to higher education for immigrants.* Retrieved from www.nilc.org/wp-content/uploads/2017/04/table-access-to-ed-toolkit-2017-04.pdf

Napolitano, J. (2012). *Exercising prosecutorial discretion with respect to individuals who came to the United States as children* [Memorandum]. Washington, DC: U.S. Department of Homeland Security.

4

Palacios, A. (2017). *Undocumented student support.* Retrieved from undocumented .georgetown.edu

Perez, W. (2009). *We are Americans: Undocumented students pursuing the American dream.* Sterling, VA: Stylus.

Plyler v. Doe, 457 U.S. 202 (1982).

Preston, J., & Cushman J. H., Jr. (2012, June 15). Obama to permit young migrants to remain in US. *New York Times.* Retrieved from www.nytimes.com/2012/06/16/us/us-to-stop-deporting-some-illegal-immigrants.html

Stepick, A., & Stepick, C. D. (2002). Becoming American, constructing ethnicity: Immigrant youth and civic engagement. *Applied Developmental Science, 6,* 246–257.

Theodorson, G. A., & Theodorson, A. G. (1969). *A modern dictionary of sociology.* New York, NY: Crowell.

University of California at Berkeley. (2017). *Undocumented student program.* Retrieved from undocu.berkeley.edu

University of Texas at Austin. (2017). *About the Longhorn Dreamers Project.* Retrieved from world.utexas.edu/undocumented/about

U.S. Congress (104th). (1996). Illegal Immigration Reform and Immigrant Responsibility Act of 1996. Retrieved from http://epic.org/privacy/e-verify/iirira-program.pdf

PART THREE

NEXT STEPS

11

A WAY FORWARD

Exploring Strategies at Multiple Levels

Andrew Gordon

Education abroad has the potential to positively affect educational outcomes for all student groups, regardless of background or area of study. As Kuh (2008) illustrates, high-impact practices, which include education abroad, are made up of a group of activities that are particularly effective in promoting students' learning, development, and educational success. Through intentional program design and pedagogy, these methods can enhance student learning and narrow gaps in achievement across student populations.

Disparities persist in education abroad participation for students from underrepresented backgrounds and other groups underserved by education abroad, including racial and ethnic minorities, students with disabilities, and students in certain majors (Institute for International Education [IIE], 2015). Previous chapters in this volume explore the factors that have precluded various underrepresented populations from fully participating in education abroad as well as possible solutions to overcoming the barriers. This chapter looks at how we might move forward in addressing such issues in terms of advocacy and action.

Over the years a number of champions and initiatives have targeted the issue of diversity in education abroad. In 1990 Johnnetta B. Cole, president of Spelman College, presented the four Fs that prevent diverse students from pursuing education abroad: fear, finances, family and friends, and faculty (Cole, 1990). A fifth *F*—fit—was later added to the other four (Council on

International Educational Exchange, 1991). Since then numerous articles and student projects have addressed the topic of diversity and education abroad. Likewise, international education offices, education abroad program providers, and government agencies have developed initiatives to diversify education abroad. Despite such well-intentioned efforts, no significant increases have been noted in participation rates among a number of under-represented groups.

One problem is that traditional approaches to expanding representation in education abroad have been driven by disjointed efforts, which do not yield scalable solutions, instead of a comprehensive strategy. To reach parity in access to education abroad and the benefits it provides, a more unified strategy is needed. It is said that Roman philosopher Lucius Annaeus Seneca wrote that if one does not know which port one is sailing to, no wind is favorable. It is true that without a collective sense of the role of various stake-holders in achieving success—a sense of direction for where one is sailing—the individual initiatives of organizations, institutions, and agencies may only ever yield modest results. This does not suggest that staff of individual international education offices should not engage in innovative activities that could result in scalable models for diversifying education abroad; in fact, such efforts are critical in expanding our understanding of what works (or does not work) in achieving our goals. By having a strategy in place at the campus or organization level as well as at the national level, the likelihood for broad-based success in tackling the issue of diversity in education abroad is greater.

Here we explore the importance of strategic development at all levels of the education abroad ecosystem and the inclusion of a diverse set of stake-holders throughout the process. The chapter begins by describing previous efforts to diversify education abroad as well as how such efforts may benefit from longer term, multipronged strategies that embed diversity and inclusion in all aspects of education abroad. Each level of strategic development, individual, institutional, and national, is then discussed. Recommendations and examples provided in this chapter are offered from work by or in collaboration with the Diversity Abroad Network.

Diversity Abroad Network

An arm of Diversity Abroad, the Diversity Abroad Network is a global consortium of more than 230 members, including education abroad program providers, universities and colleges, and other organizations, with the express goal of advancing diversity and inclusive good practices that foster equitable access to global education (Diversity Abroad, 2006). Now in its 11th year, the Diversity Abroad Network supports its objectives by consulting with and advising institutions of higher education, nonprofit organizations, and government agencies as well as through events such as annual conferences and training opportunities for faculty and professionals. All these activities provide rich and ample examples of best practices and insights in the field from a variety of institutional types. At the same time, conversations in the Diversity Abroad Network and beyond have led to the development of a broader level of thinking that goes beyond any one institution.

The Need for Sustainable Strategies

Education abroad advocates have been discussing the expansion of diversity and access to international opportunities for some time. For example, the International Academic Opportunity Act (2000) was passed by Congress to establish a scholarship to help students with limited financial means study abroad. The Senator Paul Simon Study Abroad Foundation Act (2007) aimed to send 1 million students abroad by the year 2017. Then in 2014, the IIE (2014) launched the Generation Study Abroad initiative with the goal of doubling the number of students who participate in study abroad by the year 2020. In addition to these three high-profile programs, various institutions and organizations have launched efforts to increase access and diversity in education abroad. Although these efforts should be celebrated, in and of themselves they have not led to significant or sustained change in the demographic makeup of U.S. study abroad participants. Multiple factors may help explain why this is the case.

First, recent federal, state, and institutional initiatives have been implemented for a fixed period to address one aspect of the problem. A program that is not part of a broader strategy or is implemented for a limited time can have unintentional consequences. The message may be that the goal, diversifying education abroad, is not integral to the success of the main activity of education abroad. The initiative is perceived as an add-on and not something required for the main activity. In developing a sustainable strategy, the policies and practices informed by the strategy should become normalized and integrated into the education abroad process, thus eliminating the need for separate diversification-related initiatives in the future.

Second, funding is often dependent on the political and social climate. Once funding dries up, sometimes with little notice, institutions are left scrambling to fill the gap, or they must cease their activities. This can be particularly problematic during difficult fiscal periods, as initiatives are considered temporary and extraneous. In this environment, institutional leaders may determine that continued funding is an unnecessary and unjustifiable expense compared to other priorities on campus. For example, an office may have a program designed to support peer mentors from underrepresented groups with a grant intended to fund innovative or pilot initiatives. If the program has not been integrated into other outreach activities or incorporated into the office's annual budget, it might later serve as an easy target for line-item cuts.

Third, much of the funding is targeted solely toward providing students with scholarships and grants. Financial resources are certainly desirable and can be a useful tool for attracting diverse students to education abroad. This in turn can have a multiplication effect as participants share their experiences with their family, friends, and communities. However, providing direct funding to students is neither a sustainable nor a scalable strategy as its success depends on the availability of funding, which can evaporate with little warning.

Fourth, diversity initiatives have focused consistently on compositional diversity, comparing the numbers of students from various backgrounds who participate in education abroad with their corresponding proportions in U.S. higher education, often looking specifically at race. Such an approach makes sense to an extent, as compositional diversity can be quantified and success can be tracked. However, if the compositional diversity of students is the sole focus of the initiative, the real goal is missed. Instead, we need to ensure that diverse and underrepresented students not only participate but also benefit academically, professionally, and personally through education abroad. To understand this, one must first understand the difference between diversity and inclusion. If diversity is the quantitative representation of student populations, inclusion is the quality of the climate in which students interact with staff, faculty, and experience abroad (University of Denver, 2016).

Each year, those in the field of education abroad await the release of the IIE's Open Doors report. Results and successes, particularly with respect to the goal of diversifying education abroad, are gauged by percentage increases or decreases in participation rates. At an institutional level, campus administrators use these data to assess their success in diversifying education abroad. However, the raw numbers do not reveal much about the effectiveness of advising, support, and development for diverse student populations in education abroad.

As explored in previous chapters, the notion of *inclusive excellence*, as originally defined by the Association of American Colleges & Universities (AAC&U) (Clayton-Pedersen, O'Neil, & Musil, 2007) takes into account that a community or institution's success is dependent on how well it values, engages, and includes the rich diversity of students, staff, faculty, administrators, and alumni constituents (University of Denver, 2016). In applying this definition to education abroad, it is necessary to determine the extent to which diverse students are valued and supported when assessing success. Marrying diversity and inclusion in education abroad requires a comprehensive approach that ensures that inclusive good practices are integrated throughout the education abroad process.

The reality is that the very initiatives created to support diversifying education abroad can create unintended barriers. The following analysis is intended to help policy makers and educators alike appreciate that without a sustainable strategy even the most well-meaning initiatives will be limited in their success. Developing strategies at multiple levels is required to create equitable access, diversification of participation, and inclusive support in education abroad.

The Role of Individuals

In an ideal situation, an individual's institution or office supports a strategic plan for diversifying education abroad in thought and resources. There are, however, cases where such support may not exist. Even when resources are available, it is often up to individual faculty, staff, or students to drive projects and gain traction for initiatives. For all these reasons, it is important to consider the role a single staff or faculty member might play in helping to diversify education abroad on his or her home campus, with or without support at the outset.

To be effective, individuals benefit from training to develop professional expertise in diversity and inclusion in education abroad. Organizations like Diversity Abroad, the AAC&U, and the American Council on Education provide professional learning opportunities pertaining to diversity and inclusion in international education for faculty, administrators, and staff. Additionally, professionals interested in developing skills in these areas can avail themselves of training offered at their institution. Such opportunities not only provide skills but also help professionals build a coalition of like-minded educators who believe in the value of education abroad for student success. For example, one professional at a flagship state university invited colleagues from the institution's division of diversity and student affairs to participate in a webinar on assessing diversity and inclusion in education abroad. They used this event for professional growth and relationship building among campus stakeholders.

Moreover, training allows individuals to become successful in identifying and connecting with stakeholders who are likely to be interested in diversifying education abroad, including senior-level administrators, faculty, and other staff. These stakeholders include those who work in student affairs, diversity, or multicultural units as well as academic advising or the provost's office. It can help to start small, meeting colleagues where they are, for example, in their office or for coffee or lunch, to establish a rapport. Eventually it can help to give formal presentations before one or more stakeholders on why diversifying education abroad is vital to the campus; to their unit; and, most important, for students' success. The ability for stakeholders to understand and appreciate their role in addressing such issues can directly affect their level of support and commitment. This process should be repeated with various stakeholders over time to ensure the message permeates key areas of the campus community.

Student voices are a critical piece of the puzzle. It is necessary to engage in direct outreach to students so that their needs and concerns are known and can be addressed. Further, the more students express interest and participate in education abroad, the easier it is to justify resources to support them properly. For busy professionals, additional time spent on campus to meet with student groups may not be appealing given a rigorous work schedule. Remembering why it is important for diverse students to have equitable access to education abroad may compel key stakeholders to carve out time accordingly.

Individuals can also do much through social media with photos, video, blogs, live streaming, or other channels. By sharing the experiences of diverse students, education abroad becomes more realistic for a wider array of students. Being able to see and hear firsthand how education abroad influenced a student academically, professionally, and personally reiterates the importance of diversifying education abroad. The practice of sharing success extends to faculty and staff who have taught abroad or participated in an overseas program. As colleagues become familiar with opportunities for them and others to take diverse students abroad, the opportunities for collaboration with an education abroad office increase.

Thus, whether or not a campus's leadership has shown support for diversifying education abroad, it is important to recognize that individuals have the ability to effect change. Sometimes it takes the work of grassroots efforts for administrators of an institution to recognize that more needs to be done on a campuswide level. When this happens, it is necessary to develop an institution-wide strategy.

Sustainable Strategies at the Institutional Level

The institutional level is where theory and policy can be tested, refined, and implemented. Each institution is in an optimal position to develop a custom strategy that will diversify education abroad on its campus, based on its unique mix of students, academics, administrators, and culture. Although it is necessary and useful to monitor best practices in the field, a bespoke strategy at the institutional level, with acceptance at various levels, will have a greater chance of yielding effective and sustainable results.

To develop an effective strategy for diversifying education abroad, all the stakeholders must be consulted. Depending on a variety of factors, including institutional type, what is required for stakeholders to support a strategy of inclusion in education abroad will differ. In its work with one large public institution, for example, Diversity Abroad (2010) found that one key group—faculty—largely associated increased access to education abroad with the development of short-term programs. Many expressed concern about the academic rigor of shorter programs and apprehension toward supporting such programs. During a similar project at a small liberal arts college, it was discovered that faculty who teach courses popular among students of color have not traditionally viewed education abroad as a necessity for their students. In these examples, the stakeholders are the same, but the concerns and context differ and require campus-specific strategies.

With countless initiatives and priorities being presented to campus administrators, often with limited funding, it is necessary to stress why education abroad is critical for all students and not just those who have traditionally been represented and are able to afford such experiences. Diversifying education abroad is a common objective and can mean different things for different people. In defining this concept, it is important to emphasize that the benefits to students through participation in education abroad, which is a means for developing academically, professionally, and personally while becoming better prepared to take on the challenges of the twenty-first century, must be equitably accessible to diverse and underrepresented students. It then becomes apparent that the goal is the developmental opportunities provided by education abroad and not the activity of diversifying education abroad itself. This desired outcome often resonates with various campus stakeholders, who generally agree on the need to promote student success and educational equity.

Throughout this process, it is necessary to recognize that many units on campus have their own goals and finite resources, which may act as barriers to collaboration. Developing a tailored message for departments of the ways education abroad benefits their students' success may reach individuals who often have little room in their schedule for additional commitments and may not initially buy into the notion that education abroad inherently supports student success. It might help, for instance, to share with history faculty some of the specific skills or experiences their majors and minors have gained while abroad, which might include work in an archive, an opportunity to collect oral stories, or research that will contribute to a senior thesis. The potentially vague notion of spending time abroad suddenly takes on a more concrete purpose, which aligns with departmental goals. In addition, similar messages should be crafted for others, including students, staff, senior-level administrators, and parents.

Despite their bureaucratic realities, it is important to keep in mind that higher education institutions are also hubs for innovation and creativity. Change is possible and arguably much easier at the institutional level than at the national level. Campuses can be nimbler and implement new effective practices or pivot from noneffective practices to meet a strategic goal.

Developing a Comprehensive Institutional Plan

Developing a comprehensive institutional strategy on diversity and inclusion in education abroad is much like developing any strategic plan. A number of guides, rooted in management practices, can aid institution leaders in thinking through the various steps required during planning. Diversity office staff can often provide advice along the way and may recommend preferred methods based on institutional practices and resources.

Any effective strategy builds on existing practices and should include a holistic evaluation of the institution's current diversity and inclusion practices. Tools such as Diversity Abroad's Access, Inclusion, Diversity, and Equity (AIDE) Roadmap (2015) can assist an institution in comprehensively evaluating and benchmarking their practices in the following areas: institutional profile and data collection; current diversity and inclusion strategy; campus collaboration; professional development and staffing; inclusive outreach, marketing, and recruitment; inclusive student advising; financial aid; programming offerings; health and safety; and inclusive in-country and reentry programming. In addition to the AIDE Roadmap, one might consider using the checklist of questions created by Sweeney (2013), based on the AAC&U's model of inclusive excellence. Most important, it is necessary to follow a systematic method for analyzing an institution's strengths, weaknesses, and areas for future growth.

Although going through the steps of analysis may seem labor intensive, and it may be tempting to jump immediately into action, there are real risks in doing so. For example, at one midsize, private institution that implemented the AIDE Roadmap, education abroad staff members assumed that the primary reason their students of color did not study abroad was for financial reasons, and as a result they devoted all resources to scholarship funding. To their chagrin, the scholarship did not yield a significant increase in participation of diverse students. Instead, an evaluation found that their outreach efforts and advising practices were not inclusive because they were not structured to address some of the unique concerns of diverse students. It was also noted that the office's program portfolio offered a homogenous set of programs with respect to destination and course offerings, which did not necessarily appeal to a broader range of students than typically engaged in education abroad. Armed with these data, the education abroad office developed a multifaceted and much more effective strategy focusing on outreach, advising, program offerings, and funding.

Although a road map for establishing practices and policies is necessary, an effective plan should not stifle the innovation and creativity institutions may use to pursue their goal. Instead, an ideal strategy consists of initiatives and practices that are adaptable and tailored to meet the needs of a campus community. As an institution's administrators execute the initiatives that are informed by strategy, they should also anticipate ongoing assessment and adjustment to ensure that effective practices are in place and then change course as needed.

Strategies at the National Level

As previously mentioned, because of the unique culture of each institution, a local or institutional strategy is needed to focus on the initiatives and activities that will be effective for diversifying education abroad at an institution. At the same time, broader strategies at the state and national level also play a critical role in helping to build greater public support, understanding, and funding for education abroad, particularly for underrepresented students. This is especially critical when the political or economic environment may create a backlash against efforts designed to help these students. With more than 4,700 colleges and universities in the United States, it would be nearly impossible for the federal government or any other national entity to create an approach that would directly align with the practices at each of these institutions with respect to diversifying education abroad (National Center for Education Statistics, 2016). Instead, all initiatives must be broad and adaptable enough to be implemented in varying ways on individual campuses.

The United States is unique in that there is no central ministry of planning as in most other countries. The accreditation of institutions of higher education takes place through national and regional institutional accrediting agencies that are recognized by the U.S. Department of Education. Each of these associations operates independently and has its own policies and procedures. The U.S. government does have some mechanisms elsewhere that allow influencing higher education through a mix of laws and funding. One promising government-initiated project has been capacity-building grants for study abroad (U.S Department of State, 2015). Sponsored by the Department of State and administered by a third party agency, the program has distributed grants of up to $50,000 to colleges or universities to implement strategies to diversify education abroad on their campuses. For example, a project by Lincoln University, a historically Black university in Pennsylvania, has used the funding to support international research for underrepresented minority students in science, technology, engineering, and mathematics majors. Northeast Wisconsin Technical College, another grant recipient, likewise has collaborated with institutions in Belize and China to increase the participation of male Latino, African American, and Native American students in education abroad. Although the results of the strategies funded are not yet known, this approach is encouraging.

Outside governmental projects, multiple entities have played a role in communicating a vision and support of diversity and inclusion in education abroad, much of which has come down to funding, training, and research. Funding organizations such as the Gates Foundation or Lumina Foundation, for example, have demonstrated a strong interest in equity in education, including education abroad. Recipients of the Gates Millennium Scholarship (Gates Millennium Scholars, 2017) can use their funds to study abroad, whereas the Lumina Foundation (2008) has funded projects that pertain to expanding access to education abroad. However, these examples are the exception and not the rule. There is a need for more nongovernmental organizations to invest in worthwhile projects that support diversity and inclusion in education abroad. Given the academic, professional, and personal benefits provided through education abroad, supporting such projects is in line with broader support for educational attainment and equity.

National organizations and agencies are needed to help drive diversity efforts, in part, because of their reach, high profile, and reputation. Leading such efforts demonstrates the need and urgency of such issues and eventually encourages others to join efforts to diversify education abroad. It also ensures that higher education professionals and institutions are not working in isolation and instead are developing a more effective and sustainable approach to ensure that all students have the opportunity to participate in this important educational activity.

Conclusion

The challenges of diversifying education abroad are not always easy, yet they are surmountable. To succeed, we must learn from past initiatives and campaigns, including those that were only partially successful. The field of education abroad must move beyond piecemeal initiatives solely focused on composite diversity and fully embrace the goals of inclusive excellence in education abroad. As we have explored in this chapter, to be truly successful, we must rely on strategic efforts at three levels: individual, institutional, and national. At a grassroots level, faculty and staff can do much to effect positive change toward diversifying education abroad through relationship building and using resources at hand, however limited. At the next level, institutions have a responsibility to advocate for diversifying education abroad and to work with on- and off-campus stakeholders to develop and implement comprehensive strategies. Finally, at the national level, strategies must be developed through the collaboration of multiple entities including professional, member-driven organizations in and external to education abroad, and governmental agencies like the U.S. Department of State and Department of Education. In the United States, we have done more at the individual and institutional levels; for real progress to be made, it is necessary for a broader strategy to be put in place. Finally, it is worth noting that the commitment and dedication of individuals is at the heart of any national, institutional, or individual efforts to diversify education abroad. It is this commitment and belief that all students should have equitable access to education abroad that will be the primary factor in ensuring future success in diversifying education abroad.

References

Clayton-Pedersen, A. R., O'Neil, N., & Musil, C. M. (2007). *Making excellence inclusive: A framework for embedding diversity and inclusion into colleges and universities' academic excellence mission.* Retrieved from www.aacu.org/sites/default/files/files/mei/MEI.pdf

Cole, J. C. (1990). Opening address at the 43rd International Conference on Educational Exchange, Charleston, SC.

Council on International Educational Exchange. (1991). *Black students and overseas programs: Broadening the base of participation.* New York, NY: Author.

Diversity Abroad. (2006). *About the diversity network.* Retrieved from www.diversitynetwork.org/page/AboutUs

Diversity Abroad. (2010). *International education diversity & inclusion consulting: AID evaluation.* Retrieved from www.diversitynetwork.org/page/consulting

Diversity Abroad. (2015). *Access, inclusion, diversity, and equity (AIDE) roadmap.* Retrieved from www.diversitynetwork.org/page/aidroadmap

Gates Millennium Scholars. (2017). *Frequently asked questions.* Retrieved from www.gmsp.org/faqs

Institute for International Education. (2014). *IIE generation study abroad.* Retrieved from www.iie.org/Programs/Generation-Study-Abroad/About

Institute for International Education. (2015). *Fast facts: Open doors data.* Retrieved from www.iie.org/en/Research-and- Publications/Open-Doors/Data/Fast-Facts#.VyO6pj8kGfk

International Academic Opportunity Act of 2000, H.R. 4528, 106th Cong. (2000).

Kuh, G. D. (2008). *High-impact educational practices: What they are, who has access to them, and why they matter*. Washington, DC: Association for American Colleges & Universities.

Lumina Foundation. (2008). *Institute of international education*. Retrieved from www.luminafoundation.org/grants-database/5545

National Center for Education Statistics. (2016). *Fast facts: Educational institutions*. Retrieved from http://nces.ed.gov/fastfacts/display.asp?id=84

Senator Paul Simon Study Abroad Foundation Act, H.R.1469, 110th Cong. (2007).

Sweeney, K. (2013). Inclusive excellence and underrepresentation of students of color in study abroad. Retrieved from ERIC database. (EJ1062148)

University of Denver. (2016). *Inclusive excellence at DU*. Retrieved from www.du.edu/cme/resources/inclusive-excellence.html

U.S. Department of State. (2015). *USA study abroad: Capacity building grants for U.S. higher education institutions*. Retrieved from studyabroad.state.gov/us-government-resources/programs/institutions/capacity-building-grants-us-higher-education

12

EXPANDING THE REACH OF EDUCATION ABROAD

Recommendations for Research, Policy, and Practice

Heather Barclay Hamir and Nick Gozik

As previous chapters in this volume assert, education abroad holds promise as a supporting strategy for addressing equity issues in and beyond higher education, if only we can provide access for a broader range of students. Research has demonstrated the impact of education abroad on student development and academic success, including improvement in student retention, integrative learning, global awareness, intercultural competency, independence, and adaptability (Kuh, 2008; Landis, Bennett, & Bennett, 2004; Savicki, Downing-Burnette, Heller, Binder, & Suntinger, 2004; Sutton & Rubin, 2010; Vande Berg, Paige, & Lou, 2012). These gains directly correspond to career readiness competencies identified by the National Association of Colleges and Employers (2017), which require the ability to "build collaborative relationships with colleagues and customers representing diverse cultures, races, ages, genders, religions, lifestyles, and viewpoints" (para. 6). By extension, increasing opportunities enhances the quality of educational outcomes for individual students while additionally benefiting our society and economy.

Providing access to education abroad, moreover, fits into a broader commitment in higher education to ensure that all students have the ability to take advantage of the opportunities available to them and not just those with a certain level of cultural capital and financial resources entering a college or university. For some students, it can be a major hurdle to gain admission to a college; additional activities may seem out of reach, especially those that require extra funding, do not seem readily accepting, or require time that could be used to earn money for tuition and expenses. However, in the United States, it is understood that learning is intended to go beyond the classroom. Even on campuses where the majority of students commute, programming to help engage students during the day or evening is typical. By failing to provide access to the full range of programs and activities on campus for all students, including education abroad, it can be argued that educators are not fulfilling their responsibility to serve the entire student population. We might even be faulted for replicating inequality through differential preparation of students on the same campus who receive the same diploma.

If we can agree on the necessity for broader inclusion in education abroad, we must also acknowledge that our ability to expand participation is limited by a host of factors that must be addressed for substantive progress to occur. Previous chapters make clear the complexity of this issue. Although some common factors promote or inhibit participation in education abroad across a range of underrepresented groups, other considerations affect particular groups more strongly. It is important to acknowledge the similarities and the differences. Where similarities exist, we can more easily adopt new strategies for the benefit of a larger proportion of students, keeping in mind that success with particular groups will be enhanced through more targeted approaches. At the same time, our understanding of effective strategies to promote inclusion in education abroad will evolve as new research and practices emerge.

We conclude this volume by synthesizing the common themes and key differences among the experiences of underrepresented groups discussed in prior chapters, identifying research and policy topics for scholars and practitioners to address, and suggesting areas for further consideration to improve policy and practice relative to inclusion in education abroad.

Common Themes and Key Differences

Discussions of inclusion in education abroad often begin with the identification of barriers to participation as a first step in developing effective practice. As we continue to examine these barriers, commonalities emerge that will perpetuate the existing imbalance in participation across multiple underrepresented groups if left unaddressed. Still other factors are more likely to affect particular groups, such as the influence of family and friends on the decision-making process noted in the chapters on students of color (Chapter 3) and males (Chapter 5) or the type of financial aid students receive (Salisbury, Paulsen, & Pascarella, 2011). At times, the task seems insurmountable, yet we also see successes. For example, as noted in Chapter 9, engineering students are now participating in education abroad proportionate to their enrollment in higher education, a significant accomplishment for majors who have limited curricular flexibility to accommodate education abroad participation. However, with other groups described here, success is elusive.

The contributors to this volume identify barriers, some common to multiple groups of students and others more narrowly applicable, while also suggesting strategies to mitigate these barriers. The broad themes identified here fall into three categories relative to students' experiences of education abroad: articulating value, creating a welcoming environment, and ensuring accessibility.

Articulating Value

The decision to participate in education abroad requires substantial planning and commitment. For students to invest their time, effort, and financial resources, they must first be convinced of the value of participation. Many must also be able to articulate that value in compelling ways to others who may or may not be predisposed to support their participation, as indicated in earlier chapters on first-generation college students (FGCSs), males, and students of color. This is a particularly important issue among underrepresented groups, which may not find the often cited benefits of education abroad sufficiently compelling, such as language improvement, greater cultural awareness, or the life-changing impact of participation. For Mexican American FGCSs, for example, college life already includes navigating another culture in pursuit of educationally enriching opportunities; the traditional value narrative around education abroad may seem less relevant in terms of their long-term goals.

Reframing how we present the value of education abroad is critical for expanding participation. In particular, males, FGCSs, and science and engineering majors tend to weigh the opportunity costs of participation against the perceived value. Such costs include the perception of delayed graduation and the financial impact it creates, forgoing career-enhancing opportunities such as internships, or needing to take standardized tests for graduate admissions. Education abroad must therefore demonstrate relevance in light of a broader range of educational and professional goals, including the following: timely graduation; concrete enhancements to the degree, such as the ability to study with a world-renowned faculty member or conduct unique research abroad; and the positive career impact of participation. Unfortunately, the most common ways past participants describe their time abroad—fun, amazing, or life changing—combined with images of vacation-like experiences are at odds with the necessary messages about value for these groups and, one might add, for all students. Stereotypical and superficial descriptors of education abroad undermine the academic integrity of the endeavor and signal that such experiences are reserved for the privileged.

Beyond what is offered abroad, who endorses education abroad also contributes to perceptions of value. As James M. Lucas indicates in Chapter 5, males seek messages endorsing participation from sources they trust, including faculty and peers, and particularly other males. The chapters on science majors (Chapter 8) and engineers (Chapter 9) serve as a case in point. At an institution with little faculty support for education abroad in the sciences, student interest was also low; at the same time, an institution that designed programs specifically for engineering majors, a process requiring sustained faculty support, had much higher participation. These examples illustrate the significance of aligning articulated messages with actual practice to support participation while also stressing the need for top-down support (Brustein, 2009). Removing barriers to participation in and of itself is an assertion of value and an important one if students are to persist beyond the initial inquiry stage.

Creating a Welcoming Environment

Although perceived worth is the first requirement for education abroad to convey relevance to a broader range of students, students' assessment of the environment will influence whether they pursue an interest in education abroad. This theme highlights the need for equity-based rather than equality-based strategies in overcoming concerns, perceptions, and barriers that disproportionately affect underrepresented groups. If equality means giving everyone the same resources, equity means giving students access to the resources they need to achieve the same outcomes as their peers. Within this framework, it is not enough to adopt the same approach for all students; we must employ strategies that deliberately and visibly welcome students beyond those who have historically participated.

Creating a welcoming environment occurs through inclusive marketing, outreach, and advising practices. Print and electronic images should present a diversity of students. Images should illustrate broader definitions of *value* as described previously; inclusive photos of students jumping in the air will still convey a discrepancy between the articulated value proposition and the apparent reality of the experience. Intentionally emphasizing underrepresented groups through prominently displayed resources, as mentioned in Chapter 6 on students with disabilities, is effective in defining who is expected to participate in education abroad. Similarly, ensuring that websites are compatible with screen readers indicates that the education abroad office is sensitive to the needs of students with visual impairments.

Outreach and advising practices go hand in hand with representing an organizational commitment to inclusion. Offering advising services across campus, as mentioned by Jinous Kasravi (Chapter 3), sends a signal that advisers are ready to meet students where they are, literally and figuratively. By hosting advising sessions in spaces familiar to students, the initial inquiry process becomes a much lower risk endeavor because it lacks the formality of a structured appointment at an office students may never have visited. Previous participants should ideally be used in advising (e.g., as peer advisers) as students tend to see other students as more reliable and credible sources of information (Stroud, 2017). At the same time, centers or units that choose to sponsor these events implicitly vouch for education abroad as a welcoming office and an endorsed activity. Subsequent advising can be a critical component for students' successful pursuit of education abroad, as indicated by the value FGCSs placed on advising relative to other factors as noted in Chapter 4.

Ensuring Accessibility

Conveying the value of education abroad and creating a welcoming environment for participation will succeed in promoting inclusion only if policy and practice ensure accessibility. The three main areas touched on in this volume—financial resources, academics, and physical accessibility—affect individuals and groups to different extents. Finances are a prevalent concern encompassing issues such as the inability to secure resources to fund the full cost of attendance abroad; lack of awareness of financial resources for education abroad, including financial aid and scholarships; and questioning whether potential costs can be justified. Financial aid practices can exacerbate the challenges of pursuing education abroad, although there is potential to mitigate this factor.

Issues of academic compatibility remain central to inclusion or exclusion for many students. Academic issues can create real and perceived structural barriers to participation, including credit transfer policies, course approval processes, and the availability of programs offering relevant and degree-applicable courses. For students who are intent on timely degree progress, the ambiguity of whether courses will be applicable to their degree plan becomes an unjustifiable risk, and campuses are not always able to confirm this information up front. These issues disproportionately affect students in highly structured or credentialed programs, including science, technology, engineering, mathematics, and education.

Individual students often face multiple overlapping barriers that cannot be easily untangled. Rather than simply a matter of academics or finances, a student may be dealing with both, perhaps in addition to other factors.

For instance, accessibility among students with disabilities might intersect with academics and financial resources. Students who are hearing or sight impaired need educational accommodations to succeed academically abroad; providing these services requires an investment, which many institutions have yet to formalize through policy or practice. There is a widespread sense that additional dedicated scholarships and financial resources assist in efforts to improve inclusion, although the reality of securing those resources proves challenging.

One of the impediments to broader inclusion in education abroad arises from our own partial understanding of the complex factors influencing participation. Several chapters that provide insight into inclusion for underrepresented groups likewise identify the need for additional investigation. Following are areas that we suggest need further research and examination to advance efforts toward equitable inclusion in education abroad.

Advancing Knowledge and Practice

Numerous areas for research identified throughout this volume indicate knowledge gaps that may impact the effectiveness of our inclusion practices. As research explores issues of inclusion in more depth, we will in turn be prepared to adopt new strategies and practices that further our ability to serve an increasingly diverse student population. The following sections provide an overview of areas for additional research and suggestions related to policy or practice with the potential for expanding the reach of education abroad.

Areas for Further Research

In Chapter 2, Lily Lopez-McGee, David Comp, and Eduardo Contreras lay out an agenda to support future work on inclusion in education abroad that focuses on four main areas: data, student experiences abroad, learning outcomes, and the intersection of student identities and learning outcomes. They recommend the expansion of data collection efforts to encompass more accurate and comprehensive data on education abroad participation at the institutional and national levels. They also recommend collection of more nuanced participation data to enhance our understanding of participation patterns, including additional student identity categories, destinations, and programs. Groups discussed in this book, such as FGCSs, are not tracked at a national level and are challenging to identify at the campus level.

Similarly, inclusion of gender as an identity category instead of sex in data collection would expand our understanding of participation beyond the binary approach currently used, as discussed by Lucas in Chapter 5.

In Chapter 3 Kasravi's research highlights the value of disaggregating categories among students of color as different groups can have highly diverse experiences, on campus and abroad. As a corollary to this line of inquiry, in Chapter 6 Holben and Malhotra discuss the need for additional data on students with disabilities as well as research on the efficacy of specifying student accommodations as part of contracts and agreements in terms of improved student mobility. Similar areas for examination include targeted, collaborative programming for other underrepresented groups and institution-specific scholarship arrangements to promote participation.

Subsequent recommendations in Chapter 2 by Lopez-McGee and colleagues center on deepening our understanding of student experiences abroad and their outcomes based on student identity. While there are still areas for further exploration in terms of the student decision-making process and intent to study abroad, particularly with respect to the intersection of student identities, less has been studied relative to the differences in student experiences while abroad. Moreover, more research needs to be conducted on the intersection of learning outcomes and student identity based on program type as suggested by Engle and Engle (2003). Although this volume focuses specifically on inclusion in the context of access to educational opportunities, the impact of these efforts is diminished if unsupported by research and practice that promote inclusion throughout the education abroad continuum of predeparture, on-site, and postprogram experiences.

Future Considerations for Policy and Practice

To fulfill the promise of education abroad participation for a broader population of students, we must approach issues of inclusion in new ways. The need for an inclusive orientation to marketing, advising, program design, and institutional policy have been described, yet other areas also require careful consideration. Gordon's Chapter 11 outlines advocacy strategies at the individual, institutional, and national levels. Here, we add areas for additional consideration if we are truly to move forward in our agenda of inclusion.

Campuses

The greatest impact on participation occurs through campus-level action, which may be enhanced by broader national-level activities. At the institutional level, tenure and promotion policies also influence inclusion in education abroad. Key strategies for fostering inclusion, such as participation in curriculum integration projects, faculty-led programs, and the evaluation of education abroad offerings, may fall outside the typical advancement expectations for research, teaching, and service. Teaching abroad is often an additional load on top of regular teaching responsibilities and is frequently not counted toward tenure or service. Contributions to projects that address academic barriers to education abroad may be incorporated into the category of service, assuming a committee structure is established, although this is not always a given. If institutional leaders want faculty to help promote inclusion at home and abroad, they will need to acknowledge faculty efforts in this area.

As Gordon points out, the scalability of inclusion efforts is a critical consideration in shifting participation patterns in the long term and is a commitment that requires substantial cross-divisional collaboration among education abroad offices, academic units, and offices dedicated to diversity and inclusion. Curriculum integration, which requires time and collaboration with academic departments to implement effectively, is relatively inexpensive and easily scalable. By shifting the emphasis of education abroad from location or program length and instead focusing on options that serve students well from the perspective of their major, curriculum integration can accommodate differing institutional priorities and needs. Such efforts create a shared investment between academic departments and the education abroad office, leading to greater confidence in programmatic recommendations and broader support. Similarly, the American Council on Education's (2017) multiyear At Home in the World initiative makes the case for a common agenda between diversity and multicultural offices and internationalization, in part as a means to further inclusive excellence.

Collaborative approaches require like-minded individuals, sustained effort, and time. Opportunities for more rapid change exist in the practices typical of education abroad. Every step in the process to pursue participation creates another point at which students have to navigate a system and make a decision to continue. Efforts to educate students and balance workload for staff, such as prerequirements before meeting with an adviser, can suggest an arduous process with many steps and potentially limited support. The idea that students' ability to navigate complex processes on campus reflects their ability to succeed abroad is questionable and fails to consider alternative reasons a more diverse range of students does not persist.

Eligibility criteria and the application process also require careful consideration. Criteria for participation, including a minimum grade point average (GPA), are intended as a proxy for the likelihood of student success abroad, which can mean their academic success, their likelihood of completing the program, or their engagement as a learner. However, studies demonstrate that students with low GPAs perform satisfactorily abroad (Schaeffer & Neumann, 2011; Trooboff, Cressey, & Monty, 2004), and in fact, participation for students with lower GPAs is correlated with greater than average gains in student retention (Barclay Hamir, 2011; O'Rear, Sutton, & Rubin, 2011; Willett, Pellegrin, & Cooper, 2013).

Complex application processes mirroring the university admissions process create unintended barriers. As an example, faculty references are a common requirement to shed light on a student's suitability for participation. However, this practice assumes that students understand they should cultivate relationships with faculty and that they have the opportunity to do so. According to the National Survey of Student Engagement (2016a, 2016b), 20.2% of first-year students and 23.2% of seniors reported having meaningful faculty-student interactions. Given these statistics, the odds that a significant proportion of students can secure a meaningful reference from faculty are low. On a practical level, moreover, staff in many education abroad offices find that recommendations are not informative; faculty are normally reticent to write down anything negative, and so the process of submitting recommendations becomes more of a bureaucratic task rather than one that aids in student selection.

Standard practices to improve office efficiency can also create hurdles, including required steps before students can access advising support or extensive scholarship requirements to help winnow applicant pools. Other areas for careful consideration include the timing and amount of fees, essay topics and evaluation criteria, and assumptions about what behaviors or characteristics suggest that a student is ideal or undesirable vis-à-vis participation in general. In Chapter 5 Lucas demonstrates, for instance, that males' behavior during the application process can differ from that of females; assumptions about what constitutes a good applicant may be unintentionally reinforcing seemingly immutable participation patterns. Certainly not every student is suited to every opportunity, but many more students are suited to one or more opportunities than current enrollment suggests. Evaluating inquiries and started applications versus participant demographics can establish a baseline for the evaluation of existing practices (Finley & McNair, 2013).

Most of the efforts described here do not require new funding and instead are about being intentional and efficient with the resources already allocated. That said, funding is a significant concern and must be considered by institutional leaders in developing a strategy to promote inclusion. As noted earlier, financial resources can be applied to scholarships and grants to help support students going abroad. Sometimes even a relatively small grant to cover some or all of the airfare will make enough of a difference to allow a high-need student to study abroad, especially depending on how financial aid is calculated and distributed. In development of programming, thinking about if and how financial aid can be applied is likewise necessary. A short-term program over spring break, for instance, can permit students to secure additional funding through a spring semester financial aid package, which may not be available over the summer. Institutions can also provide small grants to faculty and others for the development of programming for diverse groups of students. These are just a few ideas to illustrate how even a small stream of funding can make a significant difference on a college campus.

Federal Policy

The impact of policy and processes on inclusion in education abroad occurs at the federal level as well, largely because of the sheer volume of federal aid funds disbursed through various programs. The federal government disbursed $125.7 billion in student aid in 2016 to more than 13 million postsecondary students at all levels (Federal Student Aid, 2016a). The National Center for Education Statistics (2014) has estimated that nearly 73% of full-time, full-year undergraduates received some federal aid in 2011–2012, the last year of data reporting. With cost as a major factor in students' ability to participate in education abroad, the impact of federal aid policy cannot be understated.

Federal financial aid applies to the cost of attendance for education abroad, and when the cost of education abroad is higher than the cost of attendance on the home campus, aid eligibility can increase to federal aid award limits. Aid is disbursed no earlier than 10 days before the first day of classes on U.S. home campuses (Federal Student Aid, 2016b). When students enroll in education abroad programs that start on or after home institution semester dates, disbursements occur on a familiar time line. However, when students attend programs that start earlier than those at the home institution, aid disbursement may occur as much as two months after the program begins. Although program payments can generally be deferred until institutional aid is disbursed, this system often leaves aid-dependent students without funds for living expenses that are excluded from the program fee, which may include meals, transportation, and books. Most aid-dependent students must secure some level of upfront funding to cover costs such as application fees and deposits, passport or visa expenses, and airfare.

Even when the full cost of attendance is met through aid funds, the timing of disbursement may make participation impossible. Initiatives that address up-front costs, such as the scholarships described in Chapter 4 or the Bridging Loan Program at the University of Minnesota (University of Minnesota Learning Abroad Center, 2015), are a positive step, but broader adoption will be required to benefit a larger proportion of students. Ideally, federal aid policy would allow disbursement dates to align with the dates of attendance abroad for officially approved education abroad opportunities, which would also affect state and institutional awards as they are typically disbursed in tandem. This combination would significantly improve procedural issues in aid disbursement that impede student participation.

Another area of improvement at the federal level relates to the ability of military veterans or their dependents to use post–September 11, 2001, benefits for education abroad. More than 900,000 veterans used educational benefits in 2012 (West, 2016). The U.S. Department of Veterans Affairs (VA) provides clarification on how these benefits apply to education abroad expenses, yet policies are open to varied interpretation as each campus works with campus-based certifying officers and VA State Approving Agencies to determine which overseas programs are eligible for consideration. Whereas federal aid can be applied to the cost of attendance for any program approved by the enrolling U.S. institution, VA benefits specify the application of benefits relative to expenses, making benefit application dependent on institution-level policies, which vary widely. For example, VA benefits may be applied to participation in a program at one institution, but the same program is ineligible at another. The discrepancy can be rectified and streamlined by adopting criteria parallel to federal financial aid applicability for education abroad.

Additional Considerations

Beyond institutions and government agencies, a number of other actors have a bearing on the educational opportunities available to students. Accrediting and licensing agencies shape the structure and delivery of education for students in numerous disciplines, in part through the standards they set. Accreditation standards for business schools and engineering programs, which include criteria related to the global context of professional practice, serve as models that support participation (Accreditation Board for Engineering and Technology, 2016; Association to Advance Collegiate Schools of Business, 2016). In contrast, state-specific teacher licensure requirements can create unintended difficulties related to education abroad participation.

Although more limited in scope, institutions and foundations that offer full cost of attendance awards for undergraduates can also play a role in promoting inclusion in education abroad. Since its inception, the Gates Millennium Scholars (n.d.) program has provided funds to meet the full cost of attendance during the academic year, even when educational costs may increase because of overseas study. This guarantee of support eliminates the financial uncertainty associated with considering education abroad, essentially leveling the playing field for highly diverse, high-need scholars. Numerous institutions and foundations offer awards that cover most or all of the cost of attendance for students. Allowing funds to be adjusted accordingly for education abroad entails a relatively low financial investment, although one with a great impact on individual students' ability to go abroad.

Investing in the Future

Research and effective practice shed light on many of the hidden assumptions that perpetuate underrepresentation in education abroad, yet one overarching issue will determine our long-term success: investment, particularly at the institutional level. Are institutions invested in education abroad as a critical educational opportunity for students? The answer is somewhat mixed. There is philosophical support for education abroad, yet as we have seen, many impediments persist that we have the power to influence. The existence of these barriers serves as a litmus test for investment: Where barriers are successfully addressed, investment has typically been high; where they persist, they might suggest an underlying belief that education abroad is not significant enough to merit addressing the issue. As long as education abroad remains on the periphery of the institutional agenda, inclusion will be challenging to achieve. To expand the reach of education abroad, we must also emphasize the relevance of education abroad to the success of undergraduates while they are enrolled and beyond completion of their degrees, regardless of the type of institution.

To fulfill the promise of education abroad requires us to remain attentive to learning outcomes and educational quality. Kuh (2016) qualified earlier work on education abroad as a high-impact practice by emphasizing the need to ensure that it is a high-quality educational opportunity. Student narratives that read like vacation reminisces or *war stories*, to use Lucas's term from Chapter 5, inherently undermine these efforts. The purpose of inclusion is not limited to expanding representation; it is also the enhancement of undergraduate learning for a broader range of students. More work must be done to reorient students' expectations and reflections on their experiences abroad alongside ongoing efforts to assess and enhance the learning opportunities available to students while abroad.

Going Beyond the Numbers

The impetus to enhance learning in the international context corresponds to yet another area for further attention: an inclusive agenda with respect to the experience abroad. Just as we support inclusion on campuses, we should also promote inclusion beyond student acceptance into programs abroad, applying this lens to inform predeparture preparation, program design, and training for faculty and staff. All students bring strengths and unique perspectives with them abroad, and program directors must consider this to serve a broader range of students well. Simply admitting more students of color, for example, may not go far enough in helping these students integrate into the program and the host country if additional support and services are not provided.

Such acceptance is a particularly important consideration in immersion programs where students integrate into an entirely new host and academic culture, typically without a home institution representative on-site to translate and mediate challenges. Issues of privilege must also be anticipated as students from different socioeconomic, racial, and ethnic backgrounds may have very different experiences abroad in the local context and in programs enrolling cohorts of U.S. students. As administrators of universities have learned, it is not sufficient simply to admit increasingly diverse cohorts, it is also essential to support and embrace the unique strengths they contribute to the educational enterprise, as the AAC&U construct of inclusive excellence so aptly states (Milem, Chang, & Antonio, 2005).

Although this book focuses on underrepresented students in education abroad, the inclusive excellence framework also creates a better environment for a range of students who may need significant advising and support, regardless of their proportional representation among education abroad participants. Lesbian, gay, bisexual, transgender, questioning, and other students, for instance, may have fears or concerns about whether they will be accepted in other countries, as well as in their international program. Likewise, students from certain religious backgrounds may hesitate to go abroad if they are concerned for their own safety or acceptance. Questions might arise over what someone can say, do, or wear overseas.

The bottom line is that inclusion can and should be a benefit for all. Here, we might consider the AAC&U's (n.d.) statement on making excellence inclusive, which rests on the assertion that "a high-quality, practical liberal education should be the standard of excellence for all students" (para. 3). By valuing diversity and taking steps not only to accept but also to draw on students' unique perspectives throughout the educational experience, programs will be more pedagogically sound and culturally grounded. At the same time, word will ideally get out that education abroad is accessible and attainable for any student regardless of his or her background or major.

Concluding Thoughts

This volume is the first of its kind to bring together leading experts to explore ways education abroad participation can be expanded to include more students. Although scholars and practitioners have made presentations on this topic or published individual chapters, articles, and position papers, until now no book has been assembled on the barriers to and opportunities for including a variety of historically underrepresented groups in education abroad. However, this is not intended to be a comprehensive work. Instead, it is an opening and a call for more research, practice, and policy analysis in the United States and overseas.

If we have learned anything through this project, it is that broader inclusion in education abroad is possible and beneficial on a number of levels. Strategic and sustained efforts can yield better participation outcomes as several of the chapters illustrate, most notably in the case of engineering majors. To expand on these successes, we must build alliances, foster greater investment across a range of constituent groups, and test new strategies based on research and effective practice. It takes many actors working in sync to change long-standing patterns, yet change is possible, given time and a shared commitment to inclusion.

References

Accreditation Board for Engineering and Technology. (2016). *Criterion for accrediting engineering technology programs, 2017–2018.* Retrieved from www.abet .org/accreditation/accreditation-criteria/criteria-for-accrediting-engineering-technology-programs-2017-2018/

American Council on Education. (2017). *At home in the world toolkit: What is at home in the world?* Retrieved from www.acenet.edu/news-room/Pages/AHITW-Toolkit-Main.aspx

Association to Advance Collegiate Schools of Business. (2016). *Eligibility procedures and accreditation standards for business accreditation.* Retrieved from www.aacsb .edu/-/media/aacsb/docs/accreditation/standards/businessstds_2013_ update-3oct_final.ashx

Association of American Colleges & Universities. (n.d.) *Making excellence inclusive.* Retrieved from aacu.org/making-excellence-inclusive

Barclay Hamir, H. (2011). *Go abroad and graduate on-time: Study abroad participation, degree completion, and time-to-degree* (Doctoral dissertation). Available from ProQuest Dissertations and Theses database. (UMI No. 3450065)

Brustein, W. (2009). It takes an entire institution: A blueprint for the global university. In R. Lewin (Ed.), *The handbook of practice and research in study abroad: Higher education and the quest for global citizenship* (pp. 249–265). New York, NY: Routledge.

Engle, L., & Engle, J. (2003). Study abroad levels: Toward a classification of program types. *Frontiers, 9,* 1–20.

Federal Student Aid. (2016a). *Federal student aid, annual report FY 2016.* Retrieved from studentaid.ed.gov/sa/sites/default/files/FY_2016_Annual_Report_508.pdf

Federal Student Aid. (2016b). *Federal student aid handbook with active index, 2016–2017.* Retrieved from ifap.ed.gov/fsahandbook/attachments/1617FSAHbkActiv eIndexMaster.pdf

Finley, A., & McNair, T. (2013). *Assessing underserved students' engagement in high-impact practices.* Washington, DC: Association of American Colleges & Universities.

Gates Millennium Scholars. (n.d.). *Gates millennium scholars: 2011–2012 GMS renewal packet.* Retrieved   from gmsmichigan.files.wordpress.com/2011/08/gates-renewal-packet.pdf

Kuh, G. D. (2008). *High-impact educational practices: What they are, who has access to them, and why they matter.* Washington, DC: Association of American Colleges & Universities.

Kuh, G. D. (2016, July). *Ensuring that education abroad is a high quality high-impact practice.* Paper presented at the meeting of the Institute for Study Abroad, Butler University, Indianapolis, IN.

Landis, D., Bennett, J. M., & Bennett, M. J. (Eds.). (2004). *Handbook of intercultural training* (3rd ed.). Thousand Oaks, CA: Sage.

Milem, J. F., Chang, M. J., & Antonio, A. L. (2005). *Making diversity work on campus: A research-based perspective.* Washington, DC: Association of American Colleges & Universities.

National Association of Colleges and Employers. (2017). *Career readiness defined.* Retrieved from www.naceweb.org/knowledge/career-readiness-competencies.aspx

National Center for Education Statistics. (2014). *Percentage of full-time and part-time undergraduates receiving federal aid, by aid program and control and level of institution: 2007–08 and 2011–12* [Table 331.90]. Retrieved from nces.ed.gov/programs/digest/d14/tables/dt14_331.90.asp?current=yes

National Survey of Student Engagement. (2016a). *NSSE 2016 U.S. engagement indicator: Descriptive statistics by Carnegie classification, first-year students.* Retrieved from nsse.indiana.edu/2016_institutional_report/pdf/EngagementIndicators/EI%20-%20FY%20by%20Carn.pdf

National Survey of Student Engagement. (2016b). *NSSE 2016 U.S. engagement indicator: Descriptive statistics by Carnegie classification, seniors.* Retrieved from nsse.indiana.edu/2016_institutional_report/pdf/EngagementIndicators/EI%20-%20SR%20by%20Carn.pdf

O'Rear, I., Sutton, R. C., & Rubin, D. L. (2011). *The effect of study abroad on college completion in a state university system.* Retrieved from glossari.uga.edu/wp-content/uploads/downloads/2012/01/GLOSSARI-Grad-Rate-Logistic-Regressions-040111.pdf

Salisbury, M. H., Paulsen, M. B., & Pascarella, E. T. (2011). Why do all the study abroad students look alike? Applying an integrated student choice model to explore differences in the factors that influence White and minority students' intent to study abroad. *Research in Higher Education, 52*, 123–150. doi:10.1007/s11162-010-9191-2

Savicki, V., Downing-Burnette, R., Heller, L, Binder, F., & Suntinger, W. (2004). Contrasts, changes, and correlates in actual and potential intercultural adjustment. *International Journal of Intercultural Relations, 28*, 311–329. doi:10.1016/j.ijintrel.2004.06.001

Schaeffer, G., & Neumann, E. (2011). *Brief of program participants with a pre-departure grade point average below 2.5 & their academic performance abroad.* Goleta, CA: University of California Education Abroad Program.

Stroud, A. (2017, February). *Students at the margins: Making study abroad a possibility.* Paper presented at the Boston Intercultural Skills Conference of Boston College, Chestnut Hill, MA.

Sutton, R. C., & Rubin, D. L. (2010, May). *Documenting the academic impact of study abroad: Final report of the GLOSSARI project.* Paper presented at the annual conference of NAFSA: Association of International Educators, Kansas City, MO.

Trooboff, S., Cressey, W., & Monty, S. (2004). Does study abroad grading motivate students? *Frontiers, 10*, 201–217.

University of Minnesota Learning Abroad Center. (2015). *Bridging loan program.* Retrieved from umabroad.umn.edu/students/finances/bridgingloan

West, C. (2016). Helping military veterans study abroad. *International Educator*, 44–47.

Willett, T., Pellegrin, N., & Cooper, D. (2013). *Study abroad impact technical report.* Sacramento, CA: Research & Planning Group for California Community Colleges.

Vande Berg, M., Paige, R. M., & Lou, K. H. (Eds.). (2012). *Student learning abroad: What our students are learning, what they're not, and what we can do about it.* Sterling, VA: Stylus.

EDITORS AND CONTRIBUTORS

Editors

Heather Barclay Hamir is president and CEO of the Institute for Study Abroad, Butler University (IFSA-Butler). She has worked in international education since 1997 at public and private universities, initially as an adviser and later at the director and executive director levels. Throughout her career, Barclay Hamir has focused on increasing access for underrepresented populations in study abroad, and has been an active contributor in national discussions on this topic. During her tenure at the University of Texas at Austin (UT Austin), new initiatives undertaken by Study Abroad resulted in greater and more representative participation abroad, for which the university received both NAFSA's Senator Paul Simon Spotlight Award and Diversity Abroad's Excellence in Diversifying International Education Institutional Award in 2014. Currently, she serves on Diversity Abroad's advisory committee and served two terms on the forum council of The Forum on Education Abroad. Barclay Hamir earned her doctorate in higher education leadership from the University of Nebraska—Lincoln, two master's degrees from Oregon State University, and her bachelor's degree from Pomona College.

Nick Gozik is director of the Office of International Programs and McGillycuddy-Logue Center for Undergraduate Global Studies at Boston College. Previously, Gozik held positions in education abroad at the University of Richmond, New York University, and Duke University. He has also served as a visiting assistant professor at New York University as well as a lecturer at Boston College and Lesley University. Gozik has conducted research on identity, race, and education in France, using history-geography education on the French island of Martinique as a case study. He has contributed to research at the Social Science Research Council on internationalization, interdisciplinarity, and boundary-crossing in U.S. higher education. Gozik has been active in a number of professional organizations and is currently serving as chair of the forum council for The Forum on Education Abroad.

Gozik holds an MA in French language and civilization and a PhD in international education from New York University.

Contributors

Teri Albrecht is director of international student and scholar services at the University of Texas at Austin. Albrecht also holds a lecturer position and teaches first-year students. Prior to joining UT Austin in 1999, Albrecht held positions at St. Edward's University in Austin, Texas, and Louisiana State University. Albrecht completed her PhD in higher education administration at UT Austin where her dissertation research focused on the experiences of undocumented students in institutions of higher education. She received her BBA and MS in educational administration from Texas A&M University. Active in NAFSA, Albrecht has served in various leadership positions and served as editor for *Crisis Management in a Cross Cultural Setting*. Albrecht has presented and published on a wide range of topics affecting international education.

David Comp currently works as the assistant provost for global education at Columbia College Chicago. He previously worked for 17 years at the University of Chicago in various international education roles. He also serves as a study abroad research consultant for the Center for Global Education at California State University at Dominguez Hills. He serves on the editorial advisory board of the *Journal of Studies in International Education* (*JSIE*), as assistant/copy editor for the *Journal of International Students,* and as a peer reviewer for *Frontiers: The Interdisciplinary Journal of Study Abroad.* In addition, he has coauthored several book chapters, journal articles, and reports on international education topics. He is also a board member of the Fund for Education Abroad. He received his PhD in cultural and educational policy studies, comparative and international education from Loyola University Chicago.

Eduardo Contreras Jr. is the director of studies abroad and chair for the Collaborative for International Studies and Global Outreach (CISGO) at the University of Portland. With over 15 years in public and private U.S. postsecondary education, Contreras has experience in education abroad, access, and internationalization at many different levels. While at the Harvard Graduate School of Education (HGSE), his dissertation was on the history of education abroad in the twentieth century, and he served on the Dean's Global Education Task Force and taught a course on internationalization in U.S. higher education. Contreras has a long-term personal and professional commitment to inclusive excellence. Most recently, he has served as the conference committee chair for the annual Diversity Abroad Conference. In addition to an EdM and EdD from Harvard, he has a BA in history and an MA in Asian cultures and languages from UT Austin.

Solomon R. Eisenberg is senior associate dean for academic programs in the College of Engineering, and professor of biomedical engineering and electrical and computer engineering. He earned the SB, SM, and ScD degrees in electrical engineering from MIT and joined Boston University faculty as assistant professor of biomedical engineering in 1983. He was a visiting associate professor in the Harvard-MIT Division of Health Science and Technology in 1997. He was the recipient of an NSF Presidential Young Investigator Award 1987–1993, a 1990 Metcalf Award for Excellence in Teaching from Boston University, and is a fellow of AIMBE. He served as associate dean for undergraduate programs from 1998 to 2013, as dean ad interim of the College of Engineering for the 2005–06 academic year, and was chair of biomedical engineering from 2007 to 2015. Eisenberg has been engaged in developing the College of Engineering's study abroad programs since 1999.

Benjamin Flores joined the faculty of the University of Texas at El Paso in 1990 after receiving his PhD in electrical engineering from Arizona State University. He is a professor of electrical and computer engineering and has held a number of administrative positions including dean of the graduate school, associate dean of graduate studies for the college of engineering, founding director of the division of computing and electrical engineering, and chair of electrical and computer engineering. Flores is an expert in retention strategies for non-traditional undergraduate and graduate students in science, technology, engineering, and mathematics (STEM). He is the director of the UT System Louis Stokes Alliance for Minority Participation. In 2010, Flores was recognized by President Barack Obama with the Presidential Award for Excellence in Science, Mathematics, and Engineering Mentorship for his efforts to increase the enrollment, retention, and graduation of Latinos and Latinas in STEM.

Lynda Gonzales is director of student programs at the Texas Institute for Discovery Education in Science (TIDES) at UT Austin. TIDES was established in 2013 in the College of Natural Science and aims to catalyze, support, and showcase innovative, evidence-based undergraduate science education. Gonzales received her MEd in educational administration in 1995 from UT Austin, and, since then, has been working in positions at the university that support experiential and engaged learning opportunities for undergraduates, including research, study abroad, internships, and most recently entrepreneurship.

Andrew Gordon is a social entrepreneur and CEO and founder of Diversity Abroad. With a passion for student success and international education, Gordon founded Diversity Abroad in 2006 with a simple vision that the next generation of young people from diverse and underrepresented backgrounds have the confidence, experience, and skills necessary for success in the twenty-first-century global marketplace. As the chief national advocate for diversity, equity, and inclusion within international education, Gordon speaks and writes extensively on such topics. He has consulted for colleges and universities, non-profit and for-profit organizations, and government agencies on developing strategies for connecting diverse and underrepresented students to global educational opportunities. A native of San Diego, California, Gordon is fluent in Spanish and Portuguese and proficient in French. He is a graduate of the University of San Francisco and has studied, worked, and traveled in Africa, the Americas, Asia, Europe, and the Middle East.

Ashley Holben is a project specialist with the National Clearinghouse on Disability and Exchange at Mobility International USA, where she also serves as executive specialist to the CEO. She writes and presents on disability inclusion in international exchange and develops initiatives and resources to increase participation and inclusion of students with disabilities in international exchange. As a Rotary Group Study Exchange participant, Holben visited disability organizations and alumni in Malaysia to learn about the country's disability rights issues and movements. Holben graduated from the University of Oregon with a degree in international studies and economics and a focus in international comparative development and Africa, which led her to intern with a non-profit organization in Dakar, Senegal.

Jinous Kasravi earned her BA in French and MA in comparative education from University of California, Los Angeles (UCLA). She earned her PhD in education policy and administration from the University of Minnesota–Twin Cities. Her passion for the field of international education was ignited through her own lived experiences in several countries and education systems. In her current role as the director of program evaluation and university outreach in the Kuwait Cultural Office, Los Angeles, she evaluates institutions in the west coast of the United States to ensure that they meet the criteria set forth by the Kuwait Ministry of Higher Education for the study of Kuwaitis. Kasravi also works with university partners to establish Memorandums of Understanding with various sponsors in Kuwait. Prior to joining the Kuwait Cultural Office, Kasravi was involved in study abroad and served as director of the education abroad program at University of California–San Diego.

Lily Lopez-McGee serves as the deputy director for the Rangel International Affairs Program at Howard University. She is also a doctoral candidate at George Mason University where she is working on her dissertation, which focuses on college students perceived changes in self-efficacy as a result of participating in study abroad. Previously, she served as manager at Diversity Abroad where she managed the Diversity Abroad Network, a professional network of institutions of higher education and education abroad provider organizations. She serves as the cochair for Global Access Pipeline and helps coordinate the Conference on Diversity in International Affairs. Lopez-McGee graduated from the University of Washington with a bachelor's degree in international affairs and a master's degree in public administration.

James M. Lucas serves as the assistant dean for global education and curriculum at Michigan State University (MSU). His duties include overseeing first-year seminars, curriculum development and assessment, and global and multicultural education efforts on campus. He completed his PhD in higher, adult, and lifelong education at MSU with a focus on male engagement in education abroad. Lucas has led various study abroad programs around the world for over 15 years, and he has supervised programs for first-year students in Ireland, New Zealand, Iceland, Dubai, Cuba, and Japan. He currently leads a program to Italy for male-identified fraternity members as part of his ongoing research in the area of male education abroad engagement.

Monica Malhotra is a project manager with the National Clearinghouse on Disability and Exchange at Mobility International USA, which aims to increase participation of people with disabilities in inclusive international exchange programs. Previously, Malhotra worked for 10 years at UT Austin's international office where she assisted with admission, immigration, student counseling, ESL services, disability support, and sponsored student programs. During this time she created partnerships with the disability office and international office for ongoing cross-training and collaboration. She also wrote a chapter for NAFSA's *Crisis Management in a Cross-Cultural Setting* titled "Responding to Relationship Violence." Her past experience includes serving four years on the board for the Multicultural Refugee Coalition in Austin, Texas, and interning with the EastWest Institute in New York.

Malhotra earned her bachelor's degree in sociology from the University of Texas at Arlington and her master's degree in international studies from the University of Exeter, United Kingdom.

Margaret McCullers is the associate director of academic and special projects at the Institute for Study Abroad, Butler University (IFSA-Butler), one of the largest non-profit study abroad providers in the United States. In this role, she provides leadership in promoting inclusive excellence in IFSA-Butler programming and practices and supports the academic integration of study abroad for institutions across the country. She also oversees scholarships, chairs the Financial Need & Aid Committee, and directs the Work-to-Study program, which provides opportunities for high-financial-need students to build professional skills abroad. McCullers is cochair of NAF-SA's Subcommittee for Diversity & Inclusion in Education Abroad and was awarded a 2014 Australian Endeavour Executive Fellowship for her work on curriculum integration. McCullers previously worked at UT Austin supporting underrepresented and first-generation college students in study abroad and at the University of Georgia coordinating international programming for honors scholars. She holds an MEd in higher education administration from UT Austin.

Arelis Palacios holds an MS in higher education administration and a BA in English literature from Florida State University. Her career in education began in Miami Dade County Public Schools as a secondary English, leadership, journalism, and yearbook teacher. Within international education, she has worked at Florida State University, UT Austin, and presently at Georgetown University. As a native Nicaraguan who grew up in Miami, Florida, the realities of immigration were ever-present in her upbringing and classroom and helped to refine her interest in supporting underrepresented students along secondary and tertiary education, but specifically within international education. At Georgetown University, Palacios holds a dual role as the senior associate director of programming and advising within the Office of Global Education and as adviser for undocumented students within the Division of Student Affairs, where she continues to work collaboratively to create institutional support mechanisms for underrepresented students.

Amalia Pérez-Juez holds a PhD in archaeology and history and is the director of Boston University's study abroad programs in Spain. She oversees all the academic and personal integration of students in Spain, as well as teaches classes related to history and archaeology. She spent four years abroad as both an undergraduate and graduate student and as a visiting professor. Her passion for teaching and doing research is as vast as her passion for traveling and understanding other cultures. This makes her job as director of a study abroad program a perfect setting where she can devote time to discovering, teaching, managing, and interacting with students. Her academic background enriches the students' experience and it enables her to know the students as an administrator, a professor, a mentor, and a program director. She has been working for Boston University for over two decades.

Rosalind Latiner Raby, PhD, is a senior lecturer at California State University, Northridge, in the educational leadership and policy studies department of the College of Education where she has taught for the past 24 years and where she is an affiliate faculty for the ELPS EdD Community College program. She also serves as the director of California Colleges for International Education, a nonprofit consortium whose membership includes 91 California community colleges. Raby received her PhD in the field of comparative and international education from UCLA and since 1984 has worked with community college faculty and administrators to help them internationalize their campuses. Raby has a range of publications, with the most recent being *International Handbook of Comparative Studies on Community Colleges and Global Counterparts* (Springer, forthcoming) and *International Education at Community Colleges: Themes, Practices, and Case Studies* (Palgrave, 2016).

Gary M. Rhodes is the associate dean of international education and senior international officer in the College of Extended & International Education at California State University at Dominguez Hills (CSUDH). As associate dean and senior international officer, he is responsible for providing support for all international initiatives on the CSUDH campus. He is also director of the Center for Global Education, a national research and resource center supporting the internationalization of higher education. Rhodes' areas of expertise include the internationalization of higher education; study abroad program development and administration; integrated international learning; diversity and study abroad; and health, safety, crisis, and risk management for study abroad. He publishes articles and presents widely at U.S. and international conferences. He holds a BA in English from UCSB, an MA in international relations and an MSEd and a PhD in education from USC, and he has received Fulbright Specialist grants to India and South Africa.

Daniel Siefken is the assistant director for faculty-led programs at UT Austin's international office, where he also serves on the Longhorn Dreamers Project taskforce. Siefken has over 10 years of experience in higher education, working in various capacities within international education, student development, and admissions. During his tenure in admissions, he admitted the university's first undocumented student and helped shape the existing policies around undocumented student admissions. Siefken received his MS in global and international sociology from the University of Edinburgh in Scotland, where he wrote his thesis on barriers to accessing higher education for undocumented students. He has experience living and working throughout Central America and Europe, as well as serving as the country director for a community development non-profit organization in Guatemala and Honduras.

Sarah Simmons is assistant director of science education at Howard Hughes Medical Institute (HHMI). Within the undergraduate and graduate programs of HHMI's science education department, her portfolio includes several initiatives including the HHMI's professors program. Simmons joined HHMI in 2014 and prior to that held the position of assistant dean for honors, research, and international study in the College of Natural Sciences at UT Austin. In this latter position, she administered multiple college initiatives including honors programs, international science initiatives, and undergraduate research, in addition to teaching undergraduate science courses. She was also director and principal investigator of the HHMI- and NSF-funded Freshman Research Initiative (FRI)—a unique, large-scale program that engages undergraduates in research at UT Austin.

Michelle Tolan is the field director for inclusive excellence and research at the Institute for Study Abroad, Butler University (IFSA-Butler). In 2012, Tolan designed their award-winning First Generation College Student (FGCS) Scholarship program, which took an evidence-based approach and was the first of its kind for a study abroad organization. Since then she has designed several groundbreaking programs to better include diverse students in study abroad including the Fill the GAP fund-matching program, UpFront billing program, the Work-to-Study project grant program, and the diversity and inclusion focused website "Unpacked: A Study Abroad Guide for Students Like Me." Tolan has been active in leadership positions for NAFSA, Diversity Abroad, and The Forum on Education Abroad, where she currently serves as inclusive excellence working group chair. A "first gen" herself, she holds an MA from Indiana University, a BA from Drake University, and studied abroad as an undergraduate in Costa Rica.

disability nondiscrimination law
not sufficient for study abroad, 99,
101, 102–3, 111
overseas, 99, 101–3, 104, 107
Disability Rights Education and
Defense Fund, 101–2
diversity, vii–viii. *See also* inclusive
excellence; underrepresentation
accreditation, licensing and, 207
accrediting agencies and, 193
AIDE Roadmap for, 192–93
attempts to increase, 18, 32, 186–87
of California population, 49–50
capacity-building grants for, 193–94
collaboration barriers and, 191–92
of community college students, 116,
118, 123–24, 129
compositional, insufficiency of, 188,
193–94
comprehensive institutional plan for,
192–93
congressional legislation promoting,
187
federal aid and, 206
financial barriers and, 192–93
four Fs and, 185
funding for inconsistent, 187–88
funding promoting, 18–19, 205–6
government support for, 193–94
holistic evaluation of, 192–93
inclusion contrasted with, 188,
192–93, 194–95, 208–9
individual role in, 189–90, 195
institutional strategies for, 190–92,
195, 203–6
national and state strategies for,
193–94, 195, 203, 206–7
nongovernmental organization
support for, 194, 207
PAO promoting, 58
professional training for, 189–90,
208
reports on, 19–20
of sex, 83

stakeholders for, 189–90, 191, 195
for student development, 6
students with disabilities and, 105
study abroad for openness to, 24
sustainable strategies for, 187–89,
190–92, 204, 210
of UCSD population, 50
Diversity Abroad, 11, 30, 186, 189
AIDE Roadmap of, 192
on faculty as stakeholder, 191
UCSD and, 58
Diversity Abroad Network, 32,
186–87
DREAM Act. *See* Development, Relief,
and Education for Alien Minors
Act
Dresden, Germany. *See* Technical
University of Dresden
Durbin, Richard, 178–79

Eastern Michigan University, 106
Educator for Undocumented Students,
177
Ehigiator, K., 31
eligibility criteria, as barrier, 204
Engineering Criteria 2000
(Accreditation Board for
Engineering and Technology), 151
engineering majors, 12, 53
accreditation criteria modified for,
151
BU case study of, 14, 149–50,
151–62
culture shock approaches for,
158–59, 161–62
curricular flexibility as barrier for,
152
curriculum integration for, 153, 154,
161–62
English-language instruction for,
154, 156
field trips for, 157
foreign language as barrier for, 152,
153, 158

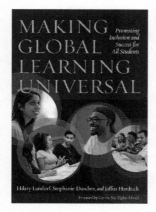

Making Global Learning Universal
Promoting Inclusion and Success for All Students
Hilary Landorf, Stephanie Doscher, and Jaffus Hardrick

Foreword by Caryn McTighe Musil

While there is wide consensus in higher education that global learning is essential for all students' success, there are few models of how to achieve this goal. The authors of this book, all of whom are from one of the nation's largest and most diverse research universities, provide such a model and, in doing so, offer readers a broad definition of *global learning* that both encompasses a wide variety of modes and experiences—in-person, online, and in cocurricular activities at home and abroad—and engages all students on campus. They provide a replicable set of strategies that embed global learning throughout the curriculum and facilitate high quality, high-impact global learning for all students.

The approach this book describes is based on three principles: that global learning is a process to be experienced, not a thing to be produced; that it requires all students' participation—particularly the underrepresented—and cannot succeed if reserved for a select few; and that global learning involves more than mastery of a particular body of knowledge.

Sty/us

22883 Quicksilver Drive
Sterling, VA 20166-2102

Subscribe to our e-mail alerts: www.Styluspub.com

Also available from Stylus

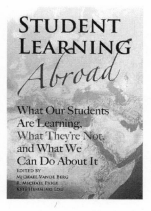

Student Learning Abroad
What Our Students Are Learning, What They're Not, and What We Can Do About It
Edited by Michael Vande Berg, R. Michael Paige, and Kris Hemming Lou

"The book is a good source for study abroad professionals and has the ability to provide direction for programs needing new life breathed into them, particularly at a time when budgets are shrinking; calls for accountability are increasing; and students deserve, more than ever, to have truly meaningful study abroad experiences."
—*The Review of Higher Education, Director Emerita,*

This book provokes readers to reconsider long-held assumptions, beliefs and practices about teaching and learning in study abroad and to reexamine the design and delivery of their programs. In doing so, it provides a new foundation for responding to the question that may faculty and staff are now asking: What do I need to know, and what do I need to be able to do, to help my students learn and develop more effectively abroad?

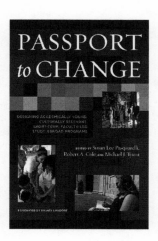

Passport to Change
Designing Academically Sound, Culturally Relevant, Short-Term Faculty-Led Study Abroad Programs
Edited by Susan Lee Pasquarelli, Robert A. Cole, and Michael J. TysonForeword by Hilary Landorf

There has been enormous growth in faculty-led, short-term study abroad programs because they offer flexibility and expand opportunities for students and faculty members who wish to study and work abroad but do not have the resources or time to spend a semester or year away. These experiential programs offer unique opportunities for university faculty to teach their disciplines abroad while engaging students in direct, authentic cultural encounters for transformative change.

This volume provides a detailed framework and guidance on how to plan and implement a faculty-led study abroad program. Seasoned faculty leaders and administrators describe an overall program development process, comprehensively identify the elements for designing the curriculum, and offer advice and solutions to unique challenges inherent in various types of programs.

(Continued on preceding page)

This book is a copublication of NAFSA: Association of International Educators and Stylus Publishing, LLC.

NAFSA: Association of International Educators is the largest association of professionals committed exclusively to advancing international higher education. The association provides leadership to its diverse constituencies through establishing principles of good practice and providing professional development opportunities. NAFSA encourages networking among professionals, convenes conferences and collaborative dialogues, and promotes research and knowledge creation to strengthen and serve the field. We lead the way in advocating for a better world through international education.

www.nafsa.org

To order this and other NAFSA publications: Call **1.866.538.1927** | Online **shop.nafsa.org**

Founded in 1996, Stylus focuses on higher education, covering such areas as teaching and learning, student affairs, professional development, service-learning and community engagement, study abroad, assessment, online learning, racial diversity on campus, women's issues, doctoral education, and leadership and administration. Stylus is the official distributor of the book programs of ACPA, Campus Compact, and the National Resource Center for the First-Year Experience and Students in Transition.

See or download a PDF of our current Higher Education Catalog at www.Styluspub.com (click on "Books" in the navigation bar and search under "Print Catalogs"), or call 1-800-232-0223.